After the Fall
American Literature Since 9/11

Richard Gray

A John Wiley & Sons, Ltd., Publication

This edition first published 2011
© 2011 John Wiley & Sons Ltd

Wiley-Blackwell is an imprint of John Wiley & Sons, formed by the merger of Wiley's global Scientific, Technical and Medical business with Blackwell Publishing.

Registered Office
John Wiley & Sons Ltd, The Atrium, Southern Gate, Chichester, West Sussex, PO19 8SQ, United Kingdom

Editorial Offices
350 Main Street, Malden, MA 02148-5020, USA
9600 Garsington Road, Oxford, OX4 2DQ, UK

The Atrium, Southern Gate, Chichester, West Sussex, PO19 8SQ, UK

For details of our global editorial offices, for customer services, and for information about how to apply for permission to reuse the copyright material in this book please see our website at www.wiley.com/wiley-blackwell.

Library of Congress Cataloging-in-Publication data is available for this book.

Hardback: 9780470657928

A catalogue record for this book is available from the British Library.

This book is published in the following electronic formats: ePDFs 9781444395846; Wiley Online Library 9781444395860; ePub 9781444395853

Set in 11.5/13.5pt Bembo by SPi Publisher Services, Pondicherry, India
Printed and bound in Malaysia by Vivar Printing Sdn Bhd

1   2011

After the Fall

Blackwell Manifestos

In this new series major critics make timely interventions to address important concepts and subjects, including topics as diverse as, for example: Culture, Race, Religion, History, Society, Geography, Literature, Literary Theory, Shakespeare, Cinema, and Modernism. Written accessibly and with verve and spirit, these books follow no uniform prescription but set out to engage and challenge the broadest range of readers, from undergraduates to postgraduates, university teachers and general readers – all those, in short, interested in ongoing debates and controversies in the humanities and social sciences.

Already Published

To
Sheona
Jessica and Jack
Catharine and Ben

Contents

Acknowledgments

I have accumulated many debts in the course of working on this book. In particular, I would like to thank friends at the British Academy, including Andrew Hook, Jon Stallworthy, and Wynn Thomas; colleagues and friends at other universities, among them Kasia Boddy, Susan Castillo, Henry Claridge, Richard Ellis, the late Kate Fullbrook, Mick Gidley, Sharon Monteith, Judie Newman, Helen Taylor, and Nahem Yousaf; and colleagues and friends in other parts of Europe and in Asia and the United States, especially Saki Bercovitch, Bob Brinkmeyer, the late George Dekker, Gordon Hutner, Jan Nordby Gretlund, Lothar Honnighausen, Bob Lee, Marjorie Perloff, Michael Rothberg, and Waldemar Zacharasiewicz. Among my colleagues in the Department of Literature, I owe a special debt of thanks to Herbie Butterfield and Owen Robinson; I also owe special thanks to my many doctoral students for allowing me to test my ideas out on them and providing me with much needed guidance. Sincere thanks are also due to Emma Bennett, the very best of editors, at Wiley-Blackwell for steering this book to completion, and, also at Wiley-Blackwell, I also wish to thank my daughter Jessica for making such a first class job of compiling the index. In Chapter 2 I have drawn to some extent on essays I have written previously: 'Open Doors, Closed Minds: American Prose Writing at a Time of Crisis,' in *American Literary History*, Spring, 2009; and 'Cormac McCarthy: *The Road*' in *Still In Print: Southern Writing Today* edited by Jan Nordby Gretlund (University of South Carolina Press, 2010). Though both essays represent earlier and briefer versions of what is developed and argued here, acknowledgements to these publications are due. On a more personal note, I would like to thank my older daughter, Catharine, for her quick wit, warmth, intelligence and understanding, and for providing me with the very best of son-in-laws, Ricky Baldwin and two perfect grandsons, Izzy and Sam; my older son, Ben, for his thoughtfulness, courage, commitment and good company; my younger daughter, Jessica, for her lively intelligence, grace and kindness as well as her refusal to take anything I say on trust; and my younger son, Jack, who, being without language, constantly reminds me that there are other, deeper ways of communicating. Finally, as always, I owe the deepest debt of all to my wife, Sheona, for her patience, her good humor, her clarity and tenderness of spirit, and for her love and support, for always being there when I need her. Without her, this book would never have been completed.

1

After the Fall

If there was one thing writers agreed about in response to 9/11, it was the failure of language; the terrorist attacks made the tools of their trade seem absurd. "I have nothing to say," Toni Morrison told what she called "the dead of September," "– no words stronger than the steel that pressed you into itself; no scripture older or more elegant than the ancient atoms you have become" (1). W.S. Merwin, in his poem "To the Words," addressed the tools of his craft directly, "When it happens you are not there" (3), he complained, as he contemplated the attack on the Twin Towers. While Suheir Hammad confessed that there was "no poetry in the ashes south of canal street./ no prose in the refrigerated trucks driving debris and dna./ not one word" (139). Philosophers, called on to make some comment, tended to agree. "The whole play of history and power is distorted by this event," Jean Baudrillard observed, "but so, too are the conditions of analysis" (*Spirit of Terrorism*, 51). And, interviewed on the function of philosophy in a time of terror, Jacques Derrida, said much the same. "We do not know what we are talking about," Derrida argued:

> "Something" took place ... But this very thing, the place and meaning of this "event," remains ineffable, like an intuition without concept ... out of range for a language that admits its powerlessness and so is reduced to pronouncing mechanically a date, repeating it endlessly ...

After the Fall: American Literature Since 9/11, First Edition. Richard Gray.
© 2011 John Wiley & Sons, Ltd. Published 2011 by John Wiley & Sons, Ltd.

a … rhetorical refrain that admits to not knowing what it's talking about. (Borradori, 86)

"The thing," "the event," "9/11," "September 11:" the vague, gestural nature of these terms is a measure of verbal impotence – or, rather, of the widespread sense that words failed in the face of both the crisis and its aftermath. Writers and other observers, as Derrida suggests here, fell back on repetition, incantation, bare facts and figures, names and dates, the irreducible reality of what had happened, the blank stare of the actual. Not quite, though: what they also fell back on was the myth of the fall – the underlying conviction that the deep rhythms of cultural time had been interrupted and that the rough beast of "a new era" (Berger, 55), "a new period in history" (Hirsch, 85) was slouching towards America, and perhaps the West, to be born.

"On that day we had our fall" (Kahane, 113): "that day," however, has always varied according to the observer. There is a recurrent tendency in American writing, and in the observation of American history, to identify crisis as a descent from innocence to experience: but the crisis changes, the moment of descent has been located at a number of different times in the national narrative, most of them associated with war. For Washington Irving, as one of his best-known stories "Rip Van Winkle" illustrates, the critical moment was the War of Independence. Rip falls asleep for twenty years and wakes up to discover, to his deep discomposure, that he has fallen into another world. "Instead of being a subject of his majesty George the Third," he learns, "he was now a free citizen of the United States" (52). "I'm not myself," the bewildered Rip complains, " – I'm somebody else;" "I'm changed, and I can't tell what's my name or who I am!" (50). For Henry James, as I suggest in the next chapter, it was the Civil War; so, too, for James's contemporary Mark Twain. Twain felt he had little enough in common with Henry James (he remarked of one book by James, "Once you put it down, you can't pick it up."[1]), but what he did share was a belief that he, along with other Americans, had fallen from a pre-lapsarian state into a post-lapsarian one. "A glory that once was," Twain ruefully

---

[1] http://www.ralphmag.org/twain.html.

2

observed, had "dissolved and vanished away" (LM, 142), thanks to four years of civil conflict; a world that seemed to be "just far enough away to seem a Delectable Land, dreamy reposeful, inviting" (TS, 29) had been supplanted, for good or ill, by "progress, energy, prosperity" (LM, 144); the romance of the past had surrendered in short, to the stern realism of the present. For Ernest Hemingway, F. Scott Fitzgerald and their contemporaries, it was the First World War that provided a savage introduction to the actual. "Here was a new generation," Fitzgerald declared of the 1920s, "… grown up to find all Gods dead, all wars fought, all faiths in man shaken" (15). For those who came of age twenty or thirty years later, it was the Second World War. So, one postwar American poet, Karl Shapiro, ends an account of his wartime experiences, in a poem aptly titled "Lord, I have seen too much," by comparing himself to Adam "driven from Eden to the East to dwell" (27), while another, Randall Jarrell begins one of his most memorable poems, "The Death of the Ball Turret Gunner," by comparing the protagonist's (and, by implication, the poet's) entry into war to falling from sleep "into the State" (609). The line continues up to the present, in terms of the reading of other, later American wars. So, in writing about his own experience as a combatant in Vietnam, W.D. Ehrhart concludes his poem, "Fragment: 5 September 1967" by confessing of himself and his comrades in arms, "After that, there was no innocence;/ And there was no future to believe in" (33); and Yusef Komunyakaa, also an active participant in that war, admits in his poem "Maps Drawn in the Dust" that, after their encounter with conflict, he and his fellow soldiers were "no longer young,/ no longer innocent," "we were wired to our trigger fingers" (13). Revelations like these – and there are many of them (think, for instance about the popularity of *Heart of Darkness* as an intertextual referent in films and fiction about the Vietnam War) – alert us to a powerful vein of nostalgia at work in American thinking. In terms of deep structure, the story or subtext moves from the presumption of initial innocence to an encounter with forms of experience that are at once dire and disorienting. Innocence is shattered, paradise is lost, thanks to a bewildering moment, a descent into darkness, the impact of crisis. This is an old story, at least as old as the American nation. And, at this moment, in

3

the national narrative, it has been fired into renewed life by the events of September 11, 2001 and after – the acts of terror that left nearly 3000 dead by the end of that day and the acts of both terror and the "war on terror" that have accounted for hundreds of thousands more deaths[2].

An old story, then, but also a new one. What is decidedly new in this chapter of the continuing tale of what happens in America after the fall, comes down to two things: the particular nature of the crisis and the specific terms in which writers have reacted to it. As for the particular nature of the crisis, that has to do with three unusual factors that might be handily summarized in terms of invasion, icons, and the intervention of the media. Prior to September 11, 2001, the last time the United States had been invaded, its borders significantly penetrated, was during the 1812 war with Great Britain, which lasted for three years. The last and, until 9/11, the only time. There had been civil war; there had been an attack on the periphery of American power, at Pearl Harbour. But there had been nothing from outside that struck at the heart of the nation. Nothing that suggested that the United States itself might become an international battlefield. International wars, apart from the war for independence and a war that might be considered its residue, had always been fought on foreign soil. To have war brought home was an unusual experience for America, to have the mainland not only invaded but attacked from the skies and devastated was not only unusual but unique. People living in Vietnam or Afghanistan or Korea, the former USSR or those

---

[2]   The number of deaths resulting from the attacks on September 11, 2001, is usually given as 2995; this includes the 19 hijackers (http://en.wikipedia.org/wiki/September_11_attacks). The number of deaths resulting from the wars in Afghanistan and Iraq is disputed. Estimates of deaths resulting from the Iraq War, for instance, vary drastically. These estimates include the ones supplied by the Iraq Family Death Survey (151,000 as at June, 2006), the *Lancet* survey (601,027 violent deaths out of 654, 965 excess deaths as at June, 2006), the Opinion Research Business Survey (1,033,000 as at April, 2009), the Associated Press (110,600 as at April, 2009), the Iraq Body Count (94,902–103,549 as at December, 2009), and the *Lancet* survey of excess deaths (1,366,350 as at December, 2009). Whatever the number, it can only increase (http://cn.wikipedia.org/wiki/Iraq_War).

of a certain generation in Europe might wonder about the reaction to 9/11. Quantitavely, the destruction of the Twin Towers and 2995 lives pales beside, say, the bombing of Hiroshima and Nagasaki or what has been called "ecoside" (Bui, 967), the devastation of natural and human life, in Vietnam. But crisis is as much a matter of perception, of feeling, as anything else. America had been impervious, either by calculation (thanks to the doctrine of isolationalism, the avoidance of entangling alliances with other, war-torn parts of the globe, especially Europe), or by fighting its wars elsewhere ("It's better to fight communism in Vietnam than in California," was a common argument heard in the 1960s), or by sheer blind luck. Then everything changed. On September 11, 2001, as the media did not fail to point out over and over again, America came under attack. It was – at least, according to the national sense of things – invaded. The homeland was no longer secure and, to that extent, no longer home.

"I never liked the World Trade Center," David Lehman wrote in 1996: "When it went up I talked it down/ As did many other New Yorkers." What persuaded him to change his mind, he says, was the attack on the building in 1993, when a car bomb was detonated at the foot of the North Tower. "When the bomb went off and the building became/ A great symbol of America, like the Statue/ Of Liberty at the end of Hitchcock's *Saboteur*," Lehman explains, "My whole attitude toward the World Trade Center/ Changed overnight" (xv). He began to appreciate the way it came into view as you reached a certain point in downtown Manhattan, or the way the two towers appeared to dissolve into the skies. It was there, for him, as a power-ful *image* of national achievement and aspiration. The reference to its cinematic presence in Lehman's poem is telling: its virtual status, this intimates, was at least as important as its existence as an actual, material structure. That distinction emerged with even more force when the presence of the Twin Towers became an absent one. The total destruction of the World Trade Center, some eight years after the car bombing and five years after Lehman wrote his poem, left what Don DeLillo called "something empty in the sky" ("In the Ruins," 39). Less than two weeks after the 9/11 attacks, the cartoonist and visual artist Art Speigelman famously produced a cover for the

5

New Yorker that showed the silhouettes of the North and South Towers in a black-on-black painting, as a way of suggesting their continuing existence as a symbolic trace, their lingering presence despite their disappearance. Even after the destruction of the World Trade Center, architectural critics betrayed a distinct reluctance to celebrate it as a material structure: one referred to it as an extreme example of "the generic postwar corporate office tower" (Wigley, 75). What they, and others, did celebrate, however, was the totemic significance of this particular downtown building complex: which was why, of course, it was targeted not once but twice by terrorists. "The attackers did not just cause the highest building in Manhattan to collapse," as Jurgen Habermas put it; "they also destroyed an icon in the household imagery of the American nation" (Borradori, 28). The loss of life was, first and last, the most terrible consequence of the 9/11 attacks. But what made this crisis new and different from other, at least equally terrible crises, was this iconic dimension.: The towers made an indelible imprint on the Manhattan skyline and on the popular imagination; they were, in the words of Habermas, a "powerful embodiment of economic strength and projection toward the future" (Borradori, 28); and, in a terrifying symbolic gesture, the terrorists had deleted them – in fact, if not from the imagination.

And the whole world was watching. That is the third factor that helped make this particular crisis unique. The collapse of the towers was a global media event. "The whole world population," in the words of Habermas, was "a benumbed witness" (28). There have been other critical events that have been rapidly broadcast throughout the world, including, in the recent American context, the assassinations of John and Robert Kennedy and Martin Luther King. The difference here, however, is threefold: witness at the actual moment of crisis, the failure of ritual and the mixing of the strange and the familiar. The destruction of the World Trade Center took place in front of what Habermas called "a global public" (Borradori, 28). The world was an eyewitness to the event, as it actually happened. As a televisual event, it could be played over and over again, which it was. The death of President Kennedy was certainly a major media event, with the news of his assassination being rapidly broadcast worldwide. But the immediate visual dimension was, famously, limited to a brief piece of long-range, poor quality film. And the deaths of Robert Kennedy and Martin Luther King took place offstage, as it were. With Bobbie Kennedy, the memorable images are before and after: the young Senator declaring his intention to go on to Chicago and the Democratic convention, the almost unbearable panic as news spreads into the crowd that there has been a shooting, the body lying bleeding on the floor. With Dr King, the visual traces are even more fragmentary, the most notable being his friends and colleagues in shock, pointing towards the place from where they believe the shots that killed him were fired. There is an absence here. The global public was witness to the consequences of the traumatic event, and the responses to it (including the civil unrest that followed the killings of Bobbie Kennedy and King), but not the event itself. With 9/11, that global public was in the unique position of watching the event as it occurred; the impact, the explosion, the fall of the towers were there for all to see in what media people like to call "real time." Not only that, every moment could be replayed, slowed down, speeded up, put in freeze frame or in a wider or narrower perspective: in short, placed under obsessive, compulsive scrutiny. One vital consequence of this, for writers, was that the traumatic moment was also an iconic one. The fall of the towers, as we shall see – and, for that matter, the fall of people from the towers – has become a powerful and variable visual equivalent for other kinds of fall. In some texts, the towers, or the people, fall over and over again, as they did on instant replay on the television. "I've seen the same thing happen so many times now," one character complains in a play set on September 12, 2001, as he watches "those buildings fall down again" on TV, "I don't even know when "now" IS anymore! It's like it's always happening!" (Wright, 32;). In others, the falling towers are caught at a frozen moment, as a distillation of terror, as again they were on television. And in some texts, the towers rise from their ashes, are returned into the Manhattan skyline, or the falling man or woman is plucked out of the sky and restored to the building from which they jumped, in a gesture that is partly a longing for redemption and partly simple wish fulfilment. "Perhaps September 11 could be called the first historic world event in the strictest sense" (Borradori, 28),

7

Habermas has speculated, because of this, the global witnessing of the event as it happened. That may be so. What is certainly the case is that this immediacy – an immediacy that was, above all, visual – was something new in the experience of crisis. And it offered writers and other artists a powerful series of symbols for an otherwise unendurable and perhaps unknowable event.

A further difference between the media event that was 9/11 and, in particular, the media event that was the killing of President Kennedy is what one commentator has called "the *political* failure of our mourning" (Brooks, 49). The distinction that Freud made between mourning and melancholia is relevant here. On the one hand, there is mourning: the use of ceremony, ritual, acting out of some kind to enable a working out of and getting through the traumatic event. On the other, there is what Freud called "the open wound" that is "the complex of melancholia," "drawing to itself cathectic energies… from all directions, and emptying the ego until it is totally impoverished" (253). The Kennedy assassination left a huge hole in the life of America – a hole that has been endlessly filled with conspiracy theories, speculation about what would have happened if Kennedy had survived, and so on – but the period of national (and international) mourning that followed his death provided, at least, some measure of release, an appropriate catharsis. With 9/11, however, the period of commemoration has been hijacked by a series of events tied to it in rhetoric if not necessarily in reality: the "war on terror," the Patriot Act, extraordinary rendition, the invasion of Afghanistan and then Iraq. "The time of memory and commemoration evolved from the start alongside the time of revenge," one commentator has observed (Simpson, 4). Or as another commentator has it, 9/11 was the moment when "trauma time collided with the time of the state, the time of capitalism, the time of routine," producing a "curious unknown time, a time with no end in sight;" "the state, or whatever form of power is replacing it, has taken charge of trauma time" (Edkins, 233). Acting out grief has been jettisoned in favor of hitting out; getting through the crisis has yielded, in terms of priorities, to getting back at those who initiated it; commemorative rituals have ceded place to the initiation of a state of emergency. The result has been, to return to that phrase, a failure of mourning: a failure that leaves an open wound, a gap or emptiness in the psychic life of the nation – the operative symbol for which is Ground Zero.

Watching the events of September 11 unfold on television, one viewer, the screenwriter Lawrence Wright, apparently declared, "this looks like a movie – my movie" (Radstone, 119). The director of the action film *Die Hard*, Steve de Souza, said something similar: "the image of the terrorist attacks looked like a movie poster, like one of my movie posters" (Radstone, 119). The events of September 11, 2001 looked to many people so strange, as to be unreadable, unintelligible, as if inscribed in a new vocabulary. But those events also looked, as one observer put it, "like something we had seen before in both fact and fiction" (Simpson, 6). On the one hand, all this was deeply unfamiliar: a demonized and, for a while, faceless enemy swooping down from the skies. On the other hand, it was all eerily familiar. A television documentary produced by the BBC early in 2002 made the point in its title: "September 11th: A Warning from Hollywood." "As millions of people watched the horrific spectacle of the Twin Towers collapsing," the documentary pointed out, "… many eye-witnesses and survivors compared the dramatic images to a Hollywood movie."[3] One writer, Jennifer Lauck, admitted that when she first heard the news about 9/11, "I thought of that stupid movie *Independence Day* where aliens blow up the White House and figured: It's a hoax" (300). "My first thought when the south tower came down," confessed another writer, Joshua Clover, "was for the film industry in crisis movies had been superceded more or less right on time" (130). Some conspiracy theorists found an appropriate cinematic reference in the satirical film, *Wag the Dog*, in which, as one of those tempted towards such theories, the essayist Sallie Tisdale, put it, "a marketing team manufactures a phony war to distract attention from a presidential scandal" (50). But the more usual, instinctive response was to see the attacks through the prism of disaster and horror movies,

---

[3] "September 11th; A Warning from Hollywood," *Panorama*, BBC1, March 24, 2002 (http://news.bbc.co.uk/hi/english/audiovideo/programmes/panorama/news. d-1875000/1875186.stm).

as a realization of the darkest dreams of the Hollywood dream factory. "For the great majority of the public, the WTC explosions were events on the TV screen," Slavoj Zizek has pointed out,

> and when we watched the oft-repeated shot of frightened people running towards the camera ahead of the giant cloud of dust from the collapsing tower, was not the framing of the shot itself reminiscent of spectacular shots in catastrophe movies, a special effect which outdid all others … ?(11)

The case of *The War of the Worlds* is instructive here. A commonly reported reaction to the attack on the World Trade Center, on the day it happened and immediately after, was desperately to hope that it was all a hoax (to use Lauck's term) along the lines of the notorious 1938 Orson Welles radio broadcast of the H.G. Wells novel. Another was to try to assimilate what had happened, to understand the sheer scale of the terror, by seeing it in terms of all those "stupid" space invader stories for which *The War of the Worlds* (1898 novel, 1938 radio broadcast, 1953 film) has provided the template. Either way, *The War of the Worlds* supplied a tool for making disaster manageable, spelling out the strange in a familiar vocabulary. Reality might be, in the words of Zizek, "the best appearance of itself" (11), but appearance was needed on September 11, 2001, to cope with the real; a depthless fiction was required for the facts to be read. Then, in 2005, came the movie remake of *The War of the Worlds*, directed by Steven Spielberg. Spielberg was in no doubt that his version of the story reflected the national anxiety generated by the destruction of the Twin Towers. "We live under a veil of fear that we didn't live under before 9/11," Spielberg said. "There has been a conscious emotional shift in this country."[4] So the peculiarly symbiotic relation between otherwise unassimilable fact and eerily familiar fantasy took yet another turn here: 9/11 perceived through the screen of an alien

[4] "New "War of the Worlds" recalls 9/11 images," *USA Today*, June 30, 2005 (http://www.usatoday.com/life/movies/news/2005-06-30-war-of-the-worlds-911_x.htm).

10

invaders movie was transposed into an (as it happens, enormously successful) alien invaders movie seen through the screen of 9/11. The unique paradox of 9/11, and its consequences, is caught in this tension between the strange and the familiar. It was a demolition of the fantasy life of the nation in that it punctured America's belief in its inviolability and challenged its presumption of its innocence, the manifest rightness of its cause. It was also a dark realization of that fantasy life, in the sense that it turned the nightmare, of a ruthless other threatening the fabric of buildings and of the nation, into a palpable reality. The most deeply unsettling events, one commentator on 9/11 has suggested, are not those that are entirely unexpected but those that are anticipated in fantasy, those in which we have a libidinal investment (Kahane, 108). The vertiginous collapse of the World Trade Center, its reduction to rubble, was just such an event. Clearly, it offered a profound and, on one level, unexpected shock to the system. The shock was all the greater, however, because, on another level, it *was* expected – or, rather, dreaded. Americans woke up to the fact that their borders were not impregnable, that there was an enemy out there prepared to kill and be killed. But it woke up, paradoxically, to the realization of one of its darkest dreams, complete with all the symbolic paraphernalia of such dreams – falling towers and flesh, dark avengers from the skies, the bodies of women, men and buildings reduced to a waste land of ashes.

One of the deeper, darker curiosities of the "war on terror" that followed soon after the terrorist attacks of September 11 was the way it sustained and even reinforced this slippage between fact and fantasy, history and (often nightmarish) dream. This was in part because of the bizarre conjunctions that the various phases of the war have generated. Habermas, for instance, noted what he called the "morally obscene" "assymetry" in the Afghan war between opponents who seemed to come from different worlds (and, in a sense did, the First and Third ones): "the concentrated destructive power of the electronically controlled clusters of elegant and versatile missiles in the air" and "the archaic ferocity of the swarms of bearded warriors outfitted with Kalashnikovs on the ground" (Borradori, 28). It was also in part due to the rhetoric of some of those who promoted the war.

Prior to the invasion of Iraq, for example, there was a great deal of talk, among those who favored going in, of a conflict that was essentially "immaterial" (Zizek, 37). On the one hand, there was the threat of invisible terrorist attacks, chemical and technological viruses that could be anywhere and nowhere; on the other, so the story went, there was the possibility of counter-terrorist retaliation that could be more or less virtual, at least on the side of the United States and its allies, with technology largely replacing direct military encounter. But the elision between the real and the artificial was, above all, the product, after 9/11, of what the masters of the "war on terror" managed with this kind of rhetoric, once the war – and, in particular the invasion of Iraq – had begun. Consider, for instance, what the *New York Times* journalist Ron Suskind was told by a senior adviser to the government during the early days of the Iraq war. "The aide said," Suskind tells us,

> that guys like me were "in what we call the reality based community," which he defined as people who "believe that solutions emerge from your judicious study of discernible reality." ... "That's not the way the world really works anymore," he continued. "We're an empire now, and when we act, we create our own reality ... and while you're studying that reality ... we'll act again, creating other new realities ... We're history's actors ... and you, all of you, will be left to just study what we do." (6)

In his novel, *Omega Point*, Don DeLillo introduces the reader to a fictional cousin of this government aide, a retired academic called Richard Elster. Elster was called in by the American Government at the beginning of the war on terror, we learn, to conceptualize their efforts, to form an intellectual framework for their troop deployments, counterinsurgency and orders for rendition. This fictional conceit, incidentally, is far less bizarre than something that actually happened in October, 2001: as reported in the press at the time, a group of Hollywood scriptwriters and directors, specialists in catastrophe movies, was set up in October, 2001, at the instigation of the Pentagon, to imagine possible scenarios for terrorist attacks and how to fight them. Elster spends much of the novel recollecting his two years mapping the reality that the architects of the "war on terror" were trying to create. As he does so, he ventures the suggestion that, for such architects, history is a dream dreamed by those who make it. Elster is unapologetic about this. "Lying is necessary," he insists:

> The state has to lie. There is no lie in war or in preparation for war that can't be defended. We went beyond this. We tried to create new realities overnight, careful sets of words that resemble advertising slogans in memorability and repeatability. Those were words that would yield pictures eventually and then become three-dimensional. The reality stands, it walks, it squats. (*Omega Point*, 28–9)

With the terrorist attacks, the real returns as a nightmarish fantasy that is also actuality; with the war on terror, it surfaces as a performance that acquires not only its meaning but also its substance from those who have scripted and perform it. Differently staged and nuanced, both chapters in this story of crisis involve a strange dematerialization of the material. The distinction between the actual and the artificial, the dreamed and the imagined, collapses; the real comes back as the artificial.

"The *return of the repressed*," Herbert Marcuse has suggested, "makes up the tabooed and subterranean history of civilisation" (xv–xvi). That is another way of reading the dreadful contradictions at work in the story of September 11, 2001 and after: contradictions that, for many writers at least, seemed to confound the possibilities of speech. Which brings us back to another exceptional aspect of 9/11, this particular moment in American history when the dark, repressed fantasies of life after the fall suddenly made their return. "I have nothing to say," Toni Morrison said. Apart from the obviously oxymoronic character of this, however, there is the not quite so obvious intertextual referent at work here. "Nothing to say" is precisely the phrase, the composer and poet John Cage uses to describe that peculiar cross between speech and silence that is his aesthetic aim. "I have nothing to say/" Cage said in one of his poems, "and I am saying it/ and that is poetry/ as I needed it."[5] What was remarkable, and arguably unique, about the response of American writers to the crisis of 9/11 was that it reignited their interest in a paradox that lies at the heart of writing at least since the time of Romanticism: the speaking of silence, the search for verbal forms that reach beyond the condition of words, the telling of a tale that cannot yet must be told. Just how individual writers pursued that interest will be one of the subjects of the chapters that follow. What is worth pointing out for now is the difference between the reaction of writers to earlier moments of crisis and their reaction to this most recent one. Disorientation is certainly a feature of writing in America after the fall. ("I'm changed," Washington Irving's most famous character confessed, "and I can't tell what's my name or who I am!"). So is a sense of loss and, occasionally, longing for a "dreamy, reposeful, inviting" pre-lapsarian world, a "Delectable Land" (to use Mark Twain's phrase) now evidently gone with the wind. Some writers, like Fitzgerald and Hemingway, clearly saw the fall experienced by their generation as also an initiation into deeper, darker and more adult forms of knowledge; they were "lost," perhaps, but they had also "grown up." Others, such as the poets of the Second World War and the Vietnam War, tended to equate the loss of innocence with the loss of hope ("there was no innocence;/" in the words of W.D. Ehrhart, "And there was no future to believe in"). There is no sense with any of these other, earlier generations of American writers, however, that they may have been silenced, no suspicion that the crisis they had encountered made words useless. A sterner, sparer language might be needed, after the fall; Ernest Hemingway certainly thought so. "I was always embarrassed by the words sacred, glorious and sacrifice and the expression in vain," says the protagonist Frederic Henry in Hemingway's *A Farewell to Arms*, set in the Great War: "the things that were glorious had no glory and the sacrifices were like

---

[5] http://www.writing.upenn.edu/~afilreis/88/cage-quotes.html. "I Have Nothing to Say and I Am Saying It" is also the title of a "performance biography" of Cage that features interviews with Merce Cunningham, Robert Rauschenberg, Laurie Anderson and Yoko Ono. See the review in the *New York Times*, May 14, 2010 (http://movies.nytimes.com/movie/80272/John-Cage-I-Have-Nothing-to-Say-and-I-Am Saying-It/overview).

the stockyards of Chicago... There were many words that you could not stand to hear and finally only the names of places had dignity" (207). But there is never the suggestion that language itself has been invalidated, that the currency of the writer's trade is counterfeit and worthless. But that suggestion, as we shall see, was made over and over again in the immediate aftermath of the September 11 attacks – and, for that matter, in response to the "war on terror" that followed. "Nothing to say" became a refrain, a recurrent theme with writers, as they struggled to cope with something that seemed to be, quite literally, beyond words.

And it is here that a link could be made, not with other, specifically American generations of writers, but with the arguments about literature that have dominated Western thought at least since the Romantics and Symbolists – and that were given an extra edge by the experience of total war and genocide in the middle years of the twentieth century. "Where the philosopher seeks certitude in the sign – the 'p' of the propositional calculus," Siguurd Burckhardt has suggested, " – and the mystic in the ineffable – the 'OM' of the Hindoos – the poet takes upon himself the paradox of the human word, which is both and neither and which he creatively transforms in his '"powerful rhyme"' (298). That offers one handy summation of a dialectic that has characterized thinking about and the practice of literature in the past two hundred years or so, in the English-speaking world and beyond. An equally handy summary was furnished by the poet Octavio Paz, when he argued that the definitive characteristic of post-Romantic literature is its vacillation between the magical and the revolutionary impulses. The magical, Paz explained, consists in a desire to return to nature by dissolving the self-consciousness that separates us from it, "to lose oneself for ever in animal innocence, or liberate oneself from history." The revolutionary demands the "conquest of the historical world and of nature." Both are ways of bridging the same gap and reconciling the "alienated consciousness" to its environment, Paz suggests; and both may be at work within the same writer (246). A century or so earlier than Paz, Charles Baudelaire actively demonstrated that vacillation by insisting both that "poetry is sufficient to itself" and that "the puerile utopia of art for art's sake,

15

by excluding morality and often even passion, was inevitably sterile" (Hamburger, 5). Literature as autonomous and autotelic or literature as referential and rooted in history, "pure" or "impure," literature as end (the path of Mallarme, we could say, who insisted, "After I had found nothingness I found beauty" (Hamburger, 29)) or literature as means (the path of Rimbaud who, famously, found the means inadequate, or of another, later French writer, Francis Ponge who declared, "People say that art exists for its own sake. This means nothing to me. Everything in art exists for men." (147)). This debate about the nature and function of literature boils down to a debate about the nature and function of its tools. It is about words and their uses – or, to be more exact, their potential usefulness or uselessness. And it was given renewed urgency by the experience of global conflict and, more particularly, the Holocaust. The Polish poet, Tadeusz Rosewicz, spoke for many when he confessed in 1960, "I cannot understand that poetry should survive when the men who created that poetry are dead. One of the premises and incentives for my poetry is a disgust with poetry. What I revolted against was that it had survived the end of the world, as though nothing had happened" (Hamburger, 249). Whether they knew it or not, American writers were suddenly, rudely awoken to this debate by the irruption of 9/11 and after; they, too, began to question their trade and its tools. And they felt compelled, not just to search for a new verbal austerity as some other, earlier generations had done, but to wonder if words were any use at all – and, to ask, quite simply, if literature could or should survive the end of *their* world.

Just how American writers have asked and tried to answer this question is the subject of this book. In the next chapter, *Imagining Disaster*, I focus on works that, in my opinion, have failed to come up with an adequate answer. My interest here is in the possible reasons for this failure: a failure that is not just a formal but also a political one. In place of a necessary imaginative encounter with disaster, and the recalibration of feeling and belief that surely requires, most of the fiction addressed in this chapter betrays a response to crisis that is eerily analogous to the reaction of many politicians and the mainstream American media after 9/11: a desperate retreat into the old sureties. Even the one novel considered in this chapter that manages to go

16

beyond this, to begin imagining what it might feel like to survive the end of the world, is not entirely resistant to the seductive pieties of home, hearth and family and, related to them, the equally seductive myth of American exceptionalism. And the other books discussed here do not just momentarily slip into or scramble after the familiar, they embrace it – and, in doing so, dissolve public crisis in the comforts of the personal. In chapter three, *Imagining Crisis*, the subject is the exact opposite to this withdrawal into the domestic and the security of fortress America: fictions that get it right, as I see it, thanks to a strategy of convergence, rooted in the conviction that the hybrid is the only space in which the location of cultures and the bearing witness to trauma can really occur. These fictions resist the challenge of silence by deploying forms of speech that are genuinely crossbred and transitional, subverting the oppositional language of mainstream commentary – us and them, West and East, Christian and Muslim. And they respond to the heterogeneous character of the United States, as well as its necessary positioning in a transnational context, by what I would call deterritorializing America. Of the books discussed in the fourth chapter, *Imagining the Transnational*, only some are directly concerned with the crisis of terrorism and counter-terrorism since September 11. But all of them address – with greater or lesser success – the fundamental issues raised by that crisis. In particular, they show, or try to, how trauma, crisis may provide an intercultural connection: one that can be written up either through the exploration of the interface between cultures in the United States (the so-called "browning of America" (Rodriguez, *passim*)), or through the mapping of America's extraterritorial expansion (the global reach of American culture and power), or both. All of them, in short, try to reimagine disaster by presenting us with an America situated *between* cultures. In the final chapter of this book, *Imagining the Crisis in Drama and Poetry,* I open out the discussion a little further, by looking at some dramatic and poetic explorations of crisis and after. The issues at stake here are, I think, basically the same as in the case of fiction. But, as I try to· suggest, they are complicated by other, related debates. With drama, those debates have circulated, among other issues, around the several functions of dramatic art, as communal commemoration, therapeutic

17

ritual, public witness and collective re-enactment. With poetry they have mostly involved the perennial, and always hotly debated question of the relationship between politics and poetry and the role of poetry as testament and therapeutic practice. With both drama and poetry, they have had to do with the potential democratization of aesthetic forms – forms associated, as a rule in the United States and elsewhere, with a relatively small, elite minority.

The basic issues at stake here are, I hope, beginning to come clear from this necessarily brief introduction. My aim is to make them clearer, and explore them in more detail, in the chapters that follow. One final point is perhaps worth making before that. Everything I try to say in this book is built on a simple premise, one that I have used the terms *convergence, the hybrid, interface* and *deterritorialization* to describe. Whether they know it or not – and, as it happens, many of them do – Americans find themselves living in an interstitial space, a locus of interaction between contending national and cultural constituencies. They are not alone in this. After all, as Fredric Jameson has argued, any social formation is a complex overlay of different methods of production which serve as the basis of different social groups and, consequently, of their world views. And in any given epoch a variety of kinds of antagonism, conflict between different groups and interests, can be discerned. One culture may well be dominant: but there will also be – to borrow Raymond Williams's useful terms – a residual culture, formed in the past but still active in the cultural process, and an emergent culture, prescribing new meanings and practices. What has made this liminal condition more radical or, at any rate, more remarkable over the past few years is the encounter with terrorism and the experience of counter terrorism. Now, more than ever, Americans find themselves caught between the conflicting interests and voices that constitute the national debate, situated at a peculiarly awkward meeting place between the culture(s) of the nation and the culture of the global marketplace – and, perhaps above all, faced with the challenge of new forms of otherness that are at best virulently critical and at worst obscenely violent. What this offers to American writers is the chance, maybe even the obligation, to insert themselves in the space between conflicting interests and practices and then dramatize the contradictions that conflict engenders. Through their work, by means of a mixture of voices, a free play of languages and even genres, they can represent the reality of their culture as multiple, complex and internally antagonistic. They can achieve a realization of both synchrony and diachrony: a demonstration of both the structural continuities between past and present and the processes by which those continuities are challenged, dissolved and reconstituted. So they have the opportunity – a better one than many other members of their society have – of realizing what Hayden White has called "the human capacity to endow lived contradictions with intimations of their possible transcendence" (17). They have the chance, in short, of getting "into" history, to participate in its processes, and, in a perspectival sense at least, getting "out" of it too – and enabling us, the readers, to begin to understand just how those processes work. Many writers, as I will try to show, have seized that chance; others, apparently traumatized by accelerating social change and political crisis, have been unable or unwilling to do so. The degree to which writers do meet the challenge, of allowing their work to be a site of struggle between cultures – and a free play of idioms and genres – will surely help to determine where American writing is twenty, thirty or more years from now, long after this particular fall.

2

Imagining Disaster

"The flower of art blossoms only when the soil is deep," that eminent Anglo-American, Henry James, once observed, "… it takes a great deal of history to produce a little literature" (23). By now, the United States has a great deal of history. In the past twenty years alone, the United States has witnessed the disintegration of its sinister other, the USSR; it has also borne witness to the birth of a world characterized by transnational drift, the triumph of global capitalism and the re-emergence of religious fundamentalism. That, perhaps, suggests several tensions this great deal of history of the past two decades has generated. American culture may have become internationally dominant but the United States itself has been internationalized; America may be the sole remaining superpower, but it is a superpower that seems haunted by fear – fear, among other things, of its own possible impotence and potential decline. In the global marketplace, it may well be America that is now the biggest item on sale; in a postcolonial world, it equally well may be that the imagination has now been colonized by the United States. But the United States itself has become what Ishmael Reed has called "the first universal nation" (55); and some of our sense of what it means now to be an American can be telegraphed in a series of numbers and names that have become almost iconic and suggest the very opposite of triumphalism – 9/11, the "war on terror," Al Quaeda, Saddam Hussein, Abu Ghraib, Guantanamo Bay.

After the Fall: American Literature Since 9/11, First Edition. Richard Gray.
© 2011 John Wiley & Sons, Ltd. Published 2011 by John Wiley & Sons, Ltd.

"The world is here" (56), Reed declared in an essay titled "America: The Multinational Society." And the world is "here," in the United States, for two seminal reasons. The first is that particular ethnic groups that have been here for centuries have gained additional presence and prominence. There has been a fourfold increase, for instance, in the past thirty years, in those claiming Native American descent; and in 1997 the Census Bureau calculated that by 2050 Hispanics would account for nearly one in four of the American population. The second has to do with that perennial seedbed of change in America, immigration. "American literature, especially in the twentieth century, and notably in the last twenty years," Toni Morrison wrote in 1992, "has been shaped by its encounter with the immigrant" (92). Since she wrote that, the growth in immigration – and especially immigration from outside Europe – has been radical. From 1990 to 1997 alone, seven and a half million foreign-born individuals entered the United States legally, accounting for 29.2 per cent of the population growth. By the middle of the twenty-first century, it has been calculated, "non-white" and third world ethnic groups will outnumber whites in the United States. And, as one commentator has observed, "the 'average' US resident... will trace his or her ancestry to Asia, Africa, the Hispanic world, the Pacific Islands, Arabia – almost anywhere but Europe" (Henry, 28). Revealing the central dynamic of Western, and in some sense global life today, which is marked by the powerful shaping force of shifting, multicultural populations, America has witnessed the disappearance of the boundary between the "center" and the "margins."[1] And

[1] On some of the general and theoretical issues raised here, see, for example, William Boelhower, *Through a Glass Darkly: Ethnic Semiosis in American Literature* New York: Oxford University Press, 1987; Iain Chambers and Lidia Curti (editors), *The Post-Colonial Question: Common Skies, Divided Horizons* London: Routledge, 1996; Partha Chatterjee, *The Nation and its Fragments: Colonial and Post Colonial Societies* Princeton: Princeton University Press, 1993; James Clifford, *Routes: Travel and Translation in the Late Twentieth Century* Cambridge: Harvard University Press, 1997; James Clifford and George E. Marcus (editors), *Writing Culture: The Poetics and Politics of Ethnography* Berkeley: University of California Press, 1986; Gustavo Perez Firmat, *Do the Americas Have a Common Literature?* Durham, North Carolina: Duke University Press, 1990; Anthony Giddens, *The Consequences of Modernity* Stanford, California: Stanford

with white Americans moving, it seems, inexorably into a minority, it has lost any claim it may have tried to make once to a Eurocentric character and an exclusive destiny. One measure of the impact such a demographic transformation has had, and might continue to have, on the social and political culture of the United States is the election of Barack Obama as President in 2008. Born in Kenya, raised in Indonesia and then Hawaii, Obama has said that his "experience of a variety of cultures in a climate of mutual respect" became "an important part of his world view." The "patchwork heritage of America," Obama observed in his inauguration speech, was "a strength not a weakness;" "we are shaped by many languages and cultures, drawn from every end of this earth."[2] And a measure, in turn, of what impact such demographic change has had, and might have, specifically on the writing of America is registered in a question asked at the beginning

University Press, 1990; Paul Gilroy, *The Black Atlantic: Modernity and Double Consciousness* Cambridge: Harvard University Press, 1993; Jurgen Habermas, *The Philosophical Discourse of Modernity* (1985) Oxford: Blackwell, 1987; Gayan Prakash (editor), *After Colonialism: Imperial Histories and Postcolonial Displacements* Princeton: Princeton University Press, 1995; Werner Sollors, *Beyond Ethnicity: Consent and Descent in American Culture* New York: Oxford University Press, 1986; Ronald A. Takaki, *A Different Mirror: A History of Multicultural America* Boston: Little, Brown, 1993; Ronald Takakai, (editor), *From Different Shores: Perspectives on Race and Ethnicity in America* New York: Oxford University Press, 1987. On the specific question of immigration and its consequences, see, for example, Jon Gjerde (editor), *Major Problems in American Immigration and Ethnic History: Documents and Essays* New York: Harper Collins, 1998; John Bodnar, *The Transplanted: A History of Immigrants in Urban America* Bloomington: Indiana University Press, 1985; Vernon M. Briggs and Stephen Moore, *Still an Open Door? U.S. Immigration Policy and the American Economy* Washington, DC: American University Press, 1994; Roger Daniels, *Coming to America: A History of Immigration and Ethnicity in American Life* New York: Harper Collins, 1990; Geoffrey Passel and Barry Edmonston, *Immigration and Race: Recent Trends in Immigration to the United States* Washington, DC: Urban Institute, 1992. Useful websites include Arizona State University Im/migration web page: www.asu.edu/class/history/asu-imm; H-Net Humanities & Social Sciences Online – H-Ethnic: www.h-net.org/-ethnic; Immigration and Ethnic History Society: www.iehs.org.
[2] Reyes, B.J. (February 8, 2007), *Honolulu Star-Bulletin* (http://archives.starbulletin.com/2007/02/08/news/story02.html); http://news.bbc.co.uk/1/hi/world/americas/obama_inauguration/7840646.stm.

of a collection of critical essays published in 2002: "What really is the language of the United States?" (Shell, 3)

And then there are the cataclysmic events of 11th September and their aftermath. These are as much part of the soil, the deep structure lying beneath and shaping the literature of the American nation, not least because they have reshaped our consciousness; they are a defining element in our contemporary structure of feeling and they cannot help but impact profoundly on American writing. One possible way of interpreting these events is in terms of trauma: a recalibration of feeling so violent and radical that it resists and compels memory, generating stories that cannot yet must be told. Trauma, a word whose origins lie in the Greek word for wound, was famously defined by Freud and his disciples in terms of an event the full horror of which is not and cannot be assimilated or experienced fully at the time but only belatedly. It is not "available to consciousness until it imposes itself again, repeatedly, in the nightmares and repetitive actions of the survivor" (Caruth, *Unclaimed Experience*, 4): a "feature," Freud observed, "one might term *latency*" (84). The first step towards recovery is testimony to a listener, an "intellectual witness" – a concept that, as Geoffrey Hartman has explained, is "without generational limit" (37). This transformation of the traumatic event into what Cathy Caruth has called "a narrative memory" (*Explorations in Memory*, 153) allows the story not only to be verbalized and communicated but assimilated – the dispersed, and in most cases repressed, pieces of the event can be disinterred and delivered into some kind of sequence. The writer, acting here as both victim and witness, with their text both symptom and diagnosis, can, in the words of another authority on trauma and recovery, "see more than a few fragments of the picture at one time, ... retain all the pieces and ... fit them together" (Herman, 2) into a meaningful story.

Certainly, what is notable about those texts that have attempted to confront the dreadful events of 9/11 and its aftermath directly is the presence of, and in fact an emphasis on, the preliminary stages of trauma: the sense of those events as a kind of historical and experiential abyss, a yawning and possibly unbridgeable gap between before and after. "These three years past since that day in September, all life

24

had become public," observes a character in Don DeLillo's *Falling Man* (182). Another character, in the lead story in Deborah Eisenberg's *Twilight of the Superheroes*, echoes that observation: "Private life shrank to nothing," he reflects, "all one's feelings had been absorbed by an arid wasteland…one's ordinary daily pleasures were like dusty curios on a shelf" (36). "Cataclysmic events, whatever their outcome, are as rare and transporting as a great love," goes one of the epigraphs in Jay McInerney's *The Good Life*,

> Bombings, revolutions, earthquakes, hurricanes, – anyone who has passed through one and lived, if they are honest, will tell you that even in the depths of their fear there was an exhilaration such as had been missing from their lives until then.

That strange, almost unsayable confusion of fear and exhilaration, resistance to and immersion in the extreme is what McInerney then tries to capture in his story of two Manhattan couples teetering on the brink of change when 9/11 happens. It is also what Ken Kalfus tries to catch in *A Disorder Peculiar to the Country*, particularly in his registering of the odd – almost obscene, on the face of it – response of one of his characters, Joyce, to the destruction of the Twin Towers, both during and after the event. "She covered the lower part of her face," when she is told about the collapse of the south tower. What she feels "erupt inside her," is "something warm, very much like, yes it was, a pang of pleasure, so intense it was nearly like the appeasement of hunger. It was a giddiness, an elation" (3). This elation, or exhilaration, has a partial if humanly speaking unacceptable explanation in the fact that her husband has an office in the south tower and they are at marital war with each other. But the explanation is, to say the least, partial. After the event, we learn, Joyce engages in casual liaisons. "They called it terror sex. Everyone needed something new, some release or payback or just acknowledgement that their lives had changed" (22–3).

Sex, love, the public and the private – and art and economics. Everything has changed, according to those writers who have offered preliminary testimony to 9/11 and its aftermath, from the material fabric of our lives to our terms of consciousness. For Wendell Berry, the changes press down on our need to shake off the illusions of late capitalism. "The time will soon come," he writes at the beginning of *In the Presence of Fear*,

> when we will not be able to remember the horrors of September 11 without remembering also the unquestioning technological and economic optimism that ended that day (1).

"This optimism," he goes on,

> rested on the proposition that we were living in a "new world order" and a "new economy" that would "grow" on and on, bringing a prosperity of which every new increment would be "unprecedented" (1).

For Berry, at least, trauma has led to intellectual clarity. We have a choice generated by a dreadful historical eruption. "We can," as he puts it,

> continue to promote a global economic system of unlimited "free trade" among corporations, held together by long and highly vulnerable lines of communication and supply, but *now* recognizing that such a system will have to be protected by a hugely expensive police-force that will be world-wide (4).

Alternatively,

> we can promote a decentralized world economy which would have the aim of assuring to every nation and region a *local* self-sufficiency in life-supporting goods (4).

Berry's alternatives are etched out with force and clarity here, as in all his work: a "total" or a "local" economy (*Art of the Commonplace*, 259), "competition" or "interdependence" (*Unsettling of America*, 47), "ownership" of the earth or "stewardship" (*Gift of Good Land*, 275, 280), the "global village" or the "village as globe" (*Standing by Words*, 61). *In the Presence of Fear* was written and published before the Bush administration had made, or at least publicly announced, their choice.

But that only adds to our sense of the prescience of this small book, and to the irony of such phrases as "a hugely expensive police force that will be world-wide." Because Berry chose the distance offered by reasonably dispassionate (if highly committed) economic and social analysis, he achieved an unusual transparency of vision and statement. He eschewed the opportunity of an imaginative encounter with the disasters of the past few years in favour of discursive argument. This came at a cost; there is not the immersion, the intimacy of experience that comes from literary testimony. But what that buys is the lucidity of witness. There is little sense here of what it is humanly like to encounter trauma. Equally, though, there is none of the confusion of feeling, the groping after a language with which to say the unsayable that characterizes much of the fiction devoted to the new forms of terror. Trauma, as one theorist of the subject has put it, is "a mind-blowing experience that destroys a conventional mind-set and compels (or makes possible) a new worldview" (Farrell, 19). Recognition that the old mind-set has been destroyed, or at least seriously challenged, is widespread in recent literature. Not all of it, however, manages to take the fictional measure of the new world view.

Another way of putting this is to borrow an observation from Georg Lukacs, that the trouble with immediacy is precisely that it lacks mediation (*Meaning of Contemporary Realism*, 19–22). What we are left with is symptom: in this case, the registering that *something* traumatic – perhaps too dreadful for words, unsusceptible as yet to understanding – has happened. *Falling Man* is beautifully structured, playing with images announced by the title that are no less resonant for being obvious. But the structure is too clearly foregrounded, the style excessively mannered; and the characters fall into postures of survival after 9/11 that are too familiar to invite much more than a gesture of recognition from the reader. Here, for instance, is one character falling back on the game of poker as his refuge:

> The money mattered but not so much. The game mattered, the touch of felt beneath the hands, the way the dealer burnt one card, dealt the next. He wasn't playing for the money. He was playing for the chips. The value of each chip had only hazy meaning. It was the disk itself

that mattered, the color itself. There was the laughing man at the far end of the room. There was the fact that they would all be dead one day. He wanted to rake in chips and stack them. The game mattered, the stacking of chips, the eye count, the play and dance of hand and eye. He was identical with these things (DeLillo, 228).

This is not the hysteria, the barely expressible disruption of the nervous system to which both Kalfus and McInerney allude. It is another form of emotional numbness. And the trouble is that the prose is similarly, symptomatically numb. The insistent repetition never gets us beyond the obvious, as outlined in the first two sentences here. One critic has suggested that *Falling Man* "sets itself the task of articulating" the condition of melancholia: that condition which Freud identified as one of emotional isolation and inertia (Versluys, 20). But it would surely be more accurate to say that the novel is immured in the melancholic state, offering a verbal equivalent of immobility, that it is symptom rather than diagnosis. The sense of *déjà vu* that both this passage and the novel as a whole inspire only compounds the problem. This account of a gambler seeking shelter from the storm in the simple rituals of cardplay lacks – to name just two writers being echoed here – both the passionate intensity of Dostoevsky and the cold eye of Joan Didion. Elsewhere, another character in *Falling Man* turns to the rituals of religion, falling prey to the will to believe in a way that Wallace Stevens would surely have understood. "She didn't believe this, the transubstantiation," we are told, "but believed something, half fearing it would take her over" (233): a compulsion that seems almost openly to recall Wallace Stevens's claim that the "final belief" is to believe in a fiction "which you know to be a fiction, there being nothing else" (*Opus Posthumous*, 163). The allusiveness is not a problem in itself, of course. What is a problem, however, is that this – the game as sanctuary, the willing suspension of disbelief – adds next to nothing to our understanding of the trauma at the heart of the action. In fact, it evades that trauma, it suppresses its urgency and disguises its difference by inserting it in a series of familiar tropes.

Towards the end of another novel set in Manhattan in the early years of the twenty-first century, *The Emperor's Children* by Claire

Messud, a character looks at the cover of a new magazine that was his brainchild. It is the projected first issue, now scuppered, as in fact the whole project is, by the terrible events of September 11. "Already with its vermilion, orange, and yellow graphic, a sunburst, a remarkable photograph of a sunburst," the narrator observes,

> the idea having been that they were exploding upon the scene, illuminating truths, and different, down to the images, from the rest; already it looked out of date and faintly forlorn, like some child's abandoned artwork (504).

It does not take a particularly subtle or intensive reading of this passage to see it as an act of recognition: that the old world has been turned upside down, altered ineradicably and the old literary forms and compulsions consequently made to look "forlorn," immature and obsolete. The reader is possibly reminded of James's claim, in his book on Hawthorne, that the Civil War "marks an era in the history of the American mind." "It introduced into the national consciousness a certain sense of proportion and relation," James explained, "of the world being a more complicated place than it had hitherto seemed, the future more treacherous, success more difficult... the good American, in days to come, will be a more critical person than his complacent and confident grandfather. He has eaten of the tree of knowledge" (135).

To that extent, what we have here is that recurrent rhythm in the cultural history of the United State mentioned in the first chapter, linking the national fate, at moments of crisis, with notions of innocence and the fall into a deeper self-consciousness, a darker knowledge. To point out that it is recurrent, however, is not to deny its significance. New events generate new forms of consciousness requiring new structures of ideology and the imagination to assimilate and express them: that is the intellectual equation at work here. And it begs the question of just how new, or at least different, the structures of some of these books are. The answer is, for the most part, not at all.

This is not an argument for simple change, always supposing such a thing were possible. What it is an argument for, though, is enactment of difference: not only the capacity to recognize that some kind of alteration of imaginative structures is required to register the contemporary crisis, to offer testimony to the trauma of 9/11 and its consequences, but also the ability and willingness imaginatively to act on that recognition. "Every age reaccentuates in its own way the works of its immediate past" (421) Bakhtin observed; and what is required by recent events, surely, is at the very least a radical reaccentuation. A book like *The Emperor's Children* may acknowledge this, by suggesting how "forlorn" texts written prior to the crisis appear to be. But it does not enact it. The irony is that, relying on a familiar romance pattern – in which couples meet, romantic and domestic problems follow, to be concluded in reconciliation or rupture – books like this, and, for that matter, *The Good Life, A Disorder Peculiar to the Country* and *Falling Man*, simply assimilate the unfamiliar into familiar structures. The crisis is, in every sense of the word, domesticated. "All life had become public," that observation made by a central character in *Falling Man* is not underwritten by the novel in which it occurs, nor in any of these novels. On the contrary, all life here is personal; cataclysmic public events are measured purely and simply in terms of their impact on the emotional entanglements of their protagonists. In the early years of the American republic, Alexis de Tocqueville warned of the dangers of a cultural condition in which, as he put it, "each citizen… generally spends his time considering the interests of a very insignificant person, namely himself" (627). In a situation where "all a man's interests are limited to those near himself," he suggested, "folk… form the habit of thinking of themselves in isolation and imagine that their whole destiny is in their hands" (653–4). If anyone "does raise his eyes higher," all they see is either "the huge apparition of society or the even larger form of the human race." They have "nothing between very limited and clear ideas and very general and vague conceptions; the space in between is empty" (627). For all the limitations of his vision, Tocqueville hit on a point that is pertinent here, since many of the texts that try to bear witness to contemporary events vacillate in just this way between large rhetorical gestures acknowledging trauma and retreat into domestic detail. The link between the two is tenuous, reducing a turning point in national and international history to little more than a stage in a sentimental education.

In another post-9/11 novel, *The Writing on the Wall* (2005) by Lynne Sharon Schwartz, there appears to be a suspicion that the turn towards the domestic may have come as a result of the perceived corruption of the public sphere, in the wake of the "war on terror." But that suspicion only leads eventually to a deliberate rejection of the public domain. The title of the novels refers to the walls of homemade posters from people seeking information about missing loved ones after 9/11 that appeared in various parts of New York. At one point, the protagonist, Renata, a linguist working at New York Public Library, is waiting for a friend in downtown Manhattan. The friend is "predictably late," and so, the reader is told,

> there's plenty of time … to study the south entrance to St. Vincent's Hospital, which has become a kind of wailing wall plastered with photos of the disappeared, the *desaparecidos*, ordinary home photos, nothing arty … along with their descriptions and *marcas corporals* … If the televised images of suited pundits have been oppressive, these notices are an antidote, so much more eloquent than the public words: hunt them in their caves, the full resources of our law-enforcement agencies, all necessary security precautions, a monumental struggle. These words – mastectomy scar, left eye turned in, feathery salt-and-pepper hair, shamrock tattoo on left buttock – scar the eyes. (147)

The subtlety of this reflection is that, while drawing a clear line between the words of the private sphere, which "scar the eyes," and the words of the public, the cant of the political administration and the media, it recognizes, through its allusions to the disputed political territory of the Middle East ("wailing wall") and Latin America ("*desaparecidos*"), the inescapability of the public realm. There is a similar recognition, elsewhere in the novel, that matters that once appeared important before 9/11 now "seem eons away, lost in pre-history" (279), as if what has occurred might involve a fall away from the "prehistoric" (145) into the awful responsibility of historical time. Such recognitions fade in the course of the narrative, however. By the final pages, Renata has achieved a tentative resolution of her emotional troubles by reuniting with her boyfriend Jack. "Nothing can ever be the way it was," she tells Jack. "You mean the world can never be the same?"

he asks. "He can be so dense, it makes her laugh," Renata thinks, then adds, "I wan't thinking on a global scale" (295). As if to underline the retreat into the domestic, Renata uses her linguistic skills in these final moments of the novel to address her boyfriend "in flawed Arabic." What she says to Jack, in such a politically charged language, makes no attempt to weave the personal and the political together, however. On the contrary, Arabic becomes the idiom of a retreat into romantic love. "Make me love you again," she tells Jack, in a language he does not understand, before putting her arm through his "for warmth" (295). "There is a connection between the public and the private," the reader is informed just before this closing exchange, "but Renata knows that this connection, just now, is merely a distraction" (294). That observation could act as an epigraph to so many of these novels of reified domesticity; *The Writing on the Wall*, it turns out, is unusual only in making the turn towards the domestic so explicit and emphatic.

A further measure of the limitations of these texts is their encounters with strangeness. With the collapse of communism, a sinister other that enabled American self-definition may have disappeared. It is a truism, however, to say that it has now been replaced by Islam. Facing the other, in all its difference and danger, is surely one of the challenges now for writers: not just because of obscene acts of terrorism committed by a small group of people but because the United States has become, more than ever, a border territory in which different cultures meet, collide and in some instances collude with each other. There is the threat of the terrorist; there is also the fact of a world that is liminal, a proliferating chain of borders, where familiar oppositions – civilized and savage, town and wilderness, "them" and "us" – are continually being challenged, dissolved and reconfigured. Many writers respond to the bigger picture, the United States as cultural borderlands, and register it in their writing: among them, Deborah Eisenberg, Mohsin Hamid, Rattawut Lapcharoensap, Cormac McCarthy and other writers who will be looked at later. When it comes to encountering the enemy, though, a kind of imaginative paralysis tends to set in, to immobilize many texts. Perhaps it is too soon, "The events of September 11, 2001, were so overwhelming," begins a brochure accompanying the exhibit "Aftermath: Photography in the Wake of September 11," "that more than four months after the fact, we are still struggling to explain and comprehend their meaning" (Lubin, "Masked Power," 124). Perhaps more time is needed, by many writers and other artists, to "comprehend," to "explain" or at least piece the fragments together. Whatever the reason writers as accomplished as John Updike and Don DeLillo (who admitted, immediately after the event, "this was so vast and terrible that it was outside imagining.... We could not catch up to it" (DeLillo, *In the Ruins of the Future*, 39)) hardly seem to scratch the surface.

Here, for example, is how John Updike introduces the reader to Ahmad, the central character in *Terrorist*,

> *Devils,* Ahmad thinks. *These devils seek to take away my God.* All day long, at Central High School, girls sway and sneer and expose their soft bodies and alluring hair. Their bare bellies, adorned with shining navel studs and low-down purple tattoos, ask, *What else is there to see?* Boys strut and saunter along and look dead-eyed, indicating with their edgy killer gestures and careless scornful laughs that this world is all there is – a noisy varnished hall lined with metal lockers and having at its end a blank wall desecrated by graffiti and roller-painted over so often it feels to be coming closer by millimetres (3).

This is brilliantly conceived. Updike uses his own undoubted distaste for the secular temper of contemporary America and a world of commodities as a kind of bridge: a way of assuming the vision of a young Arab-American boy. The banality, the casual sexuality of the girls and aggressive indifference of the boys, the sense of everything closing in: the threat here is not in Ahmad but in the world that seems to challenge and imprison him. Updike captures this: the sense, not merely of not belonging but of not feeling safe, of fearing that the world he inhabits is eating away at the very core of his belief and his self. "Islam is less a faith," we are told later in the novel, "than a habit, a facet" of the condition of young Arab-Americans like Ahmad: men and women who constitute "an underclass, alien in a nation that persists in thinking of itself as light-skinned, English-speaking, and Christian" (244).

33

Ahmad, in short, is "an outsider among outsiders," dwelling in an "underworld" (244) that middle America chooses not only not to value but not even to see. To that extent, he is a familiar, iconic figure in American literature, with such notable predecessors as Richard Wright's Bigger Thomas and Ralph Ellison's invisible man. To mention those particular literary antecedents, however, is to suggest the limits to Updike's testimony. Ahmad remains an outsider, not merely to those around him but also to the reader. We never get further than this: Ahmad's resistance to a world he never made and his consequent, confused search for a way of hitting back at that world. In both *Native Son* and *Invisible Man*, an emotional engagement that makes the prose sometimes seem to palpitate with fear is underwritten by passionate analytical insight; there is dramatic immediacy but it is rhetorically and structurally framed. In *Terrorist*, by contrast, there is neither the same degree of imaginative involvement, getting inside the skin of the victim, nor anything like a similar measure of argumentative mediation, the witnessing or explanatory piecing together of personal or cultural motive. Quite simply, this brave attempt to imagine the other never really fits together as a meaningful story.

The determining feature of trauma is that it is unsayable. What is traumatic is defined by what Caruth has called "the impossibility of ... direct access" (*Explorations in Memory*, 4). So perhaps one way to tell a story that cannot be told is to tell it aslant, to approach it by stealth. This is the strategy of Cormac McCarthy's *The Road. The Road* is Cormac McCarthy's tenth novel. It is also the first of his novels to be met with almost unanimous critical acclaim. Those who were less than impressed with his ninth novel, *No Country for Old Men*, greeted it with something pretty close to relief. Others – and these are so far in the majority among critics of *The Road* – have focused their attention, and their admiration, on what has been seen as a return to stylistic form and a return to the overwhelming questions that haunt so much of McCarthy's earlier work. In a time of literary minimalism, when so many writers seem intent on pursuing a style of scrupulous meanness, McCarthy reverted in *The Road* to the rich and even baroque rhetoric of his novels *Suttree* and *Blood Meridian*. And at a moment when the notion of a grand narrative has been dismissed and deconstructed,

McCarthy chose to continue his search in *The Road* for some answer to the overwhelming questions of life, death, meaning, and nothingness, and to address those questions in what one critic of the novel has termed "a thought and feeling experiment, bleak, exhilarating (in fact endurable) only because of its integrity, its wholeness of seeing" (Mars-Jones, 19). Like all novels – if we are to believe Bahktin – *The Road* is a curious hybrid. It is, like all McCarthy's fiction, haunted by the lives and writings of others, it is densely allusive and yet it is unmistakably the work of a fiercely original writer, swimming against the tide of literary fashion. It has the elemental quality of allegory and myth but also addresses issues that are ferociously contemporary, specific to the here and now. It declares the imminence, and perhaps the inevitability, of entropy, a world running down to inertia and oblivion, but it also offers a testament of faith in the will to meaning, the possibility of human intimacy and the simple, inextinguishable desire of the human animal to go on.

To take the allusiveness first: McCarthy has never made any secret of just how deeply intertextual he takes all texts, including his own, to be. "The ugly fact is that books are made out of other books," he declared once in a rare interview. "The novel depends for its life on other novels that have been written" (Woodward, 36). One critic has called McCarthy "a literary hybrid" (Ragan, 15). Another has remarked that reading one of McCarthy's novels is "like strolling through a museum of English prose styles;" adding that the border trilogy appears to have been written "by the illegitimate offspring of Zane Grey and Flannery O'Connor" (Pilkington, 312, 318). There is a hint of criticism here, a sly suggestion that something is not quite right with a book that is a forest of allusion. Some commentators have gone beyond hinting and openly expressed offence. "Should a novel be quite so reminiscent of other novels as this one is?" one clearly exasperated reviewer asked of *All the Pretty Horses* (Doody, 20). But such uneasiness or exasperation is surely beside the point. As a matter of principle, all literature is intertextual. McCarthy knows this. So, for that matter, do such otherwise different writers as Joseph Brodsky and Wendell Berry. "All good human work remembers its history," Berry has pointed out. "The best writing, even when printed, is full of intimations that

it is the present version of earlier versions of itself... it is a palimps-
est" (Berry, *Standing by Words*, 192). "A good poet," observes Brodsky,
"does not avoid influence or continuity but frequently nurtures them,
and emphasizes them in every possible way.... Fear of influence, fear
of dependence, is the fear – the affliction – of a savage, but not of
culture, which is all continuity, all echo" (Brodsky, 184). What matters
is not the fact of dialogue between texts, since that is unavoidable, but
the quality of that dialogue: what a writer adds to the existing monuments of literature, to use an Eliotic image, how he reaccentuates the
voices of his literary forebears in echoing them.

And McCarthy certainly, and decisively, reaccentuates the voices
of his literary ancestors in *The Road*. The novel describes the journey of two people, a father and son, "moving south" across a bleak,
devastated and sparsely populated landscape because, as the father
realizes, "There'd be no surviving another winter here" (4) where
they begin their long trek. The structure of the narrative, a continuous series of discrete paragraphs undivided into chapters or sections,
clearly repeats the rhythm of the journey, a series of short stages
moving towards something like a destination. This recasts one of the
iconic images of American literature, the journey. What the reader
is confronted with here is not the open road of, say, Walt Whitman,
John Steinbeck, or Jack Kerouac, but a route and a landscape on the
point of vanishing. The journey here is not a linear progress, from
the East to the West, a liberatory flight from the old to the new
as in the classic American Western. It is a turning back, from the
North to the South, across an unobstructed space that triggers, not
a sense of freedom but a feeling of empty immensity. This is a landscape that denies definition, distinction; and it gives the sense that
beyond the indeterminacy and vacancy of the immediate surrounds,
the grey wastes that confront father and son in the course of their
travels, there is only more vacancy, more empty space. The echoes of
Eliot, and of McCarthy's own earlier work, are inescapable here. The
world has become a waste land. That image of the waste land recurs
throughout McCarthy's earlier novels – in, say, his account of the
"neuter austerity" (247) of the American West in *Blood Meridian* and
his description of "the ancient road" across "mineral waste" (4) that

the protagonist of *All the Pretty Horses* traverses. But it is reasserted more insistently and more powerfully than ever before here. *The Road* is set in some strange, post-apocalyptic landscape. There are no birds or animals left alive. Most of the trees and many of the buildings have been destroyed, burned to extinction. And the air is filled with ash, requiring those who survive to wear face masks so as to filter the noxious air they breathe. Ash is everywhere – this is F. Scott Fitzgerald's Valley of Ashes universalized; ash is there at all times, even when it rains – as it does with great frequency. The foliage surrounding father and son "turned to dust about them" (10), we are told. Ashes, dust, and death are ubiquitous as the few human presences left on this darkling plain witness the death of both nature and culture. The reader is reminded, perhaps, not only of the T.S. Eliot poem but of the Christian funeral service that Eliot himself was echoing – although, in this case, there is no hope of recovery or resurrection.

"He ... looked out over the wasted landscape," the narrator observes of the father, the protagonist of *The Road* at one point. What he sees is a world denied the possibility of survival or redemption. There is "no sign of life" (9) here. The land, covered in ash, is grey and barren; the foliage, what remains of it, is "black and twisted" (9); the houses, what remain of them, are empty of everything but "trash in the floor, old newsprint," (18) appliances that no longer work, and furniture and fittings that are unused and falling apart. And "on the outskirts of a city," we learn, father and son come upon this:

> a supermarket. A few old cars in the trashstrewn parking lot. ... In the produce section in the bottom of the bins they found a few ancient runner beans and what looked to have once been apricots, long dried to wrinkled effigies of themselves .... In the alleyway behind the store a few shopping carts, all badly rusted. ... By the door were two softdrink machines that had been tilted over into the floor and opened with a prybar. Coins everywhere in the ash. He sat and ran his hand around the works of the gutted machines and in the second one it closed over a cold metal cylinder. He withdrew his hand slowly and sat looking at a Coca Cola. (19)

What McCarthy transmutes Eliot's *Waste Land* into is a demythologized, dystopic space that is at once America after the fall and our world, wherever it may be, after the collapse from globalism into barbarism. The supermarket evacuated of goods and customers becomes here a paradigm of a depopulated America that enjoys no myth, no narrative, no context, a place where signs carry advertisements for products that are not only gone but mostly forgotten ("What is it, Papa?" the son asks, when the father shows him the Coca Cola retrieved from the gutted machine). In an earlier novel like *The Crossing*, McCarthy's travelers encounter ruined churches and failed priests. In *The Road*, they meet with a ruined monument to consumption, which is a measure of the transformation of the world from exchange into entropy. What is at stake here is not so much loss of faith but loss of function; there is not only no apparent spiritual meaning in this particular waste land, there is no discernible meaning or purpose of any kind. This is a world that makes no sense, because the connections have gone and the signs no longer signify. The supermarket trolley is now used by the father and son to carry their few remaining possessions; the road is not so much one of the last vestiges of civilization as a place where small armies march searching for the last few humans who have not been enslaved or eaten; books lie wet and rotting on library shelves; the map the father carries has been shredded into leaves. The small bits of narrative that are retained are runic – tattoos of spiders, skulls etched with paint, patterns of rock left by the roadside. Father and son have no name; they are mostly "the man" and "the boy." Nor do any other of the characters they encounter – apart from the nearly blind, cane carrying "Ely," who, it turns out, is a chronic liar. If any of the old narratives that used to make sense of people's lives are recalled in *The Road* at all, they are recalled only to be subverted, flattened out into an absence of meaning. So Ely, in a sly reversal of Biblical narrative, takes the anti-prophetic course of declaring that God does not exist; advertisements, where they survive, are scrawled over with new messages warning of danger and imminent death; and an antebellum Southern home that father and son enter at one point turns out to have a locked basement full of human beings kept as food. The son in *The Road* has no memory of the world before it was laid waste; the father has. But both are equally trapped in the vacancy of the present. This is a fictional landscape imbued with a sense of total and irrevocable loss, inscribing what it might be like to live after the fall.

For the reader this raises the question of what kind of fall has occurred. Many reviewers of the book referred to the setting of *The Road* as post-nuclear. It is easy to see why. A passage like the following, describing a past moment dredged up from the father's memory, appears to describe a nuclear attack:

> The clocks stopped at 1:17. A long shear of light and then a series of low concussions. He got up and went to the window. What is it? she said. He didn't answer. He went into the bathroom and threw the lightswitch but the power was already gone. A dull rose glow in the windowglass. (45)

The disaster that has visited this landscape is much more generalized, however, more allegorized than this passage read in isolation might suggest; and the general contours of the landscape through which father and son travel are those, after all, of surreal nightmare – a variation, not only on the Eliotic waste land, but also on the darkness visible in the poetry of Dante and Milton and the prose of Celine. More prosaically, there are no signs of radioactivity, and none of the characters suffer from radiation sickness. The "event" that has reduced the United States – and, it is intimated, the rest of the world – to this deathly state remains resolutely unexplained. This might be the world after a nuclear holocaust, or it might not be. Some other event might have turned the world to dust. The point is that McCarthy both says and remains silent. The unnamable remains unnamed, except in its human consequences.

The reason for this indeterminacy is simple. McCarthy is dealing with trauma; and, in the first instance, with trauma of a very immediate kind. It is surely right to see *The Road* as a post-9/11 novel, not just in the obvious, literal sense, but to the extent that it takes the measure of that sense of crisis that has seemed to haunt the West, and the United States in particular, ever since the destruction of the World Trade Center. And whereas writers like DeLillo, Kalfus, McInerney, Messud, and Schwartz try to domesticate, to shepherd that sense of crisis into the realms of the familiar, McCarthy's alternative strategy in *The Road* is not to domesticate but to defamiliarize. His way of telling a story that cannot but has to be told is to approach it by circuitous means, by indirection. He translates trauma into a narrative memory that captures what it is like to live after the fall with the exactitude yet also the elusiveness of symbolism. A symbol, Carl Jung once suggested, is "the best possible expression of a relatively *unknown* fact" (Gray, 137). If that is so, then *The Road* is a symbolic narrative, a powerful but also slippery tale of something, some trauma that seems to resist telling. That same slipperiness is at work in the staple idiom and even the setting of the book. Spare, even skeletal descriptions lead up to closing passages that are rhetorically and intellectually daring; the narrative voice, at first sight, appears to be the voice of the main character, the father, but as the flow of thought and speech continues, that voice seems to segue into that of the author. So, echoing William Faulkner here, McCarthy manages to imbue the text with a sense of his own presence without deviating noticeably from a technique designed to suppress it:

> He tried to think of something to say but he could not. He'd had this feeling before, beyond the numbness and the dull despair. The world shrinking down about a raw core of parsible entities. The names of things slowly following those things into oblivion. Colors. The names of birds. Things to eat. Finally the names of things one believed to be true. More fragile than he would have thought. How much was gone already? The sacred idiom shorn of its referents and so of its reality. Drawing down like something trying to preserve heat. In time to wink out forever. (75)

A passage like this inscribes language as presence and absence – a presence made the dearer now by being only in memory, an absence made all the more harrowing as the world to which it gestures inexorably deteriorates, shrinks "down about a raw core." The author is, equally and analogously, there and not there, slipping through the verbal interstices. And a similar ghostliness or elusiveness typifies the world through which McCarthy's travellers make their way. At the beginning of the novel, for example, father and son are in an area of woods and mountains where the winters are too bitter to survive without shelter. As the two make their way south they encounter the remains of a dam, "a log barn in a field with an advertisement in faded ten-foot letters across the roofslope. See Rock City" (18); and "in the foothills of the eastern mountains" they journey across, father and son wake one morning to hear something coming. "The ground was trembling. It was an earthquake" (81–82). This is a landscape of nightmare, certainly, but it is also perhaps East Tennessee, the author's Appalachian birthplace. The journey down from the mountains occurs in a border territory, between substantial fact and surreal dream, where the author can negotiate fear. This is a map of that sense of dread, generated in the Western consciousness by 9/11, and its aftermath, which is precise in both its geographical and mental coordinates because it refuses the easy option of the immediate.

The intertextuality that is such a deep-rooted feature of McCarthy's work adds to our sense of the text as a border country. The voice of the author overlaps with the inner voice of the protagonist and in turn, the voices of McCarthy's literary forebears bleed into them; a vocal subtext resonates below the surface text, adding further dimensions of meaning. In effect, allusion becomes a form of mediation, a means of layering the narrative, catching its drift or tenor but in a nuanced, partly hidden and quietly indirect way. *The Road* brims with significances that are only partially or tentatively disclosed because, among other strategies, the echoes of other writers act both to place and displace understanding. The echoes of Eliot are there not to pin down meaning but to multiply its possibilities. This is a waste land that is determinate to the extent that it is the consequence of some disaster. But the disaster remains unlocated, and almost seems to be part of the nature of things: reminding us of what one critic said of all McCarthy's novels – that they appear to be a series of meditations on the unhomelike nature of our environment, the "scary disconnection of the human from the not-human that both Freud and Heidegger called the *unheimlich*" (Bell, 33). The narrative certainly invites us, as I

41

have suggested, to historicize its meanings, to connect it to that fear and sense of impotence that haunts the United States, and perhaps the West, in the early years of the twenty-first century. But it also compels us, through the multiple signification of the image of the waste land, to measure the gap that has perhaps always existed between the grounds of our existence and human acts and ceremonies; we are slipped the suggestion that to be human is, and always has been, to be stray and sightless, trapped in a landscape that is there in its bleak surfaces and yet not there in its deeper significances – abruptly at hand but also unseen. "We live in a world that is not our own, and, much more, not ourselves/ And hard it is in spite of the blazoned days" (Stevens, *Collected Poems*, 383): those lines of Wallace Stevens also seem to be echoed here in *The Road*, as in so much of McCarthy's earlier fiction, reminding us that it gestures towards both the historically specific – the world after 9/11 – and to the elemental and general – the world, and the human condition at any given time. This is a historical work, albeit of a peculiarly symbolic, deeply mediated kind, but also a metaphysical one – or, to be more accurate, an argument against metaphysics.

Eliot's account of the waste land concludes, famously, with an attempt to shore some fragments from the ruins of culture and a desperate gesture towards the distant possibility of faith. McCarthy's conclusions, the fragments he shores against the ruins, are rather different. There is, first, the redemptive nature of craft, doing a task and doing it carefully and well. At one point, for instance, the father tries to repair the wheel mount of the supermarket trolley that carries their few possessions:

> They collected some old boxes and built a fire in the floor and he found some tools and emptied out the cart and sat working on the wheel. He pulled the bolt and bored out the collet with a hand drill and resleeved it with a section of pipe he'd cut to length with a hacksaw. Then he bolted it all back together and stood the cart upright and wheeled it around the floor. It ran fairly true. The boy sat watching everything. (14)

Detailed, scrupulously attentive descriptions of work, activities requiring patience and skill, occur in all McCarthy's novels. They provide a still point in the turning, tumultuous world that his characters inhabit. And the echoes multiply beyond the author's own earlier texts here. The care, the precision with which the actions of the father are described echoes the care taken with the actions themselves. The father is absorbed in this moment and this activity; so is the prose and so, as a consequence, is the reader. And the precision and attentiveness of action and style echo, in turn, other, earlier moments in works by McCarthy's literary forefathers (and they are nearly all fore*fathers* here): the description of the crew working on riveting and repair to the vessel in Joseph Conrad's *Heart of Darkness* (1902), the devotion of Nick Adams to the duties of the wilderness in Ernest Hemingway's *In Our Time* (1925), Cash Bundren's loving account of the process of building a coffin for his mother in William Faulkner's *As I Lay Dying* (1930). Skill does not offer redemption for father and son in *The Road*, but it provides a temporary shelter, a moment of almost ritualistic relief. The layering, the series of echoes here, within and beyond the text, supply a richly mediated portrait of work as, if not salvation, then as a place of safety, a temporary stay against confusion.

"The Fire Sermon," the third section of *The Waste Land*, concludes with lines that appear to resonate throughout *The Road*:

> Burning burning burning burning
> O Lord Thou pluckest me out
> O Lord thou pluckest
> burning (Eliot, 72)

The allusions, as many commentators on the poem have observed, are to Buddha and St Augustine, both of whom characterized lust of the flesh as a burning fire. St Augustine in his *Confessions* singled out the eyes as filters to evil and rejoiced that God would pluck him from the snare they spread; Buddha gestured towards the prospect of all things burning free of desire with the result that the process of reincarnation would be exhausted. Fire in *The Waste Land*, as in the texts it echoes, is an agent of destruction but also of creation; it is a negative force, certainly, and at the same time a purgative and even redemptive one. Playing on this dense texture of allusion, McCarthy pursues a similar ambivalence. Fire destroys, in the post-apocalyptic landscapes of *The Road*, certainly. There is the body of a man struck by lightning that father and son encounter early on in the novel, "as burntlooking as the country, his clothing scorched and black." "One of his eyes was black," we are told, "his hair was but a nitty wig of ash upon his blackened skull" (42). There is the "burntlooking" landscape itself, where "the ashes of the late world" are "carried on the bleak and temporal winds to and fro in the void" (9–10). But fire also creates – or, if not that exactly, it offers another refuge: not the saving graces of occupation, care and craft, but the comforting hope of continuity, survival.

At several points in *The Road*, father and son comfort each other with the thought that, together, they are "carrying the fire." The reassurance they seem to gain from this is palpable, but it is not until towards the end of the novel that what they understand by this becomes clear. "I want to be with you," the son exclaims. "You cant," the father replies,

> You cant. You have to carry the fire.
> I don't know how to.
> Yes, you do.
> Is it real? The fire?
> Yes it is.
> Where is it? I don't know where it is.
> Yes you do. It's inside you. It was always there. I can see it. (234)

This fire is certainly "real" at certain moments in the narrative: when, for instance, father and son light an oil lamp found in a deserted and derelict yard. The lighting of the lamp, described in meticulous detail, is another moment of ritualistic and redemptive labor; and the lamp itself offers a literal if feeble defense against a gradually darkening world. But beyond these intimations of the saving grace of craft, and this literal dimension, there is a further, symbolic layering at work here. The resonances that the image of fire possesses – in the lighting of the fire, the carrying of the fire – recall other, earlier writers from Shakespeare ("How far that little candle throws its beams!/ So shines

44

a good deed in a naughty world" (*The Merchant of Venice*, Act V, scene i))
to Wallace Stevens. And it is in this typically, densely allusive way that
it offers not redemption, but relief.

Stevens is perhaps the closest echo here, if we are trying to identify what carrying the fire or lighting the fire might suggest or
promise. Eliot, with the tropes of fire and burning, reaches out
towards the possibility of salvation; Buddha and St Augustine, using
the same tropes, turn possibility into promise. What McCarthy
alerts us to is quite different: the chance, not of being saved, but
of surviving. Fire in *The Road* articulates no more, and no less,
than the sense of an innate human vitality, an ardency of heart, the
simple, fundamental continuation of the spark of life in a world
that otherwise seems irretrievably lost and dead. Here, McCarthy
seems to be echoing something like these lines from one of Wallace
Stevens's most famous and notable poems, "Final Soliloquy of the
Interior Paramour":

> How high that highest candle lights the dark.
> Out of this same light, out of the central mind,
> We make a dwelling in the evening air,
> In which being there together is enough. (Stevens, 524.)

Lines like these seem to echo, in turn, that moment in *King Lear* when
the mad king finds temporary refuge from the storm in a bare, fire-lit
hovel on a blasted heath. The layering of textual allusion here, back
from McCarthy through Stevens to Shakespeare, invites us to find –
not safety, still less salvation – but sufficiency in the simple human acts
of hanging on and hanging together, passing on and passing around
the will to live.

Craft, continuity, community are what, for the most part, is "enough"
in *The Road*: a source of light, however flickering and fragile, in an
irreversibly dark world. That is, until the end of the narrative; then,
something curious happens. The father dies. The boy stays for three
days by his "cold and stiff" body. Then, setting out again on the road,
the boy encounters a figure that looks and sounds as if he had stepped
out of legend:

The man that hove into view… was dressed in a gray and yellow ski
parka. He carried a shotgun upside down over his shoulder on a
braided leather lanyard and he wore a nylon bandolier filled with shells
for the gun. A veteran of old skirmishes, bearded, scarred across his
cheek and the bone stoven and the one eye wandering. (237)

The man assures the boy, "I'm one of the good guys," tells him that
he has "a little boy" and "a little girl" (the boy, he adds, is "about
your age. Maybe a little older." (239)), and promises that he and his
family "don't eat people." The man then takes the boy into the woods,
where his family is sheltering; there the boy is greeted with warmth
and affection by a woman, the wife and mother in this small, nuclear
family. "Oh," she tells the boy, "I am so glad to see you" (241). After
this initial meeting, the woman, we are told, "would talk" to the boy
"sometimes about God." The young man confesses that, when "he
tried to talk to God," he found that "the best thing was to talk to his
father." "The woman said that was all right," the narrator confides.
"She said that the breath of God was his breath yet though it pass
from man to man through all of time" (241).

What are we to make of this? It is possible that this is a bleaker
moment than it appears to be. There may be the intimation here that
humanity is about to start again along the same old road leading to
disaster – a spiraling upwards that will lead eventually to another spiraling downwards into apocalypse. There may even be the chance
that when the man reassures the boy, "we don't eat people" (239), he
is simply lying; cannibals, after all, are not given to announcing their
intentions. It is possible, but unlikely. The woman, after all, simply
puts the notion of continuity, so subtly articulated in the image of
fire, in a more emphatic and surely coarser register. She has the voice
of the great mother, calm, generous, and accepting:" "Oh… I am so
glad to see you." The man, in turn, is a reassuringly paternal figure;
with his weathered face, his assured carriage, the way he stands out
from his surroundings, his bluntness of manner, and breadth of personal experience, he also recalls any number of American heroes from
Natty Bumppo to Randle McMurphy or the characters played by

John Wayne. The family, with its "little boy" and "little girl," in their symmetry and the feelings of security they generate, seem to offer a way out, an emotional haven. It is as if, at this moment, McCarthy has withdrawn into the sheltering confines of American myth: a myth that is, in this case, a curious but not uncommon mix of the heroic and the domestic. The man is a reassuring blend of adventure and authority, the woman a source of inspiration and comfort; together, with their two children, they seem to rescue the boy from the dark passage of the road, taking him into the comforting womb of the woods and into the arms of an American form of the holy family. The whole novel could be seen, among other things, as a covert assault on American exceptionalism, but this moment temporarily drags the narrative back into the consolations of a separate and special national destiny. If this is an act of recuperation, and it certainly appears to be, then it does not work. On the contrary, it is deeply unconvincing – not least, because it is at odds with just about everything that has occurred in the novel before.

After the brief account of the several conversations that took place between the boy and the woman "about God," there is only one paragraph left in *The Road*. But it is a paragraph that returns us to the central narrative thrust of the novel, its richly mediated account of the harsh facts of the human condition and the humble shelters human beings try to construct to help them deal with or at least tolerate those facts. There is crisis here, in McCarthy's account of the unhomelike nature of the world, especially now: but there is also a sense of continuity in his gestures towards how human beings nevertheless try to build a home for themselves, or the illusion of a home, even now. "Once there were brook trout in the streams in the mountains," the narrator recalls:

They smelled of moss in your hand. Polished and muscular and torsional. On their backs were vermiculate patterns that were maps of the world in its becoming. Maps and mazes. Of a thing which could not be put back. Not be made right again. In the deep glens where they lived all things were older than man and they hummed of mystery. (241)

Characteristically, this could be a memory of the unnamed father or the elusive author or both. It hardly seems to matter. What matters is the series of tensions on which this passage, and the novel it concludes, are built: between the recognition of passing and the remembering of an ardent vitality; the specificity of a mapped and known world and the resonance of one that remains insubstantial, unknown, and unknowable; the acknowledgment of human insignificance and the assertion of at least the will to meaning. The rhythms of fall and possible recovery mark these concluding sentences, just as they leave their traces on the book they conclude; in doing so, they bear testimony to trauma but also intimate the chance of survival. That final phrase, "hummed with mystery," is a typically bold yoking together of the material and the insubstantial; the mysterious seems to take on, for a moment, bodily or at least vocal shape. McCarthy's strategies for dealing with the ghosts that haunt the twenty-first century, particularly in the West and especially in America, may not be startlingly new. Formally what is at work here, after all, is the Romantic belief in deferral (which accounts for the slipperiness of idiom), the Symbolist commitment to what Mallarme called "that part of speech which is not spoken" (21) ("the ideal is to suggest the object," Mallarme said, because it is the "perfect use of this mystery which constitutes the symbol" (38)) and the Modernist conviction that the use of what Frank Kermode called "the Image as radiant truth" might lead to the creation "out of a number of words" of "a single new word which is total in itself and foreign to language" (2, 43). But McCarthy has reworked those strategies to address contemporary pain, offering a realistic measure of its extraordinary scope, the sense of apocalypse that now seems to haunt the West, and in doing so neither to minimize that pain nor surrender to it. The experience and the knowledge flowing from it that McCarthy maps are potentially annihilating, defying speech. But McCarthy is not reduced to silence, neither do his characters surrender to despair or simply accept annihilation. In the process, *The Road* surely echoes, in its structure of feeling if not literally, Samuel Beckett's attempt to name *The Unnamable*: "I don't know, I'll never know, in the silence you don't know, you must go on, I can't go on, I'll go on" (418).

Saying and not saying. Dori Laub, a Holocaust survivor and a therapist and so no stranger to trauma, called 9/11 "a story in search of a voice" (Laub, 214). "We are still involved," she explained, "with the ongoing struggle between the imperative need to know what it is that happened to us all… and an unusually powerful urge not to know, a defensive will to deny the nature of the tear in the fabric of our lives" (204). "What is it called?" asks another observer, James Berger of 9/11. "Nothing adequate, nothing corresponding in language could stand for it;" nevertheless, "immediately people tried to name it" (Berger, 54), even if much of that naming assumed the form of the gestural ("the thing," "the event"), the coded ("9/11," "Ground Zero") or simple repetition – a repetition that, as Jacques Derrida pointed out in his meditation on 9/11, was simply a strategy for "neutralising, deadening, distancing a traumatism" (Borradori, 87) and denying powerlessness. This is the core, the key to the traumatic experience: it occupies the space between silence and speech, or, as one authority on trauma has put it, "between the will to deny horrible events and the will to proclaim them aloud" (Herman, 1). Traumatic events are "frozen and wordless" (Herman, 157), and yet they need to be articulated, released into language. The "hole in the real," to use Lacan's phrase (Stamelman, 15), a hole created by death and loss, needs to be filled, even if that simply takes the shape of words that inscribe absence, a language of gaps (the fallen towers), ghosts, and shadows (the fallen towers, the fallen dead). The contradiction at the heart of trauma, as far as speaking and not speaking it into knowledge is concerned, was memorably caught in a graphic book on the Holocaust, *The Complete Maus: A Survivor's Tale* by Art Spiegelman. During a conversation between his alter ego, Artie Spiegelman, and his psychiatrist, Pavel, the artist has Pavel, himself a Holocaust survivor, reflect that "the victims who died never tell THEIR story;" so, he adds, "maybe it's better not to have any more stories." "Uh-huh," Artie responds, "Samuel Beckett once said, "Every word is like a stain on silence and nothingness." The two speakers gaze at each other, in silence, in the next frame. Then, in the next, Artie blurts out, "On the other hand, he SAID it" (205). This is the contradiction, circling around the necessity and impossibility of saying, staining the silence that any writer imagining disaster has to confront: the challenge of turning the unspeakable into speech. "We do not know what we are talking about" (86), Derrida observed of 9/11 not long after it happened (Borradori, 86). It has, however, to be talked about. It is a story that cannot be told yet has to be told. *The Road* describes one way, at least of talking about it – of telling, and not telling, that story.

3

Imagining Crisis

"This week has changed all of us forever in ways that we can't understand" (76), observes a character, shortly after 9/11, in *The Good Priest's Son* by Reynolds Price. That is a commonplace in writing about the event, in fiction, nonfiction, poetry and drama. But – as I tried to suggest in the previous chapter – there is often a problem of register. While many novels, for example, may accommodate the claim that things have fundamentally changed since the terrorist attacks, their forms do not necessarily register or bear witness to that change. What is acknowledged is not always enacted. Crisis is recuperated in many cases, assimilated into conventional structures and a series of tropes tending to reassure the reader that nothing has determinately altered. In books like *The Writing on the Wall*, *A Disorder Peculiar to the Country*, *The Emperor's Children*, *The Good Life* and *Falling Man* the act of recuperation, as it happens, is also one of domestication. The conventions that familiarize the unfamiliar, and so suppress its urgency and disguise its strangeness, are those traditionally associated with the domestic romance. In *The Good Priest's Son*, the conventions are different, but only slightly so. Here, the trauma of September 11, 2001 is absorbed into a gently reflective narrative about a man called Mabry Kincaid coming to terms with his past. Compelled to leave New York City when he learns that his downtown loft has been devastated by the World Trade Center attacks, he journeys back

After the Fall: American Literature Since 9/11, First Edition. Richard Gray.
© 2011 John Wiley & Sons, Ltd. Published 2011 by John Wiley & Sons, Ltd.

to his native North Carolina, where he encounters and eventually lays to rest some ghosts from his familial and regional past. Perhaps, Kincaid speculates, September 11 was "the most disastrous day since the bloodiest day of the Civil War" (2) but, in this novel, it is merely the occasion for a journey back home, a return to the father that is one of the great commonplaces of Southern writing. The strange is neatly familiarized; an eruptive moment is rendered safe by being reinserted in a traditional narrative pattern.

The pattern is different again in *Extremely Loud & Incredibly Close* by Jonathan Safran Foer, but the process of familiarization is the same. Here "the worst day" (68), as it is called, becomes the occasion for a quest, in which the nine-year-old protagonist called Oskar Schell, two years after his father died in 9/11, discovers a key which, he believes, might unlock the secret of his life and take him closer to his lost father. At first sight, the novel seems experimental, disruptive, responsive to the strange. It shifts between the quest of the young protagonist, and main narrator, in twenty-first century New York and the memories of his paternal grandparents, narrated by them, that circulate around the firebombing of Dresden during the Second World War. Type settings, spaces and even blank pages give the book a visual dimension, as do the photographs that intersperse the narrative. And that visual dimension is expanded and enhanced at the end of the book. Oskar imagines that his father may well have jumped from the north tower on September 11. Identifying his father with some images of a body falling from the World Trade Center, he turns those images around so that the last one is first and the first one last. "I found the pictures of the falling body," Oskar confides, "I ripped the pages out of the book. I reversed the order.... When I flipped through them, it looked like the man was floating up through the sky" (325). This redemptive gesture is then illustrated in the series of photographs that conclude the story, which show the falling man in just such a manner, not falling but "floating," ascending. The strategy is striking but it suggests just how close to the surface the narrative experiments of this novel are. They are, in fact, not so much disruptive as illustrative. And what they illustrate is a deeply conventional if occasionally touching account of a young man growing up, coming to terms with and perhaps even transcending, ascending above loss. The "worst day" becomes, as it does in *The Good Priest's Son*, the occasion for rehearsing and replaying a deeply traditional narrative, in this case a sly but slight variation on the classic form of the initiation novel.

The determining feature of trauma is that it is, as one authority on the subject has put it, "*an affront to understanding*" (Caruth, 154). There is, as Ernst van Alphen has suggested, "the widespread conviction that the Holocaust in all its uniqueness and extremity, is unrepresentable" (van Alphen, 41). Famously, both Theodor Adorno and Lionel Trilling argued much the same. "To write poetry after Auschwitz is barbaric," Adorno insisted (Adorno, 34). "There is no possible way of responding to Belsen and Buchenwald," Trilling suggested. "The activity of the mind falls before the incommunicability of man's suffering" (Trilling, 256). There are, without doubt, significant differences between the Holocaust and 9/11: differences in scale, intensity and the sheer momentousness of the historical events and the human suffering involved. To deny this would be little short of obscene. Nevertheless, as far as this, the challenge of representation, is concerned, there is a structural connection. And many commentators have implicitly acknowledged that connection by declaring that, as one of them put it, 9/11 is "outside the bounds of language" (Edkins, 1). "As a novelist I wouldn't touch the World Trade Center, and the looming tragedy around it," the Jewish American novelist Thane Rosenbaum admitted a short time after the event, "I'm not ready to write or talk about it yet;" "silence might be the loudest sound of all", he added, the only adequate measure of the "collective numbness" caused by the "horror of what happened" on September 11 (Rosenbaum, 132). Silence is perhaps the only proper response. But silence is not really an option. "Not to speak is impossible," as one authority on trauma has observed (Caruth, 154). There is, after all, as two other commentators on trauma have put it, "the urgent necessity of reconfiguring and transforming the broken repertoire of meaning and expression" occasioned by the traumatic event (Kaplan and Wang, 12). More simply, there is also what another, in the context of the Holocaust, called "the sacred duty to bear witness" (Kremer, 27). The contradiction that is the heart of the matter here was caught in a short story, "Near November," by Lynne Sharon Schwartz published just after the terrorist attacks. In this, she describes how, in the immediate aftermath of the terrorist attack, it was impossible for the writer to move on to the "next sentence" (261). "We long to hear an intelligent word" about the event, she says. "No, we long for silence. Enough words have been spoken" (261). Schwartz is well aware that she is talking about 9/11 in talking about not talking about it – that to speak of not speaking is to speak, that to insist on silence is to break it. There is a twin imperative here for the writer, caught between what one commentator on trauma has called "the senseless-ness of the initial traumatic encounter and the sense-making appara-tus of ... narrative" (Hirsch, "Post-traumatic", 101). He, or she, has to achieve some kind of resolution, however fragile or fleeting, between the imperative of silence (since trauma is that for which there is no language) and the imperative of speech (since trauma is that which demands language as an alternative to emotional paralysis). The writer cannot write but must; words are no good but they are all she or he has; even in denying or dismissing the tools of the trade, he or she is using them. This, the speaking of silence, is, as I suggested in the first chapter, a paradox, a problem that, in literary terms, lies at the heart of Romanticism and its aftermath, as well as, in experiential terms, at the heart of trauma. The solution is either to surrender – which is not really a viable option, practically or emotionally – or to go on writing, continue trying to find some way of saying the unsayable. The nar-rator in Schwartz's short story may find it next to impossible to get beyond a litany of facts about where one was and what one was doing at the time of the attacks – a potentially endless repetition of things she and other writers "know for certain," like "I would have been there except I slept late... I got caught in traffic." (261). But getting beyond this is what she needs and has to do, she realizes. So, "we will do what is needed," she concludes her meditation. "We will write the next sentence." (262).

Writing the next sentence – and, in the process finding some means of saying the unsayable – is what the fictions I would like to concen-trate on in this chapter manage to do: *Twilight of the Superheroes* by Deborah Eisenberg, *The Reluctant Fundamentalist* by Mohsin Hamid,

Netherland by Joseph O'Neill and *The Garden of Last Days* by Andre Dubus III. What these books have in common may, on the surface, be very little. What they share below that surface, however, is the impulse to approach the contemporary crisis by roundabout means, using indirection to find historical directions out. To write, Gilles Deleuze and Felix Guattari have argued, one should "form rhizomes, expand your own territory by deterritorialisation" (203). These works, in their different ways, pursue just such a strategy of deterritorialization; they present post-9/11 America as a transcultural space in which different cultures reflect and refract, confront and bleed into one another. *Twilight of the Superheroes*, for instance, is a series of lucidly disjunctive short stories. The title story oscillates between a young man called Nathaniel, who is drinking champagne with his roommates in their sublet overlooking the site of the former World Trade Center, and Nathaniel's middle-aged uncle Lucien, in his office above his art gallery on the other side of New York City. Nathaniel recalls witnessing the 9/11 attack from the balcony of his apartment. He also recalls what became known as Y2K: the widespread belief that the world's computers would malfunction at the dawn of the new millennium, leading to disaster – with, among other things, planes falling out of the sky. Disaster did occur, he reflects, not, however, on January 1, 2000 as anticipated but a little over eighteen months later. "*You see,*" he thinks, "*if history has anything to teach us, it's that … we poor humans cannot actually think ahead, there are just too many variables.*" So, he concludes inconclusively, "*when it comes down to it. It always turns out that no one is in charge of the things that really matter*" (4). That sounds the bass note of this story: the random, fragmentary nature of things is registered in the apparently random structure of the narrative, which occupies a few minutes in present time as it vacillates between Nathaniel looking forward to possible futures and Nathaniel and Lucien, in their separate ways, looking backward to a series of impossible, unbearable pasts – pasts that include 9/11 and the family experience of oppression in Europe, World War, emigration, and exile.

Images of buildings operate ironically throughout this remarkable story – Nathaniel is an architect – to suggest the vulnerability of human structures and plans: as the events of 9/11 illustrate, after all, even the most evidently solid of artefacts can suddenly melt into the air. So do images of theatricality and artifice. "It was as if there had been a curtain, a curtain painted with the map of the earth… with Lucien's delightful city," Lucien thinks. "The planes struck, tearing through the curtain of that blue September morning, exposing the dark world that lay right behind it, of populations ruthlessly exploited, inflamed with hatred, and tired of waiting for change to happen by" (32–3). Those images perhaps connect up with the figure Albert Camus famously used to describe the discovery of absurdity: the moment when, as Camus put it, the stage sets collapse and we discover that the human enterprise is fundamentally artificial and absurd (Camus, 22). There is also a telling connection here, closer to 9/11, with Slavoj Zizek's contention that what "took place in New York on 11 September" introduced "its citizens to the 'desert of the real,'" the material reality of Third World oppression usually concealed behind the screen of "digitalised Third World" opulence (Zizek, 3–5). Both connections are relevant, since what is at stake here is an irruption of the real: a "tear in the fabric," to quote one commentator on 9/11 (Laub, 204), that allowed a "real reality" (Zizek, 2) momentarily to displace a virtual one. And what is also at stake is the extent to which this story reflects a suspicion that, after the terrorist attacks, "private life shrank to nothing" (36) because of what that day exposed and initiated. The sense of being implicated in a larger, global politics is there, despite the fact that, as Lucien observes, "money is flowing a bit again" and "most of the flags have folded up." "Once again," Lucien notes, "people are concerned with getting on with their lives." "The curtain has dropped." Except that people "seem a little bit nervous, a little uncomfortable, a little wary" (37). If they try to be cheerful, the cheerfulness seems "cranked up to the level of completely unconvincing hysteria" (36). If they are more serious, they appear "sullen and dogged." The problem is that "you can't help sort of knowing that what you're seeing is only the curtain;" also, "you can't help guessing what might be going on behind it" (37). What has been going on, and what is going on now is, the narrative indicates, easy to guess in any event. There are "all those irrepressibly, murderously angry people" (35) for whom getting on with their lives in any tolerable way is impossible. And there are "the wars in the

East" (33) triggered by a "president capering about in military uniform" (35): wars only partially, imperfectly hidden "behind a thicket
of language: *patriotism, democracy, loyalty, freedom*" (33). If those words
refer to anything, it is intimated, rather than being just camouflage,
"they all might refer to money" (33).

A memorable moment in *Tender is the Night* (1934) by F. Scott
Fitzgerald describes the elaborate machinery of production – and,
implicitly, the blood, sweat and tears – required to keep the central
female character, Nicole Diver, in the manner to which she has become
accustomed. "For her sake," the narrator of that novel observes, "...
dreamers were muscled out of patent rights... these were some of the
people who gave a tithe to Nicole and, as the whole system swayed
and thundered onward it lent a feverish bloom to such processes of
hers as wholesale buying" (224).

The strategy of Eisenberg here, if not the same, is similar. Behind
the curtain, the reader learns, behind the thicket of political rhetoric,
behind the glitz, glamour and gaiety of a slowly recovering New York
City is the stark reality of oppression and consequent rage, an economic
empire (Eisenberg also plays with allusions to earlier imperial powers,
such as Rome), a series of tottering structures built on the basis of
money being in certain hands. This sense of a potentially fatal fissure between what lies in front of the curtain and what lies behind,
and the fear, the sense of dread that fissure engenders, is the closest
this story comes to an epiphany. Which is, of course, no epiphany at
all: Eisenberg has said, in fact, that what she is after in her stories is
reverse epiphanies.[1] And that is certainly what we have here. *Twilight
of the Superheroes* ends in paralysis, its protagonists trapped between
an unimagined (because unanticipated) past and an unimaginable
(unanticipatable) future, their emotionally frozen state being a precise
register of a larger, national sense of losing the plot, being in a strange
new world without a map. This is all by way of saying that, in this
story, the personal *is* the political; what happens to characters like
Nathaniel and Lucien – and, on the surface, very little happens – is
indelibly linked to what has happened and is continuing to happen

---

[1] Interview at http://www.beatrice.com/interviews/eisenberg/.

elsewhere – in America, in Europe and in "the East." In his spare time, we learn, Nathaniel likes to draw cartoons that have as their anti-hero a figure called Passivityman. Not sure where to go with Passivityman after a while, Nathaniel reflects, "Huh, well, I guess he's sort of losing his superpowers" (23). It is not hard to catch the resonance of this sly reflection, how it echoes a suspicion felt by most of the characters in this story – and, we surmise from the drift of the story, by America.

The personal is equally the political in *The Reluctant Fundamentalist*. This short novel is set in Old Anarkali, a district of Lahore in Pakistan, on an evening in spring. A bearded local man introduces himself to a visiting American ("Excuse me, sir, but may I be of assistance?" (1)), and proceeds to tell him what he claims is the story of his life. The author, Mohsin Hamid, has said that *The Reluctant Fundamentalist* is "a half-conversation, a-half story" because the reader is "asked to provide the other half of the novel's meaning."[2] The American never speaks, we never know his name. Who is he? And what are his reasons for being in Pakistan? Is he a businessman, a tourist or (as is occasionally hinted) an agent of some sort? There is a curious bulge in the clothes near his shoulder that might be a gun or, for that matter, might be a security pouch for his valuables. Who is the bearded man who does all the talking? His speech is almost surrealistically elegant, as if he were descended from an ancient line of storytellers. His name, Changez, might be a pun on "changes" or "Genghis Khan" – reviewers have suggested the first, Hamid himself has referred to the second[3] – or it might be simply that, a name, one of the few provided in this narrative, a story that hovers curiously between the confessional and fable, the history and fairy tale. For that matter, what are we to make of all that Changez says? Is he a reliable narrator? He tends to insist that he is, but admits that he is "telling ... a history," "and in history ... it is the thrust of one's narrative that counts, not the accuracy of one's details" (118). Towards the end of his monologue, Changez observes that the American even appears convinced that he

---

[2]   Interview at http://www.themanbookerprize.com/perspective/articles/101.
[3]   See http://www.guardian.co.uk/books/2007/mar/03/featuresreviews.guardian review20; http://www.themanbookerprize.com/perspective/articles/101.

is an "inveterate liar" (181). Perhaps that conviction helps account for an uneasiness in the demeanour of the American, which Changez recurrently notes, taking pains to reassure the American of his good intentions in a tone that does not entirely reassure. Although this is only a "half-conversation," a monologue, what we experience has the quality of a verbal fencing match, as speaker and silent interlocutor seem to circle around one another in a game that becomes increasingly threatening, full of dangerous if unfulfilled potential. Even the question of just who Changez is talking to remains blurred. Is it the American? Is it ourselves, the readers? Is it both? The indeterminate character of the "you" here is a vital ingredient in the indeterminacy of the novel. *The Return of the Fundamentalist* thrives on the blurring of boundaries. It is set at a crossroads: a Muslim stronghold and an agency of American power. Changez himself, so he tells us, has vacillated between American and Muslim cultures. And the narrative itself situates the reader at a crossroads – in a border territory where we are invited, or rather compelled, to help draw the map.

Old Anarkali, we are told in the course of the story, is a district named after a courtesan who was imprisoned for loving a prince. And Changez quickly announces himself as a lover too: "a lover of America" (1). Born in Pakistan, educated at Princeton and then recruited by a firm called Underwood Sampson, a ruthless consultancy firm that does its bit for globalization by facilitating hostile takeovers of businesses around the world, Changez by his own account refashioned himself as completely and successfully as James Gatz did when he reinvented himself as Jay Gatsby: a process that seems complete when he visits the house of his boss, Jim, located in the Hamptons – "a magnificent property" (43) that made him think, Changez confesses, of Fitzgerald's most famous book. As in *The Great Gatsby*, too, the economic is interleaved with the pursuit of the erotic. Changez explains that he fell in love with an American girl called Erica: "stunningly *regal*" with "her hair … piled up like a tiara on her head" (17) and from a wealthy but liberal patrician family, she appears to embody the American Dream to the point of parody. But the dream has its dark underside. Erica has a tragedy in her past: a childhood sweetheart and only previous lover, named Chris, who died from cancer while still in his teens. Erica was unable to forget Chris, Changez recalls. And their only moment of real physical intimacy comes when Changez asks Erica to pretend, while they are making love, that he is her childhood sweetheart and, in fact, to call him Chris. It is a further stage in self-fashioning: a reinvention of identity – and, for this instant, a renaming – that, in a way curiously similar to Gatsby's, only underwrites the barriers, of class in one case, culture in another, and the barriers of wealth and power, by attempting to erase them.

The turn in this process of reinvention comes with 9/11. Changez is in the Phillippines, working for Underwood Sampson and attempting as he puts it, to be "like an *American*" (65), when he sees the destruction of the Twin Towers on the news. And, "despicable as it may sound," he confesses, "my initial reaction was to be remarkably pleased" (72) – not by the terrible loss of life but by the belief that "someone had so visibly brought America to her knees" (73). So begins a turnaround that is as curiously ambivalent as everything else in this book. Changez later learns about some soldiers known as the janissaries. Janissaries, he is told, were Christian boys trained by the Ottoman empire to fight against their own people. "I was a modern-day janissary," he observes, "a servant of the American empire at a time when it was invading a country with a kinship to mine" (152). The link between different forms of imperial power, the military and the economic, past and present, may be clear and unambiguous. But Changez's not so surprising conversion, which involves mainly growing a beard, giving up his consultancy job and leaving America for Pakistan is less so – and not only because Changez is our sole source of information. Even as Changez describes it, his repudiation of America is a curiously frictionless affair. It has, as Hamid himself has pointed out, next to no religious element; and it is marked by considerable doses of *ex post facto* wisdom. "I had always resented the manner in which America conducted itself in the world," Changez now claims to his American interlocutor and to us, "your country's constant interference in the affairs of others was insufferable. Vietnam, Korea, the straits of Taiwan, the Middle East and now Afghanistan" (156). If so, then both the silent American and we the equally silent but necessarily active readers might respond that, up until this point, Changez has kept remarkably quiet about this resentment. Some critics of *The Reluctant Fundamentalist* have lamented what they see as the fluctuation of the narrative between tale and essay, as Changez now attacks what he sees as the American "project of domination" (156), laments the "self-righteous rage" (94) and desire for revenge of the United States after 9/11 or explains how finance is "the primary means" by which "the American empire" (156) exercises its power.[4] But this is to ignore the remarkable fluidity of the novel, the way it operates through irony and in the interstices between cultures, between individuals, and between different versions of history and variant notions of the truth. And it is to ignore such simple facts as that, even by the end of the novel, we do not know whether Changez is the hunter or the hunted or neither. We do not know, in short, precisely what is going on in this latter-day version of the colonial encounter. Changez still seems oddly in love with the culture of America, constantly referring to or invoking it, even while he rages against it. And even his repudiation of America and return to Pakistan is fraught with potential irony. Is this a "genuine" conversion, whatever that may mean, or is it the superior opportunism of a highly trained appraiser of failing companies, who thinks he knows which way the wind is now blowing, and where the real power is now headed?

The slipperiness of the novel is also caught in a further series of elisions, between the personal and the political as well as between different forms of the will to power. His relationship with Erica gradually died away, Changez tells us, as her preoccupation with her own past became a disabling obsession. "She was disappearing into a powerful nostalgia" (113), he recalls, a disappearance that becomes literal as mental breakdown leads first to hospitalization and then what looks like suicide (although, appropriately, her body is never recovered). The end of the love affair with Erica coincides with the end of the love affair with America. "It seemed to me," Changez recollects, that, after 9/11, "America, too, was increasingly giving itself over to a dangerous nostalgia" (114). The blurring that is taking place here between Erica

---

[4] See the review at http://www.independent.co.uk/arts-entertainment/books/reviews/the-reluctant-fundamentalist-by-mohson-hamid441392.html.

and (Am)erica is plain to see, even without the slippage of the names. On both the personal and the political level, there is love turning to loss for Changez. On both, there is a fraught relationship with the past – "Chris' clearly alludes to Christopher Columbus" and the moment of European discovery and conquest. On both, too, there is a perceived failure to engage with the other, with the new, in short with changes/Changez: unless, that is, the other persuades by masking its otherness – by going to Princeton, pursuing the American Dream, or calling itself Chris. The play with names involved here might seem mechanically allegorical at first sight, until we recognize what matters here is the play, the elision rather than any particular meanings we may elicit from it. This is a novel set in and about a liminal world, a proliferating chain of borders, where characters and cultures cross and recross the landscape, dissolving and reconfiguring what might once have seemed a series of static oppositions: past and present, Muslim and American, East and West. The verbal slippages, such as Erica/(Am) erica, Changez/changes and Chris/Christopher Columbus are a vital part of this, inviting us into a verbal world where even the primary act of naming turns out to be partial and provisional, constantly open to later acts of renaming.

Even the title of the novel reflects this. From that title, and from the increasing tension between Changez and the unnamed American, the expectation is that Changez is moving towards a revelation that, "reluctant" though he might have been to do so, he has embraced Islamic fundamentalism and is even orchestrating some act of violence against his interlocutor. But the ending leaves that open. An unnamed "waiter" is certainly "closing in" when Changez and the American stop to say goodbye, perhaps to seize, maim, or kill the American, perhaps with the assistance of Changez. But perhaps not. Meanwhile, the American seems to be reaching into his jacket for something with "a glint of metal." Is it a gun or, as Changez tries to reassure himself in the last words of the narrative, a "holder of ... business cards" (184)? Is this the prelude to an act of violence or an exchange of names and intimacies? Is there a terrorist here and, if so, is it Changez or the American who is the agent of terror? For that matter, is it, as the reader has possibly assumed, Changez who is, or rather who has become, the fundamentalist? Or is it the American, a recruit perhaps in the fundamentalist project of a war on terror, a fight against the axis of evil? Or is it neither? Is it rather a global capitalism that seeks to dominate the world with its own form of economic fundamentalism – a project signaled by the injunction Underwood Sampson, Changez's former employers, had (we are told) chosen for their motto, "Focus on the fundamentals" (14)? There are no certain answers to these questions, since what we are presented with, constantly, is limited, equivocal evidence, partial disclosures and evidential traces – all of them occurring, verbally, in a "half-conversation" and, spatially, in a liminal territory. That territory is further problematized by a kind of geographic and historic layering. When Changez comments on the American flags that suddenly proliferate in New York City following 9/11, for instance, he wonders "what manner of host would sally forth from so grand a castle" (79), so mapping the triumphalist militarism of the United States over the ruined glory of the Mughal empire. And when he arrives in Manila, as a representative of Underwood Sampson, he informs us that he "expected to find a city like Lahore." "What I found instead," he confesses:

> was a place of skyscrapers and superhighways. Yes, Manila had its slums; one saw them on the drive from the airport: vast districts of men in dirty white undershirts lounging idly in front of auto-repair shops – like a poorer version of the 1950s America depicted in such films as *Grease*. But Manila's glittering skyline and walled enclaves for the ultra-rich were unlike anything I had seen in Pakistan. (64)

So what we have here is a multiplicity of perspectives: the comfortable frame of reference provided by Lahore, the glittering luxury of downtown Manila, the sealed, denatured bubble of airports, airport highways, and international finance, the global reach of popular culture available to anyone who wants to claim it. The terrain Changez traverses, in Manila and elsewhere, is, as this passage suggests, spongelike, a place where different cultures do not so much engage with as absorb each other. This is a peculiarly hybrid space, which seems to subvert the binary oppositions on which so much traditional thinking about culture – and, for that matter, most political discourse – is founded.

In *The Location of Culture*, Homi K. Bhabha offers a critique of what he takes to be inadequate "essentialist" readings of nationhood – readings that attempt to define and naturalize Third World "nations" by means of the supposedly homogeneous, holistic, and historically continuous traditions that falsely define and ensure their subordinate status. Nations and cultures, he argues, must be understood as "narrative" constructions that arise from the "hybrid" interaction of contending national and cultural constituencies. "It is in the emergence of the interstices," he suggests,

> – the overlap and displacement of domains of difference – that the intersubjective and collective experiences of *nationness*, community interest, or cultural value are negotiated... Terms of cultural engagement, whether antagonistic or affiliative, are produced performatively. The representation of difference must not be hastily read as the reflection of *pre-given* ethnic or cultural traits set in the fixed tablet of tradition. The social articulation of difference, from the minority perspective, is a complex, on-going negotiation that seeks to authorise cultural hybridities that emerge in moments of historical transformation. (2)

The "interstitial perspective," as Bhabha calls it (3), replaces "the polarity of a prefigurative self-generating nation 'in itself' and extrinsic to other nations" with the notion of "cultural liminality *within the nation*" (148). "The liminal figure of the nation-space would ensure that no political ideologies could claim transcendent or metaphysical authority for themselves. This is because the subject of cultural discourse – the agency of a people – is split in the discursive ambivalence that emerges in the contest of narrative authority between the pedagogical and the performative" (148): that is, between the status of the people as "historical 'objects' of a nationalist pedagogy" and their ability to perform as "'subjects' of a process of signification that must erase any prior or originary presence" (145). Hybridity, liminality, "interrogatory, interstitial space" (3) are the positives Bhabha opposes to a retrograde historicism that, in his view, continues to dominate

Western critical thinking, a "linear narrative of the nation," with its claims for the "holism of culture and community" and "fixed horizontal nation-space" (142). Such thinking, he insists, with its facile binary oppositions, must be replaced: so that, instead of stressing the opposition between, say, First and Third Worlds, West and East, the colonizer and the colonized, we concentrate on the faultlines themselves, on border situations and thresholds as the sites where identities are performed and contested.

This is the work that narratives such as "Twilight of the Superheroes" and *The Reluctant Fundamentalist* perform. Works like *Falling Man* and *The Writing on the Wall*, *The Good Priest's Son* and *Extremely Loud & Incredibly Close* locate crisis in terms of opposition – them and us, the personal and the political, the private and the public, the oppressor and the victim – and then attempt to accommodate the series of binary oppositions they construct into a traditional narrative and mythic pattern in which, so it is hoped, those oppositions can be resolved and reconciled. Eisenberg and Hamid, however, pursue a different course: locating crisis in an interstitial space, where such oppositions are contested: a site where a discourse founded on either/or distinctions is interrogated and even subverted. The New York City of "Twilight of the Superheroes" and *The Reluctant Fundamentalist*, along with the other territories encountered in these fictions (Manila, Lahore, Europe at war) are culturally hybrid spaces where engagements between different cultures, "whether antagonistic or affiliative," are performative and identity is open to constant negotiation and renegotiation: so that, for instance, the questions, "Who is the terrorist?" "Who is the fundamentalist?" are less easy to answer here than at first appears. The historical layering that characterizes both narratives, the geographical fluidity (in the sense that both stories flow uninterruptedly between diverse geographical spaces), the equivocal, interrogatory approach both take to issues of just what is happening in the contemporary crisis and why: all these are symptoms of a shared impulse towards an investigation of faultlines – on the actual sites where identities, both personal and national, are contested. The disjunctive, fragmented, antilinear structure of Eisenberg's story, and the "half-conversation" that characterizes Hamid's novel, have their part to play here too. Formally, the narratives themselves become interstitial spaces – or, perhaps more accurately, a series of interstitial spaces: here, as it were in the spaces between the tale being told, the reader is required to intervene, to engage with a continuing production of meanings that are necessarily partial and provisional. Meaning, signification, along with identity, becomes performative. Our assumptions about the agencies and identities at work here are constantly dislocated, necessitating a continual process of reinterpretation, a process of questioning that, theoretically at least, is without end because it is precisely that, the process of questioning, the performative character of historical truth, that is the point. According to Bhabha, hybridity and what he calls "linguistic multivocality" (148) have the potential to intervene and undermine the process of colonization through the reinterpretation of political discourse. Linguistic multivocality is also the key to these two stories. And its function and achievement here is precisely to intervene and undermine, if not the process of colonization then the process of *thinking* about colonization – and the terms in which we understand the current crisis.

A similar multivocality is at work in *Netherland* by Joseph O'Neill. At first sight, *Netherland* appears to belong to what Zadie Smith has rather dismissively referred to as the school of lyrical realism (1). It is true that, from a surface view, *Netherland* could be seen as a member of that school. But, without resorting to the claim of Georg Lukacs that "realism is not one style among others, it is the basis of literature" (*Meaning of Contemporary Realism*, 48), there is the surely more substantive point that some of the most innovative, and subtly interrogative fictions of recent years could be described in similar terms – at least, at first glance and while attending to surface detail. *The Corrections* (2001) by Jonathan Franzen chronicles the lives of members of a Midwestern family and the network of dependence and blame, affection and resentment that is the pattern of their daily lives. It is about an America where life has come to be "lived underground" (9), and where the affluent surfaces only partially conceal an almost bottomless disaffection and disquiet. *Look at Me* (2001) by Jennifer Egan is a densely layered analysis of individual lives lived "under the pressure of so many eyes" (415) and a corporate world "remade by circuitry" (390) that transforms gaze into economic power. It is about America as a surfeit of commodities. *The Time of Our Singing* (2003) by Richard Powers intercalates the stories of a family of mixed race with the story of race in the United States in the twentieth century. Turning a famous remark of Ralph Waldo Emerson on its head, it shows biography as enlarged history. To label these novels realistic, because of their attention to the empirical details of a particular society and individual psychology, is to say what is probably the least interesting thing about them. So it is with *Netherland*, which has at its center a character called Hans van den Broek, a Dutch banker married to an English lawyer, whose marriage starts to collapse when the destruction of the World Trade Center drives him, his wife, and his son Jake out of their Tribeca apartment and into the polyglot, bohemian refuge of the Chelsea Hotel. Soon after the family relocate, a trial separation occurs. Hans's wife, enraged by the policies of the Bush administration and unhappy with what she sees as the strange lassitude of her husband, departs with her son to London. "Can't you see this isn't about personal relationships?" she later tells Hans when settled back in England:

> Politeness, niceness, you, me – it's all irrelevant. This is about a life-and-death struggle for the future of the world. Our personal feelings don't come into the picture. There are forces out there. The United States is now the strongest military power in the world. It can and will do anything it wants. It has to be stopped. Your feelings and my feelings ... are not on the agenda. (95)

Hans does not disagree with much of this, but he does not strongly agree either; quite simply, he cannot share his wife's passion. And he is left stranded in a world turned immaterial, phantasmagoric. "Life itself had become disembodied," Hans reflects. "My family, the spine of my days, had crumbled. I was lost in invertebrate time" (28). Every other weekend he visits his family, hoping "that flying high into the atmosphere, over boundless massifs of vapour or small clouds ... might also lift me above my personal haze" (35). He is afloat, a dangling man both when in the air and when on the ground. And that is a condition he seems to share with many others in

New York, "a city gone mad" (20): whose inhabitants, Hans tells us, are unsure whether they are living "in a pre-apocalyptic situation" ("like the European Jews in the thirties" (21–2)) or one that is "merely near-apocalyptic" ("like that of the Cold War inhabitants of New York, London, Washington and, for that matter, Moscow" (22)). All this is the wisdom of hindsight, to an extent; Hans is telling his story some time later, after he has moved back to London (from where he and his family departed in 1998) in pursuit of a reconciliation with his wife. "Wisdom," however, seems too vital a word for Hans as either narrator or protagonist. For most of the narrative, Hans remains damaged, in a state of suspended animation. And, as he describes his old self wandering in a state of disconnection through the streets of the city, his terms of description wander too: the prose is melancholic, indeterminately ruminative, always gently hesitant. Phrases such as "in a way," "in some sense," "I wish," "I like to believe" and "who knows?" recur; and Hans persists in reflecting on his own reflections, apparently pursuing an authenticity, a truth (of action, of narration) that eludes him. "You're like a child," his wife Rachel tells him. "You don't look beneath the surface... Same thing with America" (160). That, like many of the things the characters say in this book is true and not true. Hans the protagonist may roam in an almost somnambulist state over the surfaces of life in post-9/11 New York. Hans the narrator does, however, attempt to probe beneath those surfaces. The trouble is that, just like Nick Carraway, the narrator of *The Great Gatsby*, he can never be sure when, if at all, he succeeds. The poignancy of this is caught in the closing sentences of the book, when Hans is reunited with his family in England. "Look!" his son Jake says, "pointing wildly. 'See, Daddy?'" "I see, I tell him," Hans discloses, "looking from him to Rachel and again to him. Then I turn to look for what it is we're supposed to be seeing" (247).

What Hans sees back in New York, after the departure of his wife and son, constitutes the other strand of the narrative. That strand introduces us to a postcolonial variation on Jay Gatsby, the complement to Hans's version of Nick Carraway. It also introduces Hans himself to a world that, safely ensconced in the comfortable milieu of international finance, he has hardly ever encountered or known. Hans meets and befriends a mysterious, charismatic figure called Chuck Ramkissoon, a Trinidadian of South Asian descent, an ambitious entrepreneur and a small-time gangster. Through Chuck, whose eventual, unexplained and violent, death provides the catalyst for Hans's story, O'Neill maps the heterogeneous territory of New York City – not only the affluent neighbourhoods but the "outer boroughs" (147) of Queens, Staten Island, and what Chuck calls "the real Brooklyn" (141). Chuck's story, which he tells Hans, is in many ways reminiscent of the story of that paradigm of the American Dream, Jay Gatsby. His motto, "think fantastic" (130), suggests this. So does Hans himself, as he rehearses that story for the reader. "He told his own story constantly," Hans recalls, "and the autobiography might succinctly, and clankingly, have been called *Chuck Ramkissoon:Yank*" (128). The irony lurking in this observation is characteristic – there is a holding back, a wariness, in just about everything Hans says – but so, too, whenever the subject of Chuck is raised, is the hint of slightly bewildered, slightly incredulous admiration. "His legend was transparently derived from the local one of rags to riches," Hans concedes, but then adds, with what almost sounds like deference, that Chuck, after all, "couldn't afford the luxury of knowingness" (128). It had to be simple, in other words; subtlety and self-consciousness were not something for which Chuck, intent on reinventing rather than investigating himself, really had the time – or, for that matter, the emotional reserves. So far, so like Gatsby; the Trinidadian dreamer is even like the American one in having his own version of Meyer Wolfsheim, a business colleague called Abelsky who provides him with an entrée into the Jewish neighbourhoods where he hopes to make a killing in property development. Like Gatsby, too, Chuck even meets with some success, the emblems of which are buildings and women. Unlike Gatsby, though, this story of success takes place on a fully globalized terrain. "It's a people business," Chuck declares of his life as a property developer, "I ran a team of Bangladeshi cement guys. I had Irish painters – well, the main guy was Irish… his men were Guatemalans. I had Russian plasterers, I had Italian roofers, I had Grenadan carpenters" (129). Hans travels with Chuck to the outer boroughs, on drives that seem to go on forever. These, as it turns out, not only make the banker an unwitting accessory to Chuck's shady business deals and his involvement in illicit gambling, they also draw the attention of Hans, and the reader, to the New York of immigration and, more generally to the United States as a site of multiple ethnic and cultural encounters. "We travelled the length of Coney Island Avenue," Hans remembers of one of these jaunts,

> ... a shoddily bustling strip of vehicles double parked in front of gas stations, synagogues, mosques, beauty salons, bank branches, restaurants, funeral homes, auto body shops, supermarkets, assorted small businesses proclaiming provenances from Pakistan, Tajikistan, Ethiopia, Turkey, Saudi Arabia, Russia, Armenia, Ghana, the Jewry Christendom, Islam: it was on Coney Island Avenue ... that Chuck and I came upon a bunch of South African Jews, in full sectarian regalia, watching televised cricket with a couple of Rastaferians in the front office of a Pakistani-run lumber yard. (141)

This catalogue of the sectarian and the surreal asks us to attend to a world that exists beyond the binary oppositions of nationalist rhetoric. This is a hybrid, heterogeneous space that resists the discourse of "us-versus-them" on which the verbal currency of terrorism and counter-terrorism depends. This is a very different kind of immigrant encounter from the one mapped in *The Reluctant Fundamentalist*. But, like Hamid's book, O'Neill's invites us to inspect the faultlines, the interstitial spaces, beyond a boundary, any boundary laid down by the linear narrative of nation.

Beyond a Boundary is the title of a book by C.L.R. James on cricket, the game that polyglot audience encountered by Hans and Chuck in the front office of a Coney Island Avenue lumberyard were watching on television. Which leads us to a vital strand, arguably the core of meaning in *Netherland*. "There's a limit to what Americans understand," one character comments in the book. "The limit is cricket" (167). And it is a limit that is tested here. Cricket, as James observes in *Beyond a Boundary*, is more than just a game. Or, as James puts it in the preface, "What do they know of cricket who only cricket know." Deeply implicated in the workings of intra- and international politics, cricket is fundamentally unimaginable outside the context of British colonial rule, much in the same way that West Indian colonialism and postcolonialism – in other words, the colonization and after of Chuck's birthplace – are unimaginable without cricket. "The cricket field," James argues, is a "stage on which selected individuals" play "representative roles … charged with social significance" (66). Cricket was and remains both a legacy of imperialism and a means of resistance to it; the roles played out on the cricket pitch are an agency, an instrument of social ideology and political transformation. What we have in the game of cricket, James suggests, is a balancing of complicity and resistance, in which, in order to turn a residual colonial practice into a subversive anti-colonial one, the cultural practice must first be learned and assimilated according to the terms of the dominant colonial order. Cricket, on these terms, is a paradigm of the colonial and postcolonial encounter. It is about collusion and conflict between the colonizer and the colonized, oppressor and victim; in a word, it is about power.

O'Neill has said as much in an interview. "I think if you're writing about cricket you're writing about power," O'Neill has observed, "because cricket is such a loaded sport … And in this country it's a sport of the powerless."[5] Hans loves cricket, finding in it to begin with a refuge, and a reminder of happier days in the Netherlands and England, when his family leave him and he finds himself lost and directionless in New York. On alternate weekends, the ones when he does not fly over to see his family in London, he plays cricket on Staten Island, the only white man in a cricket club that also includes Chuck. Chuck has a dream that circles around cricket. He wants to build a cricket stadium, to create a "Bald Eagle Field" (15) in an abandoned field in Brooklyn. Cricket, for Chuck, is or could be the true American game: "NOT AN IMMIGRANT SPORT" (101) is the subject line of one of the many unsolicited e-mail messages that, in his enthusiasm for his project, he sends to business associates and friends. It is "not an immigrant sport," since what we have here is the relocation of the American Dream, the dream of Gatsby

---

[5]   Interview at http://www.guardian.co.uk/books/2008/sep/07/celebrity.

and so many other American heroes, in a deterritorialized America. Chuck reckons, he tells Hans, that there are "maybe" a million West Indians in the New York metropolitan area. That is not all, "that's not the exciting part," he goes on. "The Indian… population has grown by eighty-one per cent in the last ten years;" on top of that, "the Pakistani… numbers have gone up by one hundred and fifty per cent, and the Bangladeshis, wait for it, five hundred per cent. In New Jersey, they're overrun with South Asians" (75). Chuck's figures may be suspect, but there is no doubting his commitment, or his belief that the new Americans from South Asia, the West Indies and elsewhere, could provide the basis for turning cricket into the national sport of the United States. It may be a utopian dream – Chuck also believes that cricket will supply a "lesson in civility" (204) to all Americans – but it is one founded on the indelible fact of a transformed America: a hybrid territory, like the one Hans encounters on his car trips with Chuck into the outer boroughs of New York.

A word of caution is necessary here. The utopian dream of Chuck is just that, the dream of a deeply compromised character. In the end, like Gatsby's, his rage for order – in this case, what he sees as the civility of cricket – ends in violence. Chuck, it turns out, is capable of violence in pursuit of his business aims; and eventually his dead body is found in a canal, hands tied behind his back. "Chuck Ramkissoon was involved in things categorically beyond my knowledge of him" (242), Hans concludes. And those "things" lead, apparently, to his death at the hands of business rivals. What *Netherland* maps, in its representation of cricket, is not the geography of civility – Chuck's belief that "all people … are at their most civilised when they're playing cricket" (204) – but the geography of heterogeneity and power, or, to be more exact, of the intricate series of power relations that what Hans calls "an intercontinental cast of characters" engage in on the field and off. Talking about the sport at one point in the novel, Hans comments that "the communal, contractual phenomenon of New York cricket is underwritten" by a "kind of homesickness," and "by the same agglomeration of unspeakable individual longings that underwrites cricket played anywhere." They are, he explains, longings concerned with horizons and potentials sighted or hallucinated and in any event lost long ago, tantalisms that touch on the undoing of losses too private and reprehensible to be acknowledged to oneself, let alone to others. I cannot be the first to wonder if what we see, when we see men in white take to a cricket field, is men imagining an environment of justice. (116)

It is this, not a field of dreams but a field of encounter, that the metonym of cricket offers in *Netherland*: a field that includes the dream of "justice," certainly, but also the reality of loss and longing, antagonism and affiliation, opposition and amity. What cricket, and for that matter the novel as a whole, disclose is a series of faultlines, the interstices that exist between individuals and cultures as they go about the business of living and coming to terms with each other in an environment where all the borders, all forms of demarcation are porous and negotiable. To that extent, O'Neill too could have justly named his novel, *Beyond a Boundary* – that is, if the title had not already been taken.

Unlike *Netherland*, *The Garden of Last Days* begins and ends in the world of the underclass; there is no diversion from the marginalized into metropolitan glitz here. This is the terrain of dirty realism: Mobil Stations, industrial parks, and lap dancing clubs, where people are down on their luck most of the time and, most of the time too, don't know why. This is an America that corresponds to Jean Baudrillard's notion of it: a landscape of "surface intensity and pure meaninglessness" (28) existing in "a perpetual present of signs" (*America*, 63). And, appropriately perhaps, the linguistic multivocality of this novel is more on the surface here too: the narrative is written in the third person subjective, moving rapidly between several characters whose experiences and responses appear to be recorded as they happen, described as they pass. The past tense may dominate, but there is a feeling of instantaneity about everything, as if the events rehearsed in this novel are being caught on a verbal equivalent of a hand-held camera, snatched momentarily from oblivion. The thematic and tonal character of *The Garden of Last Days* is established in its opening pages, when we are introduced to a young stripper named April Marie Connors – known under the stage name of Spring in the Puma Club where she works. She is driving to work with a scalding cup of coffee between her thighs. Behind her in the car is her pre-school daughter Franny. April is a single mother; the woman, called Jean, who normally looks after Franny while April works, is having tests for heart trouble and so cannot babysit; without a fall-back sitter, April has been forced, for the first time, to take Franny to the club, to be looked after by the "house mom" (16) Tina. And, as she drives through the rundown terrain of urban Florida, a sprawling development strip that is as seedy as it is ephemeral, April tries to convince herself that everything will be alright. "It was all just a show," April tells herself now, "it was just a different kind of show business and Franny'd have to be backstage just this one time and she'd be fine" (14). Then, forced to make an "illegal U-turn through the median strip" to get to the club, April turns too quickly, "splashing the hot coffee through her jeans onto her thigh." Her thigh is burned, and her half-hearted attempt to nerve herself up for the day, and for her life, collapses into a mix of panic and venom. "At this moment," we are told,

> she hated this car, and her ex-husband for buying it, she hated Jean and her weak heart, she hated Tina … for being the one to watch over her Franny, she even hated Florida and its Gulf Coast … but most of all she hated herself … for doing what she was about to do, for breaking the one rule she swore she'd never break, pulling out onto the macadam, then driving into the crushed shell lot of the Puma Club for Men, her daughter Franny right there in the car with her. (15–6)

This brief opening sequence is symptomatic. Andre Dubus III presents us with characters who are driven into corners. They make choices that somehow seem mysterious to them, because those choices are the products of circumstances over which it seems they have little control. Having embarked on a course of action – almost, it appears, without an act of volition preceding it – they are hurried along to the eventual consequences like feverish sleepwalkers. Hoping for the best, they usually encounter the worst: that spilled cup of coffee is a painful reminder that, even if planning were an option (and, on the whole, it is not here), things rarely if ever turn out as they are planned. It seems unlikely that Franny will be "fine;" as it happens, she is not; still, having wiped the hot coffee off her thighs with a tissue, April careers on towards the club and disaster. There is no time for reflection ("*Shit!*" (15) is her only articulated response to the spillage and burning), still less for turning back; she just turns into the "crushed shell lot" and the next stage in a series of events in which, it appears, she has no agency. If there is someone or something in control here, it is certainly not her.

That is the case with the other characters in this novel, most of which is set a few days before 9/11. So, one of the other major players in this game *The Garden of Last Days* describes – a game without clear rules and little opportunity for choice – is A.J., a heavy-equipment opera- tor who feels misunderstood by his boss, his wife (from whom he is estranged) and the stripper whom he visits obsessively at the Puma Club. A.J. dreams of living in the Everglades with his son Cole, "the two of them swinging in a hammock, eating roasted gator and bobcat… like naked warriors. And no women" (160). A.J. is visiting the club on the night April feels forced to take her daughter there. Unhappy that the object of his desires will not see him when she has finished work, A.J. makes the mistake of touching her arm, violating the club rules. A bouncer ejects him, in the process breaking his wrist. After buying a pint of Wild Turkey to console himself and alleviate the pain of the broken wrist ("That and his F-150 were his only companions tonight," we are told, "the only ones he could count on." (110)), full of rage and a sense of grievance A.J. returns to the club. His aim, evidently, is some kind of revenge. But he comes across Franny, unattended, in a back room. His first instinct is to protect her. Then, confused by drink, by resentment that he cannot get near his own child now that he is separated ("They'd never let him see Cole again." (78)) and by the thought that he has already compromised himself by paying close attention in the back of a strip joint to a three-year-old girl he does not know, he embarks on res- cuing Franny from her seedy surroundings. What exactly he intends to do is unclear, even to himself; however, he ends up with Franny in the back of his pick-up truck. "He looked at her in the rearview mirror," we are told, then he is off with her. "The high, terrified cries of this child only he could save" pierce the night air, but he drives on, trying to reassure himself that he is on a mission of mercy. "He disciplined himself to keep his eyes looking ahead," the narrator discloses,

> to not look back up in his mirror at the crying girl, to just wait for the Econoline in front of him to pull out of the lot, this fallen shithole of a place this child was lucky to get out of, lucky A.J. Carey had come along and found her just when he did. (197–8)

At certain moments, his brain engages enough with what is happening for him to realize that nobody is going to believe that he was just trying to help the small girl, that this is not an abduction. But the die in this particular part of the game is already cast. Almost without knowing it, certainly without deliberate choice, A.J. has embarked on a course of action that will lead him to jail. Franny, eventually, is recovered, after a panicked A.J. leaves her in a parked car. But A.J. will end up serving a long sentence. This time, the consequences – both for A.J. and for April – are more than just spilled coffee.

Things happen to these people, and most of the time for the worse. They are clearly bewildered by their status as victims, but the bewilderment leads nowhere; they seem, for the most part, to be spectators rather than agents – spectators of their own lives. They appear, in fact, to be part of what Guy Debord christened the society of the spectacle. In such a society, Debord argued, authentic social life has been replaced with its representation, a "social relation between people that is mediated by images." "Spectacle," as he put it, "is the historical moment in which we are caught" and "*separation* is its alpha and omega." "The more he contemplates," Debord says of the spectator, "the less he lives, the more he identifies with the dominant image of need, the less he understands his own life and desires."[6] People like April and A.J., to that extent, stand outside not only all the lives they observe, they stand outside their own. Unable to determine the grounds of their own being let alone heal the divisions of their existence, they stand apart; things happen, while they watch, sometimes

---

[6] Guy Debord, *The Society of the Spectacle* (*La societe du spectacle* (1967)). Translation at http://www.bopsecrets.org/SI/debord/1.htm, chapter 1, theses 4, 11, 25.

with a scarcely comprehending rage, sometimes with a kind of disbelief. This is a peculiar kind of loneliness, in which the self is isolated not just from others but from itself.

"Acts, emotions, ideas suddenly settle within a character, make themselves at home and then disappear," Jean Paul-Sartre once observed of the typical figure populating the fiction of John Dos Passos, "without his having much to say in the matter. You cannot say he submits to them. He experiences them. There seems to be no law governing their appearance" (91). Much the same could be said of the typical figure inhabiting *The Garden of Last Days*, and for similar reasons. Sartre talked of the "annihilation of consciousness" (96), Debord of spectatorship. For both, what they were talking about was a specifically social crisis, a symptom of (post)modernity and (late) capitalism. And this, surely, is what Dubus's startling novel is talking about too: an environment where people do not have lives in the traditional sense – instead, they have what Sartre termed "destinies" (91). It is no accident that the action of *The Garden of Last Days* centers on a place of spectacle, a club where sight is substituted for touch, looking and longing replace contact and (it seems almost ludicrous to use the words in this context) communion and community. The Puma Club is the site of watching, the impotent gaze: a synecdoche for which, along with the club itself, is that moment in the novel when one of the minor characters, Lonnie the club bouncer, follows his nightly routine after work of surfing through the channels on his cable television. "You've got … two hundred stations," Lonnie laments to himself, "but there's never anything that holds your interest." So "you" surf backwards and forwards: "a lion eating the cubs of the lioness he intends to mount; a set of knives that will cut through Sheetrock before slicing your tomatoes with one stroke; music videos" (249) and so on. Lonnie watches, then goes to work, then watches again, an object among objects. He seems lost in surface; he sees, and is a part of, the blank materiality of his environment.

And then there is Bassam al-jizani, a young man from Saudi Arabia. Dubus has said that the origins of *The Garden of Last Days* lie in an image that occurred to him of money on a dresser. He began a short story about one of the strippers who, according to report, had entertained one of the hijackers three nights prior to 9/11. He wondered how the stripper might feel when she learned the true identity of the man from whom she got the money. But as he wrote, Dubus has said, it became clear to him that the short story would need to be a novel and that the voice of the hijacker would have to be heard.[7]

Curiously, this account of origins bears a resemblance to William Faulkner's famous account of the origins of *The Sound and the Fury*: which also began, Faulkner later explained, as an image – of the "muddy seat of a little girl's drawers" (Meriwether and Millgate, *Lion in Garden*, 245; Gwynn and Blotner, *Faulkner at University*, 71), the girl perched in a pear tree while her brothers gazed at her from down below. This image, too, Faulkner said, inspired a short story that then gradually grew into a multi-perspectival novel, a narrative told in a series of voices all circulating around the "little girl," then later the young woman who seems throughout that narrative to be there and not there, an absent center haunting the memories of those around her. If there is a similar absent center in *The Garden of Last Days*, it is not Bassam, whose perspective is given ample narrative space. It is not, in fact, a person at all but an event, the crisis of 9/11 to which Bassam and the narrative are hurtling, although the reader never encounters those events directly: we leave Bassam, towards the end of the novel, making his way through airport security, then we and other characters simply learn of the hijacking and its consequences, and Bassam's participation, via images on the television screen. The unspeakable remains unspoken; the crisis is witnessed only circuitously, by indirection. The focus is primarily on the before, not primarily (if at all) in terms of causes or even motivation but as a succession of events that lead, eventually and it seems inevitably, to something that remains resolutely beyond the borders of the narrative – to which that narrative gestures but which it does not even begin to describe. From the standpoint of the Freudian notion of trauma, in fact, what is remarkable about *The Garden of Last Days* is that it remains, for most of the

[7] Interview at http://bostonist.com/2008/07/23/interview_with_andre_dubus_iii_the.php; review by John M. Formy-Duval for About.com Contemporary Literature at http://contemporarylit.about.com/od/fiction/fr/gardenLastDays.htm.

time, in the stage of latency. The story of 9/11 is resolutely not told; it occurs to the reader as a series of fragments – and fragments antici-pated rather than remembered. Several critics have remarked on how, in Faulkner's novels, the sense of loss *precedes* any actual experience of losing. The fear, the moral panic engendered by 9/11, in turn, appears to *precede* that terrible event in the narrative present of *The Garden of Last Days*. It is haunting the characters even before it has happened. Happened in the story, that is; it has, of course, happened outside the narrative; the reader is experiencing the before of the characters afterwards. Unlike Bassam and the others he shares a night with in the Puma Club, we, the readers are looking backward, over the rup-ture in time that is 9/11; and we are asked, if not compelled, to act as witnesses – and, as far as possible, to piece its fragments together, and to link them, by the end of the narrative, into some sort of sequence that makes sense.

Things scarcely make sense to Bassam. Like the other characters in and around the Puma Club, he appears to be groping towards a revelation, looking for an epiphany that never occurs. At the club just before he embarks on the hijacking for which, in the past few months, he has been training, Bassam is drinking heavily, smoking and spending money as if there were no tomorrow. He hires April, or Spring as he knows her, for a private dance in the Champagne Room. And, once he has her there, he appears to be driven by curiosity about her: her real name, which he eventually persuades her to reveal, the scar on her body, which he longs to touch, why she does what she does in the club. April/Spring is not so much an elusive object of desire for Bassam as a mystery wrapped in an enigma, to adopt a famous phrase once used by British orientalists to describe the other-ness of the Orient: the enigma and the mystery being precisely the otherness of April/Spring to him, the otherness of a culture that he is both drawn to and loathes, that he finds seductive, sympathetic in some ways, but that he also hates and wants to destroy. Bassam is not an entirely successful character. Dubus, apparently, researched Islamic culture before writing this novel and the research sometimes shows, the learning is not carried lightly enough. Sometimes, too, the attempt to give Bassam an Arab-inflected language is as unsuccessful as a similar attempt made by John Updike in *The Terrorist* to find an appropriate speech for his Arab-American protagonist: what is meant to sound different but authentic too often comes across as artificial, even stereotypical.

Where Dubus succeeds with Bassam, however, is where he succeeds with all the other characters: that is, in catching Bassam's confusion, as he vacillates between resolution and panic, commitment and uncertainty, the conviction that he has embarked on a course of action that he wanted and the scarcely tolerable suspicion that he is being carried along by the rapid, remorseless, and irreversible logic of events. "What he never would have known as he hardened and purified himself in training, as he prayed steadfastly in tents and motel rooms and autos," Bassam reflects, is "that he would *like* these kufar, that he would like… this April who calls herself Spring" (259). Which is not the whole truth, of course, he also loathes, fears, and despises these people, including April/ Spring. The point is in the see-saw process of his impressions and emotions, not in any coherent articulation of thought and motive. Things happen to Bassam; experiences flow through him, while he and the reader watch.

Which is not to say that Dubus makes the terrorist blameless. Bassam is complicit in the events that occur to him. He is not simply a victim of circumstance. He is, as a result, as responsible for what happens as April is when she takes Franny to the strip club and A.J. is when he then takes Franny away. If you put hot coffee between your thighs while you are driving, then execute an illegal u-turn and burn your leg, you have, in the end, only yourself to blame. In so far as there is an ethic at work in this novel, however, a gauge of responsibility, it is existential: right and wrong are measured behaviourally, in terms of action, what each character does as he or she becomes immersed in the stream of events. That stream is never fully understood by any of them; still less do they enjoy more than partial control. They can behave more or less well or badly, but that behaviour does not lead to moral assessments that venture beyond the momentary and conditional. Judgement in *The Garden of Days,* like character, is fluid; more exactly, it is performative, the product of a constant negotiation. Haunted by crises that have not yet occurred but hover over them like a thundercloud, people like April, A.J. and Bassam struggle to enact their identities; there are differences here, of gender, ethnicity, political affiliation, and so on, but the differences are a matter of superficial definition, or rather their reduction to historical objects. What matters is their shared location, in an interstitial space between stream of events and stream of consciousness: a territory where the distinctions between terrorist and stripper, stripper and abductor, or between different forms of subordination, while indisputable, receive far less emphasis and focus than the interface, the spaces where the characters thereby distinguished meet and engage. Here, at this interface, characters watch each other and themselves and struggle to fathom and perform their natures. They try, like Bassam, to work out what it is that is happening to them, what it is that they and those around them are doing, what it means to be faced with things that it seems impossible to assimilate, let alone understand.

That struggle, that attempt, it has to be said, is, for the most part, unsuccessful. Meaning remains mostly latent for the characters in *The Garden of Last Days*; they watch, they witness but they do not work out. April ends up finding a new life with Franny, A.J. ends up in jail, Jean ends up living by herself, Bassam ends up dead. These are all endings of sorts but they are inconclusive to the extent that, implicitly, the streams of events and consciousness continue to flow, the vagaries of things happening go on. With the obvious exception of Bassam: his erratic course has reached a terminus of some sort. But even here, the conclusion is inconclusive to the extent that the verdict on him remains open. Asked by Jean what the terrorist she entertained was "like," April says simply, "Like a boy. Just some drunk and lonely boy" (526). Which says everything and nothing. What we are left with is what we have encountered throughout the novel: a resistance to the kind of holistic, homogeneous, and historically continuous narrative on which ideas of nation and nationality depend. The reader, as she or he pieces the fragments of this story together, is compelled to bear witness to what Bhabha would call a "hybrid" interaction between competing and contending cultural constituencies: to make sense of what happens by recognizing how these characters occupy an intersubjective space where questions of value, interest and identity are constantly negotiable, where the game persists in remaining open. That April, A.J., Bassam and others at the

Puma Club are from the underclass is precisely the point, the reason for telling their story. They occupy a terrain quite separate from that of the dominant culture. As a result, they, or rather the narratives of their lives, provide an interstititial, interrogatory perspective on the narratives of nation and crisis – and the narrative of a nation in crisis. We see those narratives beyond a boundary in a different way from *Netherland, The Reluctant Fundamentalist* and "Twilight of the Superheroes," but one that is no less revelatory: that is, from a position that is deterritorialized by being shifted beyond – and, for that matter, below and between – the verbal maneuvres, the rhetorical masks of conventional political discourse.

In the weeks following 9/11, a New York paediatric surgeon reported an alarming number of cases involving adolescent girls all with identical symptoms (Greenberg, 26). Each of them arrived at hospital having lost an alarming amount of weight as a result of being unable to swallow. All of them believed that the reason for this was that some unidentified debris from the fall of the Twin Towers had got caught in their throats and caused a blockage. On examination, it emerged that there was some kind of physical constriction in the throat but, equally, that there was nothing there, no debris or other matter apparently causing it. The identification of these young women with the scenes they had witnessed was so powerful that it had appeared to enter their bodies. They had transformed a collective external experience into an internal one; in the process, their bodies had testified to the fact that what they had witnessed was, quite literally, impossible to swallow. 9/11 may be, as one commentator has put it, "the most photographed disaster in history" (Hirsch, "I Took Pictures," 69). But it is also one that, in terms of visible icons, functions most memorably as an absence: the towers that are no longer there, the empty skyline, the "scar of the spirit" (Hartman, 7) that is Ground Zero. Acres of print have been devoted to the terrorist attacks, among them the report of the National Commission on Terrorist Attacks Upon the United States (9/11 Commission) issued on July 22, 2004. And schemes like "The September 11, 2001 Oral History Narrative and Memory Project" sponsored by Columbia University's Oral History Research Office promise even more in the way of verbal evidence. But still all we have are what one commentator has called "incomplete fragments of meaning" (Greenberg, 19). The story of that day continues, either metaphorically or literally, to stick in the throat.

What the writer has to do in the face of all this, surely, is to pursue some form of mimesis that dips above and below the discourses of nationalism, combining closeness and distance, registering at once the communal tragedy (the devastation wrought on a particular place and people) and the structural connections to tragic experiences elsewhere (the devastation wrought on other particular places and peoples in other parts of the globe). As the books I have been looking at in this chapter suggest, trauma may provide an intercultural connection and, issuing from this, the possibility of social transformation. Or, as one authority on traumatic experience has put it, "in a catastrophic age ... trauma itself may provide the very link between cultures: not as a simple understanding of the pasts of others but rather within the traumas of contemporary history, as our ability to listen through the departures we have all taken from ourselves" (Caruth, 4). At basis, what the novels of Eisenberg, Hamid, O'Neill, and Dubus III – along with other work to be looked at later – all share is a sense of *convergence*, and a belief in the hybrid as the only space in which the location of cultures, and the bearing witness to trauma, can properly occur. It is this that allows these narratives to make the turning point in American history that is 9/11, if not understandable, then at least susceptible to understanding through a strategy of deterritorialization. It is this that transforms crisis into a story that can be accurately and adequately told.

4

Imagining the Transnational

The events of September 11, 2001 opened up a sometimes bitter debate between writers of the First and Third Worlds. At one extreme has been the British novelist Martin Amis. In a response to the terrorist attacks written just a week after they occurred, Amis was among many observers to describe 9/11 as a "defining moment" with the glint of the second plane as it crashed into the tower offering "the worldflash of a coming future." Even at this stage, Amis was not inclined to be temperate or measured in his response. "All over again," Amis insisted, "the west confronts an irrationalist, agonistic, theocratic/ideocratic system which is essentially and unappeasably opposed to its existence." But this invocation of a return to holy war – a curiously inverse image of the rhetoric of Osama bin Laden – was at least balanced by a plea for a viewpoint to recent events that would be "over and above nationalisms, blocs, religions, ethnicities." There is a recognition here of what Amis terms the "insidious geographical incuriosity" of the United States: which leads him to ask how many Americans "know, for example, that their government has destroyed at least 50% of the Iraqui population." This incuriosity, and the triumphalist insularity that possibly goes with it, is something that Amis, at this stage, saw as a threat to world peace at least as serious as Islamic fundamentalism. And it led him to call, not for revenge, but for what he termed "species consciousness." "during this week of incredulous misery," he declared,

After the Fall: American Literature Since 9/11, First Edition. Richard Gray.
© 2011 John Wiley & Sons, Ltd. Published 2011 by John Wiley & Sons, Ltd.

"I have been trying to apply such a consciousness... Thinking of the victims, the perpetrators, and the near future, I felt species grief, then species shame, then species fear."[1] Gradually, however, this measured response was jettisoned. In subsequent commentary, Amis's opinions hardened into prejudices. Within nine months of the attacks, Amis was ready to declare that September 11, 2001 was "a day of de-Enlightenment" announcing a war, not just between "opposed geographical areas, but also opposed centuries or millennia." On one side was the West, the source of rationalism and sound government. On the other was the East, offering "a landscape of ferocious anachronisms: nuclear jihad in the Indian subcontinent; the medieval agonism of Islam, the Bronze Age blunderings of the Middle East."[2] In a piece published four years after this vision of apocalypse, Amis went even further, insisting that moderate Islam had surrendered to Islamic fundamentalism, "a pathological cult" or "cult of death" that was at once profoundly inimical and incomprehensible to the West. To seek reasons for terrorism or as he called it "horrorism," Amis declared, was not just pointless and counter-productive but a sign of weakness. The only appropriate response, would be something "like an unvarying factory siren of unanimous disgust."[3]

At the other extreme from Amis is the Indian writer Pankaj Mishra – who while, quite rightly, describing Amis's commentary as "a bold and arrogant display of prejudice and ignorance,"[4] appeared to dismiss the possibility that Western commentators had anything worthwhile to say about events outside the West. More extreme still were those middle-class Turks in Istanbul who told the Turkish writer

[1] Martin Amis, "Fear and Loathing," *The Guardian* 18 September, 2001 (http://books.guardianco.uk/departments/politicsphilosophyandsociety/story/0,,553923,00.html).

[2] Martin Amis, "The Voice of the Lonely Crowd," *The Guardian* 1 June, 2002 (http://booksguardian.co.uk/review/story/0,12084,725608,00.html).

[3] Martin Amis, "The Age of Horrorism," *The Observer* 10 September 2006 (http//observer.guardian.co.uk/review/story/0,,1868732,00.html).

[4] Pankaj Mishra, "The Politics of Paranoia," *The Observer* 11 September, 2006 (http://books.guardian.co.uk/departments/politicsphilosophyandsociety/story/0,,1874132.html).

Orhan Pamuk on 9/11 that the terrorists had done the "right thing." Reflecting on his compatriot's callous reaction, Pamuk observed that such callousness was perhaps the result of something the very reverse of ignorance. An ordinary citizen of the non-Western world, Pamuk suggested, is now more conscious than ever before of his own disadvantaged condition. Thanks to global communications systems, he or she is acutely aware of "how insubstantial is his share of the world's wealth; he knows that he lives under conditions that are much harsher and more devastating than those of the "westerner" and that he is condemned to a much shorter life." The East sees the West, according to Pamuk. The West, however, does not see the East. "The western world," Pamuk wrote, "is scarcely aware" of the "overwhelming feeling of humiliation that is experienced by most of the world's population."[5] The internet and the faster movement of capital in a free global market may not have accelerated or added to knowledge of other countries and cultures, in the United States or the West generally: the Wall Street bankers in *The Good Life* by Jay McInerney are not alone in regarding "the world beyond Manhattan primarily in terms of investment and vacation opportunities" (72). It has, however, made the peoples of the Third World unwilling witnesses to their own disadvantages, their (relative or absolute) poverty. The screen concealing the "real reality" of Third World oppression and deprivation from the sight of the 'digitalised First World" (Zizek, 3–5) is perhaps more accurately described as a one-way mirror. Some in the Third World, perhaps most, can see through it, obliged to gaze at a consumer paradise, a world of surfeit that is determinately not theirs. The result, obscene though it might seem, is that some of them, at least, have ended up by responding to the events of 9/11 not with the disgust that Amis recommended to the Westerner but with something not far short of delight.

"After a couple of hours at their desks on September 12, 2001" Amis commented sardonically shortly after 9/11, "all the writers on

---

[5]   Pankaj Mishra, "The End of Innocence," *The Guardian* 19 May, 2007 (http://www.guardian.co.uk/books/2007/may/19/fiction.martinamis).

earth were reluctantly considering a change of occupation."[6] This is, of course, an exaggeration. Many writers had intuited that political and religious extremism, having devastated large areas of the world, would eventually target the wealthier and more protected societies of the West. Some may initially have seen silence as the only adequate response to an event that, as DeLillo claimed – in an essay published shortly after it occurred – "changed the grain of the most routine moment." (DeLillo, *In the Ruins of the Future*, 40). But they soon felt the obligation to write the next sentence. If a writer like Amis has felt paralysis, it might be due, not just to the trauma of the event itself, but also to the series of warring opposites in which he has chosen to think about it – and which, arguably, have paralysed most of his thought and writing on 9/11. In turn, if other writers have managed to move beyond this, it is surely because they have pursued a recalibration of feeling about the event, sometimes venturing beyond the narrow category of "9/11 fiction" to do so. They have recognized, instinctively it may be, that, in a world of fluid ethnic and geographic boundaries, where every day is a crossing of borders, the opposites on which writers like Amis depend do not work – that they need to be challenged, reimagined, and reconfigured.

"I shuttled between identities" (77) observes the title character in *Jasmine* by the Asian American writer, Bharati Mukherjee; and that sense of the improvizational, making up an identity, is a feature of many of the more interesting texts that have appeared in the past ten or so years, as writers attempt to deal with their liminal condition, their position between historical borders and cultures. This returns us to the United States as 'the first universal nation" (Reed, 56). Bearing witness to the culturally other may, for entirely understandable reasons, remain a problem for many of those writers struggling to confront the trauma of a post-9/11 society. But just such a bearing witness is at the heart of those fictions offering variations on the immigrant encounter: writing about and, in many instances from, a position of liminality, the perspective of what one critic has called "new strangers in paradise" (Muller). "To migrate is

---

[6]   Martin Amis, "The Age of Horrorism," *The Observer* 10 September 2006 (http//observer.guardian.co.uk/review/story/0,,1868732,00.html).

certainly to lose language and home," Salman Rushdie has written, 'to be defined by others, to become invisible, or, even worse, a target, it is to experience deep changes and wrenches in the soul." "But," he goes on, "the migrant is not simply transformed by his act; he transforms his new world" (210). Books about these new strangers show us this act of mutual transformation, by showing people renewed and renamed out of a frequently savage encounter between their several pasts. They also, very often, enact that same mutuality, that reciprocity of influence, by offering narrative moments, and a narrative momentum overall, that are responsive to the syncretic character of American culture. They reconfigure language, the themes and tropes of American writing in terms that go way beyond bipolar, biracial models. In the process, they become a lexical equivalent of the immigrant encounter, transforming their literary environs just as they are transformed by them – and, in effect, force us to rethink 9/11.

Take the case of the American South. In the past twenty or so years, the South has experienced a flood of immigration, from, among other places, the Hispanic world and South East Asia. And the several waves of emigration from Cuba to Florida alone have produced a literature of expatriation that includes *Raining Backwards* by Roberto Fernandez, *Dreaming in Cuban* by Christina Garcia and *The Perez Family* by Christine Bell. "I need a map," admits one exile in *The Perez Family*, which tells the story of a "family" that, strictly speaking, is not a family at all, but a group of refugees put together to gain priority for sponsorship. Needing a map to chart their way through the strange land of southern Florida, these characters offer a different angle of vision on their new American surroundings, turning them sometimes into dreamscapes. Here, for instance, is Miami as seen by one of the members of the Perez family, the self-appointed leader and matriarch called Dottie:

> Miami in the afternoon sun is crayola and bright. Like a child's drawing, the city is imaginatively colored and unimaginatively out of proportion. Slender palms stand in disbelief against giant lego constructions. Soft clouds float by the garish concrete. Rows of aqua and pink houses insult the shimmering sea and the sky they frame.

The streets themselves parallel and intersect with the simple logic of a child's board game. Miami fit Dottie's idea of freedom perfectly – it was simple, gaudy and close at hand (40).

As this passage suggests, many of the characters in these novels find a means of locating themselves in their new American space by relocating the emotional baggage they carry with them. In the process, they offer a fresh, Hispanic spin on a cluster of tropes, gathered around the notions of a lost childhood and a dreamlike paradise, that is as old as the first European encounters with America. It was an English pamphleteer of the early seventeenth century, after all, who tried to encourage emigration to the New World by calling it a "Virgin Countrey," designed to show those who journeyed there "what a brow of fertility and beauty the world was adorned with when she was vigorous and youthfull" (Williams, 19). Characters like Dottie echo and reaccentuate these myths of emigration. Needing a map, they make one for themselves, one that recharts their new home, using fresh but somehow familiar coordinates. In the process, they offer altered geographies, another perspective on the mixed, plural medium that Americans now inhabit. And the books that tell their stories give another spin to the old national narrative of exile from paradise and possible return: dramatizing, in the process, that vocal rhythm of innovation and restitution, escape and recovery that turns every day into a meeting with T.S. Eliot's "familiar, compound ghost" (38), an encounter with something strange and yet somehow known.

What is striking about stories of the immigrant encounter, in fact, is what tends to be missing in many novels of 9/11 and its aftermath. There is a strategy of deterritorialization at work here, just as there is in "Twilight of the Superheroes," *The Reluctant Fundamentalist*, *Netherland*, and *The Garden of Last Days*. Books such as *The Perez Family*, like those of Eisenberg, Hamid, O'Neill, and Dubus III, present America as a transcultural space in which different cultures reflect and refract each other. So also, perhaps even more so, do those books that bear witness to the encounter of South East Asians with America: where the strategy, very often, is to read the United States through American wars waged on foreign soil as well as to show the reader what it is to be American by exploring American spaces and places from extrinsic vantage points. One book that bears this kind of witness is *The Foreign Student* by Susan Choi, which tells the story of a shy young Korean boy called Chuck who arrives at a small college in the Tennessee mountains. Choi uses the controlling trope of translation to suggest the intricate cultural negotiations the boy must initiate before he can even begin to cope. There is always, Chuck reflects, an "inevitable shift of meaning" in the course of translation, "the drift of thought from its mooring once the word that had housed it is gone" (81). Previously a translator himself for the United States Information Service in Korea, Chuck finds himself adrift between words and meanings, unable to escape his memories of the Korean War or to catch with precision the social protocols of his new environment. Like some early explorer, he tries to fall back on figurative or literal likeness between his old world and his new. "Korea is a shape just like Florida. Yes?" he observes. "The top half is a Communist state, and the bottom half fighting for democracy!" (51). "You maybe don't believe it," he adds later, "but Korea, the land, looks very much like Tennessee" (53). So fiercely does he try to believe this, we are told, that sometimes "he woke in the morning and just for an instant was sure he was home. The mist coming out from the mountains. The soft hills" (53). But the likeness is a forced one, and he cannot always translate his present into his past.

Sometimes, the result of that failure of translation is comic: as when he shakes hands "with the coloured table servant at formal Friday dinner" because the servant's "grave demeanour and immaculate dress seemed to dictate" (15–6) such a gesture. Sometimes, it is more tragically serious, leading Chuck to feel like a visitor from "outer space" (6), who seems "to be pushing a ripple of silence ahead of himself" (12) everywhere he goes. It seems appropriate that the professor who befriends him at college offers him as a gift a Roget's Thesaurus, advising him to learn "a few new words a day," and "slip them in sideways, when your mind isn't working" (165). And it seems even more appropriate that the girl with whom he becomes involved, called Katherine, gives him a copy of the Robert Penn Warren novel, *Band of Angels*, which has at its center a woman, Amantha Starr, caught

91

between two worlds when she discovers that, while her father was a white plantation owner, her mother was black and a slave. "Oh, who am I?" (1) Amantha insistently asks; and, in his own way, Chuck is constantly formulating the same question – or trying to. For him, however, the terms of his divided identity are much more fluid, much more difficult to verbalize than they are for the classic figure of the tragic mulatto or mulatta. The difficulty, the problem Chuck has in trying to find words to break the silence around him, to fill the lack and to shape his identity, is registered even in the moment Katherine offers him her gift. "You must believe that I bought this for you," she tells him. "I was browsing the campus bookstore not expecting to find anything ... But here this was, like a message in a bottle, washing up on a desert island." "What do you mean, *browse*?" Chuck asks her. "It's what you do when you look at my books," Katherine replies. And, characteristically, Chuck's mind wanders off with this cue into contemplation of this new word. "As they walked to the car," we learn,

> he tried to make different weddings for the word, but he could come up with only one match. "I browse the shelves," he said. It had a languid, elongated shape in his mouth. The limitation made the word seem luxurious.(144–5)

That is a small paradigm of Chuck's struggle to make sense of his liminal condition by forging an appropriate vocabulary – finding the right words that will make his own limitations, if not luxurious, then at least tolerable and known. By the end of the novel, Chuck has found a place of sorts for himself, working for his own support with the black kitchen staff (led by the man whose hand he once tried to shake): people with whom "he got along well," we learn, not least because "they never peered into his thoughtful silences" (324). But, just in case we are inclined to sentimentalize this, by making an easy connection between two different versions of the marginalized, Choi draws us back in the last sentences of the book: reminding us of the legacy – of war, dispossession, and departure – that is peculiarly and painfully his. The final image is from his Korean past, of him working in the USIS offices "until the cease-fire, translating wire – consuming

it, as if it could give him a new frame for thinking, a new lexicon."
(325). That task of translation still preoccupies him, the implication is,
shadowing his American present as much as his Korean past. He is still
trying to forge or find a vocabulary to describe his position between
different races and cultures. So is his creator, Choi. So, for that matter,
are those fictions that bear witness to the consequences of another
American war waged abroad and sandwiched between the Korean
and Iraq wars – and similarly set in the American South: *Lost Armies*
and *Prisoners* by Wayne Karlin, *A Good Scent from a Strange Mountain* by
Robert Olen Butler, *Boat People* by Mary Gardner and *Monkey Bridge*
by Lan Cao. What is at stake in these books is the lives of Vietnamese
Americans, rather than Korean Americans like Chuck and Hispanic
peoples such as Dottie. But, as in *The Foreign Student,* the United
States is seen from a doubly extrinsic vantage point here, as the major
characters attempt to negotiate both the hybrid territory of their new
surroundings and their memories of an American war fought outside
the United States. And, as in both *The Foreign Student* and *The Perez
Family*, the major characters occupy an interstitial space *between* cultures. What boundaries there are here, supposedly separating those
cultures are, in any event, fluid, permeable to the point of invisibility. And these fictions, recalling that Deleuzian image of rhizomes,
establish roots in the broader terrain of different literary and cultural
histories that are numerous and adventitious – and so demonstrate
deterritorialization with a vengeance.

More than a million Vietnamese and native-born Americans of
Vietnamese descent now live in the United States, the vast majority
having come over either just after the fall of Saigon in 1975 or as the
so-called "boat people" in the second wave of emigration in 1978.[7]

[7] For the historical context mentioned here, see, for example, Paul James Routledge,
The Vietnamese Experience in America Bloomington: Indiana University Press, 1992;
for some of the larger cultural issues, Jeffery J. Folks and James A. Perkins, *Southern
Writers at Century's End* Lexington: University of Kentucky Press, 1997 and A. Robert
Lee, *Multicultural American Literature: Comparative Black, Native, Latino/a and Asian
American Fiction* Edinburgh: University of Edinburgh Press, 2003; for further analyses
of the fictions discussed here, Richard Gray, *A Web of Words: The Great Dialogue of
Southern Literature* Athens: University of Georgia Press, 2007; Sharon Monteith and

And about 300,000 of these have gathered in the southern region of the country. The attraction of the South, and especially Louisiana, Florida and Texas, for Vietnamese refugees is not hard to fathom. As a Vietnamese character in *A Good Scent from a Strange Mountain* puts it, "in the flat bayou land of Louisiana, ... there are rice paddies and ... the water and the land are in the most delicate balance with each other, very much like the Mekong Delta, where I grew up" (60). And then there is the obsession with family and ancestry, the compulsion to look backward to a past that seems to have been consumed, over and over again, by war. "*And that of course was the beginning of the far-flung web that I'm still caught in today,*" reflects a character in *Monkey Bridge*, as she recollects a past in which, she recalls, "*we never had peace.*" (234). The reflection, and even the image of the web used to describe what one of the characters in William Faulkner's *Absalom, Absalom!* terms the "pattern" in "the rug" (127) – that is, the complex weave of relations that constitute history: all this sounds distinctly southern. So does the narrative spine of so many of these novels, in which a character attempts to return to the past, by making peace with their ancestors or even returning briefly to the ancestral home. Robert Penn Warren located the central impulse of so many southern stories when he spoke of "the long compulsion and the circuit/Back" to a place where "the father waits for the son" (283). These stories are similarly governed by compulsions of restitution and recovery: as characters try to establish – to borrow a notion from Allen Tate – what degree of devotion to give to the dead. Sons seek out fathers or, more often, daughters seek out mothers, and texts seek to find a place where the past and present can feed and nurture each other.

This, however, is the problem, giving a new spin to an old story. The South is not Vietnam, for all that the characters in these books

---

Nahem Yousaf, "Making an Impression: New Immigrant Fiction in the American South," *Forum for Modern Language Studies* 40 (2004), 214–224, Maureen Ryan, "Outsiders with Inside Information: The Vietnamese in the Fiction of the Contemporary American South," *South to a New Place: Region, Literature, Culture* edited by Suzanne W. Jones and Sharon Monteith Baton Rouge: Louisiana State University Press, 2002.

may seek to find a mirror of their past in their present. "Clearly he did not know his own mind," we learn of a character in *Boat People*. "That was not unusual for Vietnamese in America, who stood between two cultures" (215). Some of the characters in these novels may give themselves wholly to their American surroundings, or at least try to – so giving what one character in *Monkey Bridge* calls "a new spin, the Vietnam spin, to the old immigrant faith in the future" (40). Others, we are also told in *Monkey Bridge*, "hang on to their Vietnam lives ... in a way not much different from amputees who continued to feel the silhouette of their absent limbs" (61) – so offering another kind of "Vietnam spin," this time not to American dream but to south-ern memory; like all those Faulkner characters who have been told and remember too much, they suffer a kind of shadowy life-in-death, unable to separate yesterday from today. But the majority are like the narrator and protagonist of *Monkey Bridge*, Mai Nguyen, and the central Vietnamese character in *Prisoners* called Kiet or K-K: only too aware of their divided destiny and, as a result, unable either to give themselves wholly to their new world or hang on convincingly to their old one.

"My dilemma," Mai Nguyen explains, "was that, seeing both sides to everything, I belonged to neither" (88). Mai Nguyen sees her-self, in a haunting phrase, as "the outsider with inside information" (212) in American society. So does Kiet, whose sense of division is acutely sharpened by the fact that she has a Vietnamese mother and an African-American father from the US military whom she has never known. "She goes looking for her father" (125), one char-acter observes of Kiet. Seeing herself as "half-a-dink, half-a-splib" (13), caught between her Asian and American selves, for most of the novel Kiet is forced to witness American normalcy from the outside: a perspective painfully illustrated by the moment when, on the run as usual, she stops for a moment to stare through "the bright rectangle of a window" at what she calls "a TV family" – a "man, woman, two children" who "sit in front of the rectangle of the tube" (113). She is apart from all this, the families on TV and the families watching TV; like the "nigger" she feels in part she is, and has been told she is, she is marginalized, reduced to the classic position of the African American in white narrative, a watcher and a commentator, someone to whom – according to the prescribed stories that get told – life does not happen. The lost child, carrying with her the burden of a past, the pain of a father who denies her; the outsider, forced to observe a white "normality" from which she feels excluded; the figure worn down by the weight of double consciousness, what W.E.B. Du Bois called "two souls, two thoughts, two unreconciled strivings" (52) in one body: Kiet, and those like her, is a character who is simultaneously old yet new. This is giving the story of the African American in American narrative another coloration, an unfamiliar inflection and fresh meaning. In the process, it is also connecting two bleak moments in American history, linking the colonialism of two different centuries and, to a degree, two different empires.

Two features of these fictions are particularly worth attention, relating to their representation of place and time. The characters in these stories share a liminal condition, as outsiders with inside information, with the places and histories in which they find themselves situated. Which is to say that the mapping of place and the narrating of history here construct both as a matter of relation. Spatial and temporal settings are seen from an interstitial perspective that resists any oppositional grid of either/or distinctions of the kind that writers like Amis – or some of the more conventional readings of 9/11 – would like to lower down upon them. *Monkey Bridge*, for example, continually crosses the bridge between past and present; as it does so, the reader learns how its main character Mai Nguyen escaped Saigon at the age of fourteen, with Mrs Nguyen then following her. Mai's father, Mrs Nguyen's husband, was already dead when they left. But they had hoped that Mai's maternal grandfather, Baba Quan, would come to America with Mrs Nguyen. He did not. Baba Quan and Mrs Nguyen, as the novel puts it, "missed each other at their place of rendezvous on the 30th April, 1975, and the preapproved car that was supposed to take both of them, along with a few other Vietnamese, to an American plane, had to leave without them" (4). Haunted by the loss of Baba Quan, terrified by what she sees as the impermanence of America, Mrs Nguyen longs to return to what she calls "the country" (69), her homeplace in Vietnam. Mai is haunted too. "What happened to my grandfather?" (10) she asks herself more than once during the course of the story. Like all of Faulkner's sad young men, Mai is pursued, it seems, by a ghost, a thin membrane of memories that are only a little hers personally – and that she can hardly bring to consciousness, let alone understand. In Little Falls, Virginia, both Mai and her mother are surrounded by still other, more local phantoms. "All around us," Mai reflects, "ghosts of a different war lingered, the Battle of Fredericksburg, the Battle of Bull Run, the Confederate victories secured by Robert E. Lee's Army of Northern Virginia" (31). This immeasurably complicates the clash between cultures that both mother and daughter experience. There is an old world of wars and phantoms, certainly, and a new world of what Mrs Nguyen calls "the great brand-new" (60). But there is also the world, the territory that seems to occupy a liminal space between the old and the new, remembrance and forgetfulness: which is their chosen place of exile.

What happens in *Monkey Bridge* is, in fact, remarkable: the "old" and the "new," the "East" and the "West," Vietnam and Virginia end up by mirroring and metamorphosing each other, creating a transcultural space for both the text and its protagonists. What the Vietnamese characters in *Monkey Bridge* believe in, most of them, is karma. And "*karma*," Mrs Nguyen writes in her notebooks, "*is the antithesis of Manifest Destiny, the kind of Manifest Destiny they teach my daughter in her history book about the great American West*" (55). "There is a luminous motion between us and our ancestors," Mai Nguyen recalls her grandfather once telling her, "and this history can never be taken away from you" (53). "*Our reality, you see, is a simultaneous past, present, and future,*" Mai similarly remembers her mother writing. "*The verbs in our language are not conjugated because our sense of time is tenseless, indivisible, and knows no end*" (252). "*Karma, my child,*" Mrs Nguyen instructs her daughter,

> is nothing more than an ethical, spiritual chromosome, an amalgamation of parent and child, which is as much a part of our history as the DNA strands. One is already the face of the other. Even as I write this, the shared facts of our lives continue to thread their way through our flesh. (170)

What is learned from all this is the erratic fatefulness of life, the necessity for stoicism and the sheer impossibility of evading or exorcising the past. "*I fear our family history of sin, revenge, and murder,*" Mrs Nguyen confesses, "*and the imprint it creates in our children's lives as it rips through one generation and tears apart the next*" (232). But "there is no escaping it" (28); the past, with its phantoms, is a compulsion not a choice. So is the condition of constant wariness that karma inevitably entails. "One wrong move," Mai Nguyen learns from her father, can alter and has often altered the seamless web of events, generating personal and historical catastrophe for generation after generation. It is a counsel against optimism, the ingrained American belief in boundless possibility, the benevolence of destiny, the power of pluck and luck: which is why, Mai supposes, "in the United States, there was no such thing as 'one wrong move'" (27). No such thing in the United States as a whole, maybe, but certainly in the South, where the notion of "one wrong move" – with all the freight of rehearsing, regretting but also reverencing the past that notion carries with it – is almost a regional trademark. Mai may feel "torn between two worlds" (165), the Vietnam of her past and the America of her present, but the two worlds remain tied by a kind of umbilical cord to each other – and not just by what they have seen and suffered in common, the scars that America has left on the body of Vietnam and the bodies of the Vietnamese (Mrs Nguyen, it turns out, was indelibly scarred during an American bombing raid). They are tied, too, by a subtle web of repetition and resemblance, the "shared stories" (53) of Vietnam and the United States that make *Monkey Bridge* one of the most significant reworkings of territorial preoccupations in recent times.

In *Prisoners*, Wayne Karlin takes the strategy of deterritorialization even further. The main Vietnamese character, Kiet, has a habit of running away, sometimes looking for her long-lost American serviceman father, sometimes aimlessly, without apparent motive or direction. On one occasion, she ends up in Washington, at the site of the Vietnam Veterans Memorial, which she has seen before only on television. By day at the Memorial, she encounters "VC homies … selling hot dogs and egg rolls and copper Washington Monuments and Sno-Globes (turn them over and shake them and napalm falls on a thatched roof village), and t-shirts saying *tough shit yeah we're here now*" (92). By night, she slips into a bamboo cage that has a sign over it: "AMERICANS ARE STILL HELD CAPTIVE BY ASIA: POW's NEVER HAVE A NICE DAY" (93). And she looks closely, attentively at the Memorial itself. "The Wall took the high yellow out of my face and gave it to me black, black with the white names scrawled all over it," she recalls. "I had walked along it slowly, letting the names write themselves across my skin, if my daddy's name was there it would have stayed on my skin when I turned from it" (99). This attempt to attend to, almost to touch the past – and, in particular, those who have fought and died in a war that has helped shape both region and nation – offers a ghostly reflection, a repetition in another key of all those other, earlier American elegies dedicated to those who have died in conflict, among them "Ode to the Confederate Dead" by Allen Tate and "For the Union Dead" by Robert Lowell. This time, though, it is one of the new people of the South who is reaching back, trying to come to terms with a common, conflicted history. And, as Kiet runs "down into the black V" of the Memorial at night, this time it is a new kind of Southern identity that is being born. "The moonlight is bright," Kiet tells us, "and I can see my reflection flowing wavy around the white shocks of the names." The names of the fallen dead seem to "give little tugs and pinches" as she runs. "My Ma's name is my face reflected in the polished stone," she goes on. "My daddy writes his name on my forehead but whenever I try to see it another name nudges it and replaces it." Pausing for breath, Kiet feels that she is falling into the Wall as she leans her head against its "cool stone." As a cloud covers the moon, blotting out her reflection, she feels more, as if she is merging with it. "I disappear into the wall," she confesses. "Black into black. I push like I'm pushing into the cold skin of water. It seizes me, my nose and ear openings and eyes and all my hollows filling with black. Disappearing." She has sunk into the past. Then comes the rebirth, the re-emergence. "I tear myself away," she concludes, "and move up towards the light, feeling myself being named and born out of the black living wedge of the dead." (99–100)

The feeling of rebirth, renewal is only momentary, as it turns out. Kiet still has plenty of running away and searching for her father ahead of her. The running away returns, for her and us, in the narrative present of Maryland. And the search will, in any event, probably last the whole of her life: even though, by the end of the story, she has destroyed the false father who abused her and found a kind of temporary surrogate father in an African American Vietnam vet called Baxter. "*I'll be whatever you need, old man,*" Kiet tells or intimates to Baxter in a strange ghostly conversation. To which Baxter simply replies: "*Just live, child. That's all you need do*" (146). The conversation echoes other ghostly interchanges between generations in *Absalom, Absalom!* and Toni Morrison's *Beloved*. And what it tells us, or rather intimates, is that what Kiet needs to do, and what her father and her past need of her, only reaches its terminus in death. To say that the rebirth is momentary, however, is not to negate its significance. Nor is it to underestimate the degree to which this moment in *Prisoners* – to use those figures of Brodsky's and Bakhtin's again – echoes earlier moments in American literature but with a difference, offering a re-sounding of the past that is also a reaccentuation. In this revisiting of a sacred site in American fiction and poetry, a site dedicated to those who died for a cause that failed, Wayne Karlin rewrites the ticket of admission. This is a new way into the monumentalized past and, given Kiet's fleeting sense of recovery and re-emergence, a new way out. Kiet sees her Vietnamese mother's face in her own fleeing reflection, reads her father's name in the myriad names of the American fallen. And then, merging herself with the past, surfaces in the present, "named and born" in an act that is not only deeply dreamlike but darkly ritualistic, personal to her but also shared with the whole "living wedge of the dead." *Prisoners* shows us an act of mutual transformation, by showing us a young Amerasian being born and named out of the savage encounter between her Vietnamese and American pasts. It also enacts that same mutuality, that reciprocity of influence, by offering narrative moments, and a narrative momentum overall, that are responsive to the syncretic character of the United States. This is a story that reconfigures the language, the themes and tropes of American writing in terms that go way beyond the bipolar, biracial model. In the process, it transforms its literary environs just as it is transformed by them.

At the end of *Prisoners*, Karlin allows the revisiting of old battle sites and memorials to take another direction. A Vietnam vet, Brian Schulman, returns to Vietnam, to help in the search for the remains of American combatants missing in action. The book began with him digging for the remains of one war, the Civil War, on a "wedge of land between the Chesapeake bay and the entrance to the Potomac" (3); it ends with him digging for those of another, later one. The two wars have shadowed each other throughout the narrative; and, with the close of the novel echoing its opening, they continue to do so. And, just as the American South was read through the prism of Vietnam for most of the story, now Vietnam is read through the prism of the South. Or, to be more exact, the Vietnam to which Brian returns, and which he feels has "enveloped him again" (153) is another ghost-haunted landscape. There are the ghosts waiting for Brian, of course, when he finds himself "back in Vietnam to find out what was left behind of and by his generation" (157). And there are the ghosts preying on the Vietnamese, already there and bearing the scars of war. The Vietnamese woman who acts as guide and interpreter to Brian and his team, Dao Thi Cam, is just such a haunted character. As Brian looks at Cam, recalling "the mini-ball and bayonet splintered skeletons of Confederate Civil War prisoners he'd unearthed near the Potomac" at his last dig, he wonders if she in any way shares his feelings, "still saw her city filtered through the dust of the war" (154). It turns out she does: not because she has anything like his memories – she was, after all, in the People's Army and he was the enemy – but because she cannot close her eyes to the horrors she has witnessed, the suffering she has seen and shared. Recalling a particularly fierce bombing near Khe Sanh, for instance, Cam tells Brian:

> I just remember hearing a great noise, outside but also inside my head, like my mind was being ripped in two. And then I woke up and all the trees were gone and all the trucks and men and my friends and I was alone in the middle of a crater and everywhere I could see were craters and everything was silent and my country was gone. So, for a while, for days until I found people again, I thought I was alone in the world, that you had finally peeled my country from the earth. That I was a ghost. (170)

101

The landscape devastated by a ruthless enemy, the sense of ghost-liness and haunting, the wounds, the divisions that are both "out-side but also inside," and the framework of indelible memories, mind and spirit scarred beyond repair: all these are tropes familiar to any reader of classic Civil War narratives transported and transformed in the process – this time, because it is "the enemy" who is speaking and she is making Brian and us see things through her eyes. Karlin has, in effect, taken a traditional language of combat and used it here as an access to understanding, a way of ensuring that otherness – not just Vietnamese immigrants but the Vietnamese who stayed at home – is both named and known. During the course of his work at battles-ites in Vietnam, Brian uncovers relics of the Mongol invasion of the country: "We didn't know about the Mongol invasion," Brian reflects, "We didn't know anything" (168). Earlier, back at home in Maryland, he is visited by a young cousin just out of the Israeli army and notes the "migratory flocks" of American troops taking off from the local army base "to disappear into the Gulf" (125). "I don't really believe in closure," Brian admits towards the end of the narrative. "Whatever's been covered can always be uncovered or even sometimes uncovers itself" (161). Karlin evidently does not believe in closure either. That is clear enough from the narrative strategies of *Prisoners,* a novel that, like *Monkey Bridge,* uses a kind of spatial and temporal layering to uncover and investigate the faultlines between cultures.

The project of books like *Prisoners* and *Monkey Bridge* is renewal not repetition. Kiet may be drawn to an African American ex-soldier in *Prisoners,* perhaps seeing in her own alienation, her sense of exile and oppression, an echo of his, but the repetition is in a different key. And her connection with him, as it turns out, is expressed in the ghostliest of dialogues and is as fragile as it is fleeting. A Vietnamese character in *A Good Scent from a Strange Mountain,* in turn, may feel "a kinship" (81) with African Americans, but he is also aware, acutely, of difference. An Amerasian character in *Boat People* may observe that "Black people came here by boat too. Just like us," but she is quickly corrected by a friend. "People *bought* them," the friend points out about those early Africans brought to America. "They had to work for the people who bought them" (254). The connection between two dispossessed peoples, and the wars and memories associated with them, fails at a certain point. So these novels explore other analogies, other connections, to try to locate just where on the national and regional maps the Vietnamese – those living embodiments of a more recent American nightmare – really are. And they search for ways of enacting the savagely specific encounter between Vietnamese past and American present from which all these characters suffer – and, more positively, of registering that mutuality, that reciprocity of influence that those characters experience in their new surroundings. Tropes of ghostliness and haunting, shadows and memory are often deployed: to describe a condition that the young narrator of *Monkey Bridge* rehearses and regrets when she talks of "a phantom that could no longer offer comfort or sanctuary" (32) that is her heritage and that she longs to flee. So too is the structural principle of repetition, with a difference, and return. So, in *Prisoners*, the "blood of the dead and living … mingle" (2) to the point where the Civil War, the Vietnamese War, the first Gulf War and other conflicts offer the spectacle of a "Massive Seepage" (104) into one another. Wars recall and rehearse other wars here, in a narrative responsive to the accumulative, syncretic rhythms of American history. And in *Monkey Bridge*, in turn, the project of crossing between cultures is announced in the title. A monkey bridge, the reader is told, offers an imperfect but necessary form of transit. A *"thin, unsteady … uncommanding structure,"* a narrow walkway made out of bamboo and vines, the secret of using it is a matter of intuition, cunning, and courage – or, as the novel puts it, *"the ability to set aside the process"* of crossing *"in favour of seeing the act whole and complete"* (179). *Monkey Bridge* constructs just such a narrative bridge itself, working through an elaborate counterpointing of war, remembrance, and forgetfulness – Vietnamese immigrants, we learn, are "an awkward reminder of a war the whole country was trying to forget" (15) – that manages both to mirror and subvert common themes and tropes, some of them national and some of them regional. In the process, it both describes and enacts the condition of being "in between:" that is, of living on a borderline or threshold – a site, both cultural and personal, where identities are performed and contested.

Consider, for instance, what the central character and narrator of *Monkey Bridge* learns about her past and the way she comes to learn about it. What she learns is the truth of a tragic history. The man she believed was her grandfather, called Baba Quan, was not her grandfather at all, but a man who, back in the Mekong Delta – "the lushest, most tender, most compelling part of Vietnam"(69) – colluded in adultery by arranging for his wife to sleep with his landlord; Mai Nguyen and her mother are the eventual and immediate issue of this arrangement. Mai Nguyen learns all this from a letter her mother writes her just before committing suicide; her mother, in turn, learned the truth from some "*raw, hard numbers,*" "*lists of names and dates*" in what is called "*the book of debts*" (232) – that is, the account book of the family plantation. What both women also learn is that Baba Quan was not only someone who gave his wife in return for the cancellation of his debts but also a murderer. "*The world, for him, narrowed and converged into one dark shaft of revenge,*" (234) Mai learns; and during the Vietnam War, he took advantage of the general confusion to emerge from "*an underground of tunnels*" (250) to kill his landlord. Learning about what her mother calls "*the karma that has pursued our family like a hawk chasing its prey*" (251), Mai Nguyen has encountered a secret, suppressed history. With this knowledge, she may quite possibly be able, not to exorcise her past nor even evade it, but simply accept it, in all its ugly reality and move on. "We had inherited the same flesh," she observes of herself and her mother, "like the special kind of DNA which is inherited exclusively from the mother and transmitted flawlessly only to the female child – the daughter" (259). Mai will, she says, "follow the course" of her own future, but "a part" of her mother "would always pass itself" (259) through her.

Monkey Bridge retells the tale of genealogies: of a character returning to a place where, to rephrase that remark of Warren's quoted earlier, the mother waits for the daughter. In doing so, it revisits not only the male narrative of repetition and recovery but also the work of such otherwise different writers as Willa Cather, Alice Walker, and Toni Morrison, for all of whom the return of mothers to daughters or daughters to mothers becomes a kind of synecdoche for repairing historical and generational rupture, in a (not unproblematic) act of restitution. It sets in tension the experience of exile with the compulsions of home, family, and tale-telling. That, in turn, is a kind of echo, and a transformation, of all those American texts preoccupied with how to turn space into place, how to use storytelling or blood ties or both to make a sense of home in the world, even when it seems determinately alien and unhomelike: texts as unlike in other ways as, say, *The Autobiography of Miss Jane Pittman* by Ernest Gaines and *The Crossing* by Cormac McCarthy. It also weaves together some of the classic tropes of American and Southern writing, familiar to any reader of, say, *Absalom, Absalom!* or *Go Down, Moses*: the lost garden paradise, the family curse revealed in some ledgers, the sense of doom (here associated with the idea of karma), the false father, a repressed, subterranean history that is at once sexual and social. And it weaves them into a new pattern. "*If you believe a pebble dropped into a pond makes circles after circles of ripples, you are a believer in the forces of karma*" (170) we are told in *Monkey Bridge*. That is a haunting rewriting of a controlling image used to describe destiny, the repetitions and revisions of history in *Absalom, Absalom!*: "*Maybe nothing ever happens once*," we are told there, "*but like pebbles on water after the pebble sinks, the ripples moving on spreading*" (261). The point here is not that Lan Cao may, or may not, have deliberately adopted a classic image in Southern writing, in order to bend it to her own aims. It is much simpler. In novels like *Monkey Bridge*, what *Absalom, Absalom!* terms "*the resonant strings of remembering*" (213) are being played in a new key. The stories that help to make up the regional and national narratives are being echoed but with an intriguing, crosscultural difference: a difference that, to return to that injunction from Deleuze and Guattari, hinges on expanding the territory of American writing by radical deterritorialization.

Two books that explore the faultlines between Vietnamese and American cultures outside the South, and share a similar deterritorializing project, are *The Gangster We Are All Looking For* by le thi diem thuy and *Grass Roof, Tin Roof* by dao strom. *The Gangster We Are All Looking For* works in terms of fragments. It recreates the life of a Vietnamese family who come as boat people to the United States as a skillfully shaped mosaic. In the first fragment, "suh-top!," the narrator tells the tale of her life after arriving in California as a six-year-old with her father, known as "Ba," and four men whom she describes as uncles although they are not related to her. Her "Ma" has been accidentally left behind, shouting out for help that could not be given, as the boat taking them from Vietnam departs. The title of this opening segment is "stop" as pronounced by the narrator's uncles. It recollects the mother's desperate cries from the water; and it also recalls another incident later in the United States, when the childish narrator attempts to release a butterfly from the middle of a paperweight owned by her host by throwing it against the wall, much to the horror of Ba and the uncles (who cry "suh-top!" (35) in a futile attempt to halt her). The paperweight shatters the glass doors of a display cabinet in which numerous ornamental animals are kept: an act which leads them all to be thrown out of their initial haven in America. An intricate web of imagery circulating around water and flight is woven into these opening pages, as the narrator and her companions struggle with their feelings of strangeness and estrangement. The narrator is the only Vietnamese child in her new school. She finds the everyday sights and events of her new American life – the supermarket, the school crossing patrol, the lights of the city at night – wonderfully odd. She also finds it difficult to disconnect her Vietnamese past from her American present. Does the water over which she travelled to her new home – and in which her mother was left crying out not to be left behind – unite or separate the two halves of her life? She wants to go to the beach, she tells her father, because "Ma's there ... You told me she was at the beach." That was "the beach in Vietnam," her father testily responds. "What was the difference?" (12–13) the child wonders.

The difference is investigated further in the second fragment of this gently elusive narrative, "palm." "Ma" makes her way to the United States, and is reunited with her small family. Together, they drift between various temporary domiciles. One place where they stay, an apartment complex, has a swimming pool. On hot days, the narrator recalls, the boys would jump, flying through the air from the second storey, into the water. After watching a kung fu movie with her mother, the narrator reflects, "I wanted to fly" (47), like the people in the movie and those boys. The chance is lost, at the apartment complex at least, when the landlord, outraged by the boys' behavior, has the pool filled with rocks and cement – with a "squat baby palm" (53) planted on the surface of the rubble, a decorative token that seems to mock the dreams and desires of the narrator, her longing to fly away across the water to some place where she can find wholeness and release. By the time of the third and pivotal narrative segment, which gives the book its title, the narrator is older. She focuses more sharply now on the father whom she adores and her brother, lost by drowning in Vietnam, when he jumped from boat to boat, risking his life just like those boys in the apartment complex. Memories are mediated through photographs here. "Vietnam is a black-and-white photograph of my grandparents sitting in bamboo chairs in their front courtyard" (78), the narrator observes. There are other photos helping her to recollect how her mother, a Catholic schoolgirl, married Ba, a Buddhist gangster. "When I grow up," the narrator confesses, "I am going to be the gangster we are all looking for" (93) just like her father. The mobility, the dangerous freedom that ambition articulates, is, however, stymied by her continued feelings of difference and disconnection. Photographs both link the narrator to her Vietnamese past, as substantial images, and, as messages from another place and time, confirm her separation. Ironically, the narrator's mother cannot digest this paradox. So, when the family is yet again evicted, Ma cries when she suddenly remembers that she has left the photograph of her parents behind. "We've left them to die," she declares. "Take me back" (98). For her, the photograph of her parents *is* her parents; the present *is* the past. By now, the narrator knows differently. "Who has seen this?" (90), she asks of the world in which she and her family live. There is, it seems "always a fence" (97) separating that world from their Californian present and, for that matter, from their Vietnamese past. She herself is still an outsider, aware that it is other children who are voted "Most Popular, Most Beautiful, Most Likely to Succeed" at school. "Though there are more Vietnamese, Cambodian, and Laotian kids at the school," she reflects, "we are not the most of anything" (89).

In the fourth fragment of the narrative, "the bones of birds," the narrator runs away from home to the East Coast. Memory and

107

movement are interlaced here, and in the fifth and final fragment, "nu' o' c," as she negotiates her recollections of her lost brother and her feelings for her parents, so different from each other and from her and yet so intimately connected. What this negotiation comes down to is, like the book itself, a delicate weaving together of connection and separation, closeness and distance. The imagery that closes the book signals this. It describes the memory of a time when, during their "first spring together in California" (157), the narrator and her parents went down to the beach. "The beach was covered with small silver fish whose bodies gave off a strange light," the narrator recalls. "Up close their little mouths moved busily, as if they could not get enough of the cool salt air" (158). That image, at once dreamlike and delicately ironic, of other wayfarers stranded in strange surroundings and seeking a voice, quickly gives way to another. "As my parents stood on the beach," the narrator remembers, "leaning into each other, I ran, like a dog unleashed towards the lights" (158). The lights here are the "small, luminous bodies" (158) of the stranded fish. Running towards them, the narrator is seeking commonality, a revelation of the secret these various strangers on the shore of a new world share with each other. While the parents lean into each other, seeking comfort and consolation, their daughter, still very young, is already obeying the impulse that will lead her eventually to leave, in search of her own place and voice. Voice is linked with water in this book. The link is, on occasion, quite explicit, as when we are told that the voice of the narrator's father "is water moving through a reed pipe in the middle of a sad tune" (10). More often, it is implicit. The narrator recalls parroting the vocal sounds, the pronunciation of her American neighbors ("I laughed to myself, thinking, You bird. You parrot. You Polly. I mouthed the words Polly, Polly, Polly as I walked…" (72)). Her father, in turn, remembers the voice of his wife as part of a chorus of voices coming from the water as his boat pulled away from Vietnam: the chorus like "a seawall between Vietnam and America" or like "a kind of floating net, each voice linked to the next by a knot of grief" (105).

Voice is imitative, it is performative, it is fluid, it is a process of continual negotiation and renegotiation. Like the waters between Vietnam and America, it joins and it separates; existing in between states; it brings together and it divides. States of being, that is, and also states in a more commonplace sense. "In Vietnamese," le thi diem thuy informs us before her novel begins, "the word for *water* and the word for *a nation, a country,* and a homeland are one and the same: *nu'o'c.*" One commentator on 9/11 has asked whether the attacks would, as she puts it, "cause us to widen our conceptions of home or to build tighter gated communities" (Greenberg, 34). What *The Gangster We Are All Looking For* does is to answer that question by going for the first option. While necessarily acknowledging the "fences" that divide one community from another, or for that matter Vietnam from the United States, the past from the present, it offers a vision of uninterrupted flow – or, to change the image and register the terms in which this extraordinary narrative is constructed, a mosaic. Nation and national community are redefined in resistance to any kind of holistic narrative that would seek simply to divide our understanding of them into warring opposites – and in obedience to an impulse that underwrites linkage, the fluid and connective. What is on offer here is what Homi Bhabha would call a condition of "cultural liminality" (148): a condition imaged in that "floating net," the watery chorus in which different voices meet. The narrator, and the novel itself, negotiate a space between nations and cultures – and, in the process, register a different, which is to say a fresher, fuller and more fluid notion of home.

In *Grass Roof, Tin Roof* dao strom treads a different, if sometimes parallel, narrative path. Told from different perspectives, sometimes in the first person, sometimes in the third and sometimes in epistolary form, the novel begins by introducing us to a young woman called Tran living in war-torn Vietnam. She bears two illegitimate children: the father of one being a French war correspondent whom she knows only as Gabriel, the father of the other a Vietnamese newspaper editor for whom she writes. The editor, who is also her mentor, is a man who, we learn, "took no side wholeheartedly when it came to the subject of war," since he believed both the Communist and the American systems to be "flawed" (9). The position of Tran seems as interstitial as that of her Vietnamese lover. She is no friend of the Vietcong, but she is hounded by the Vietnamese authorities because of her unsparing accounts of the corrupt political environment she inhabits. And then there is the problem of language. Conversant with both Vietnamese and English, Tran teaches her French lover some Vietnamese words, only to realize as she does so "how arbitrary and tenuous the association between an object and its linguistic representation could be, in some cases absurd, even." "Language," she observes, "was a thing that relied on faith" (6). She is caught between the signified and the signifier, just as she is caught between the warring sides in Vietnam. For that matter, she is caught, not just between Vietnamese and American speech but between Vietnam and America. She is drawn to the United States. But what she is drawn to is a representation, a sign that is as slippery as all other signs. The "drama of the America in her mind" (15) is coextensive with the dramatic or rather melodramatic version of America she has learned from *Gone With the Wind*, a novel given to her by Gabriel. She is resistant to Vietnam, even though she is deeply implicated in its past and present. But she cannot help seeing it through the prism of the newspapers she assiduously collects and the Vietnamese version of Civil War romance that she hopes one day to write. Small wonder, then, that when, many years later, her younger daughter, Thuy comes across her notebook, all that the daughter finds in it is "one line, not even complete." "The rest of the notebook," Thuy notes, "was empty" (123). Tran is trapped in the fissures between languages and cultures; and, it seems, when it comes to trying to do more than record the stream of time passing (which is what she does as a correspondent), reduced to paralysis.

Tran does, however, escape with her two children to the United States during the 1975 airlift. Language then becomes a slippery means of mediation again when, settled in California, she writes about her experiences in a Sacramento newspaper. Her story is read by a Danish immigrant, Hus Madsen, a survivor of the Second World War. Sensing a connection, Hus writes to her. Both of them, Hus suggests, have come from a "*structured society*" to one "*so elastic it can afford permanent outsiders.*" The secret of living in this elastic environment, he advises is "*not to think of yourself as an outsider*" (159). The advice eventually acquires a deeply ironic tinge: once Tran and Hus are married, after a brief courtship conducted mostly by letter, their shared dream of belonging falls apart. "Our mother," Thuy recollects, "did not look anything like the other mothers;" Tran feels out of place in the United States just as she did in Vietnam. And Hus, after his hopes of building a dream home in gold rush country proves as illusory as an earlier generation's dreams of finding a fortune in the hills, turns to alcohol – and, even worse, racially abusing his wife. "They had both agreed the past would be something best gotten over" (56), Thuy says of her mother and stepfather. They learn that the past, and its relation to the present, is much more elusive and, at the same time, much more indelible, than that. Like naming, it combines the arbitrary with the inescapable. That is a lesson also painfully learned by Thuy herself, her sister Beth and her brother Thien: who also find themselves caught between cultures: separated from their American present by their difference ('so you folks Chinese or Japanese?" one neighbor asks them (69)) and from their Vietnam past by temporal and spatial distance (her Vietnamese grandfather, Thuy remembers, looked, when she met him, "like *National Geographic* photos I'd seen of people from other – lesser, I'd thought then – parts of the world" (104)). Thien, the son of Tran and Gabriel, keeps his Vietnamese name and refuses the name Tim, although his stepfather tries to persuade him that it is "a nice enough alternative" (58) as well as a pathway to acceptance in America. He also tries to confirm his allegiance to his Vietnamese past, his sister Thuy notes, by "dating only other people of color" (154). But his connection to Vietnam is tenuous to the point of invisibility; his knowledge of the country, and the conflict that brought him to America, is also heavily mediated. That is measured by the moment when he goes to see the movie, *Hearts of Darkness*, about the making of *Apocalypse Now*. Watching a film about making a film about the Vietnam War – a film that, as Thien later observes, was in fact made in the Philippines – is about as close as he gets to the country he persists in trying to think of as home and to the conflict that tore it apart. Thien recalls an interview when, Francis Ford Coppola, the director of *Apocalypse Now*, insisted that his movie "is not about Vietnam. It is Vietnam" (131). The memory is appropriate, since for Thien, too, the mediated version of his birthplace is the reality; the signifier has supplanted the signified and *is* Vietnam.

111

"I was born on the fringes of several wars" (161), Beth, the daughter of Tran and Hus, reflects. The Vietnam War, however, is only a shadowy presence in her mind, "that other war" (189) she calls it; she is even unclear about the year her mother fled from Vietnam, it all seems so distant. What is closer to her is the first Gulf War. "*When the Gulf war struck I was seventeen*" (164), Beth recalls. The closeness, however, is only relative. Walking through the halls of her high school, on the day George Bush Sr declares war in the Gulf, Beth feels "dazed with the idea" that she is now "walking about in a world at war." But, then she reflects, "I was even more dazed by the lack of change war had brought about" (190). Even this war seems removed from her, and from America. "I realised, as I sat through the rest of the day's classes," she confesses,

> that it would always be as it was yesterday, war or not, at least for us, at least in America. The traffic lights would never stop, and if they did they would never be irreparable ... I was beginning to feel ill. I wished for explosions, fantastic crashes, vanishings – anything to mark it. I wanted to see the news here, now; I was tired of distant feeds, third-hand information. (191)

Grass Roof, Tin Roof was published two years after 9/11; and the irony of this reflection could hardly be lost on the reader. The irony for Beth, however, at this present moment in the narrative, is that she is alienated from both the American normalcy that surrounds her and the war-torn landscapes of the present and past. Her only moments of intimacy, at this time, come from a brief friendship with the one Muslim student in the school, who suffers racial abuse ('saddam-fucker!' "Go Home!" (172)) once war is declared. But even here the intimacy is limited. The modesty of the Muslim girl's traditional dress, for instance, makes Beth feel momentarily embarrassed about her own Westernized clothes – with the "red dress" she is wearing looking, she fears, "like a scalding blush, a flaming stain" (172). Caught in the interstices between cultures, Beth feels trapped. All she seems to have is a mediated relationship with every culture she encounters, "distant feeds, third-hand information."

112

At the end of the novel, Thuy returns to Vietnam to meet her mother's family. In stark contrast to other narratives like *Monkey Bridge* and *Prisoners*, however, the metaphorical return to the mother and the literal return to the motherland provide little relief, little sense of personal or cultural continuity. "*I never felt as I belonged there, no*" (204), Thuy recalls of Vietnam after she is back in the United States. Many of the people she meets there find it hard to believe that she is Vietnamese. "Why no speak Vietnam?" they ask. "All Vietnamese speak Vietnam" (213). "What are you?" (209), Thuy confides, is a question she is constantly asked in the United States; and the question now returns to haunt her in Vietnam. That is a question she cannot answer, because it requires an act of naming she cannot achieve; she cannot fathom or perform her nature. She has two names. There is Thuy, the Vietnamese name given to her by her mother; there is also the name April, given to her by her stepfather. She may prefer, most of the time, to go by the former. But she is shaken to her core when she discovers, during this trip back to her mother's country, that, as she puts it, "*Thuy* is a word usually paired with another to mean something" (226). Depending on pairing and accent, it could mean boundary or water or a kind of bird or abyss or drowning or burial at sea or amphibious – and so on. "I don't know which Mom was thinking of when she named me" (227), Thuy confesses. "I don't know what my name is anymore" (225). She is lost among floating signifiers; the primary act of identification, articulating her identity by finding an appropriate word or series of words for who she is or at least who she thinks she is, is denied her. This is the condition of fluidity, of being immersed in cultural process, described and dramatized in *The Gangster We Are All Looking For* perceived now, not as potential, but as a problem. The characters in *Grass Roof, Tin Roof* inhabit the border territory between cultures with a distinct sense of unease. None of them understands the implications of the discovery that Tran makes, at the beginning of the book when she is teaching Vietnamese to her French lover, and that her daughter Thuy makes at the end, when she is scouring the dictionary for the multiple possible meanings of her name. That the act cultural identification, like the act of naming, has to be continuous and performative – and, to that extent, "arbitrary

113

and tenuous." Hus said as much in that first letter he wrote to his future wife, when he suggested that in an "*elastic*" society like the United States, to be an "*outsider*," to live outside the parameters of strict, fixed cultural definition, is inevitable. To be an outsider is to be an American, Hus told Tran, the secret is "*not to think of yourself as an outsider.*" It is a secret the full meaning of which neither he nor his family ever really comprehend.

The cultural work novels such as *Grass Roof, Tin Roof* and *The Gangster We Are All Looking For, Monkey Bridge*, and *Prisoners* all perform is to interrogate the assumptions on which the either/or discourse dealing with 9/11 and the war on terror is based. Such novels do so by mapping a territory between cultures, responding to intercultural exchange in terms that are themselves genuinely intercultural, that hybridize. There are a number of novels in which the immigrant encounter is more immediately related to 9/11 or the war on terror or both: among them *Once in a Promised Land* by Laila Halaby, *Harbor* by Lorraine Adams, *Self Storage* by Gayle Brandeis and *The Kite Runner* by Khaled Hosseini. To a greater or lesser degree, however, these novels are flawed – and for reasons not unconnected to the reasons why fictions like *Falling Man* and *The Good Life* largely fail. There is a process of recuperation at work here. Difference is diminished, crisis is distanced or even suppressed by being accommodated to familiar and often conventional narrative structures. This is true of even a relatively nuanced novel like *Once in a Promised Land*. Halaby sets most of her story in Arizona and focuses on one couple. Jassim Haddad is a hydrologist from Jordan; his wife Salwa is, as the book puts it, "Palestinian by blood, Jordanian by residence, and American by citizenship" (70). Although she was brought up mostly in Jordan and lived there prior to setting up home with Jassim in Tucson, she was born in the United States. She was, she feels, tied to America by "invisible threads" even before she went to live there. "America pulled and yanked on her from a very young age, forever trying to reel her in," we are told:

> Only the America that pulled at her was not the America of her birth, it was the exported America of Disneyland and hamburgers, Hollywood and the Marlboro man, and therefore impossible to find. (49)

114

Once in America, Salwa searched for this commodified, globalized dream of America but could find it nowhere. But she continued to "hope that she would one day wake up in the Promised Land" (49). The nagging feeling of a split between the promise and performance of America widens into a fissure with news of 9/11, "a day that changed everything" (5). Ironically, the couple hear of the attack first from relatives who telephone them from Jordan. The initial assumption is that "there is no need to worry" because "New York is on the opposite side of the United States. It is nowhere near Arizona" (13). Very soon, however, Salwa begins to think, "We cannot live here anymore" (50). She hears hatred for "Mahzlims" (56) preached on the radio; she is unnerved by the sight of flags everywhere; she is even more unnerved by the suspicious looks she receives from people in the office and on the street. "All those years of schizophrenic reaction to American culture" (54) – all those times of vacillating between the belief that the United States was a place where anything from "a house in the foothills to sex with a co-worker" (50) was possible, and the fear that "wishes don't come true for Arabs in America" (184) – come to a head with what Salwa calls the "crazy suicide" (12) that destroys the Twin Towers, and its aftermath.

Things coagulate even more critically for Jassim. He becomes the target of an FBI investigation, simply because of his origins. That investigation leads him, eventually, to lose his job. What exacerbates his situation is that he also becomes involved in a serious car accident resulting in the death of a young boy. He is not at fault, but the fact that he is an Arab and that the young boy he kills "hated Arabs" (231) after 9/11 – and had a sticker declaring "terrorist hunting license" (231) on the skateboard he is riding when Jassim's car runs him over – only adds to the suspicions of the FBI agents and his own anxious mood. Lalaby is initially skilful in weaving together the personal and the political here. Jassim acts strangely and so arouses suspicion partly because he knows that, as an Arab, he is being watched after the terrorist attacks but also partly because he is traumatized by the fatal accident and feels incapable of telling anyone close to him, including Salwa, about it. The couple drift apart in the wake of 9/11, because of the climate of fear that surrounds them. There is the intimation, however, that they have never been as close as they imagined themselves to be in their shared American Dream. Jassim keeps secrets from Salwa. Salwa, in turn, keeps secrets from Jassim. She stops taking birth control pills and does not tell him ("My husband did not want a baby," she later explains, "and I did" (188)). She becomes pregnant, then has a miscarriage, and does not tell him. Finally, she embarks on an affair with a co-worker that eventually ends in violence and with Salwa being hospitalized.

It is here, however, that the narrative begins to buckle under a weight of detail that is simultaneously domestic and melodramatic. Some of the characters tend towards the stereotypical, among them a blue-collar waitress with a heart of gold in whom Jassim confides. Some of the time, Lalaby shifts her characters around like chess pieces: so, when she has no further use for a character called Jack, an ex-Marine who is one of the people who sets the FBI on Jassim's trail, she has him suffer a sudden fatal heart attack. And some of the plot developments, such as having Jassim's young victim in the accident declare shortly before his death that "he wished he could kill an Arab" (201) smack of the contrived. All this comes to a head with Salwa's demon lover, who is not only flaky and a drug addict but also, as it turns out, violently abusive. Her lover's attack on her, when she goes to say goodbye before returning to Jordan for a while, leads to the beginnings of a new understanding between Salwa and Jassim and the prospect of marital renewal and reconciliation back in Jordan. At the time of his car accident, Jassim, we learn, desperately told the friend of the young man he had killed, "'It's going to be all right'… saying words he did not believe, trying to make that ultimate jump into American life, the one that promises a happy ending for everyone if you just believe it hard enough" (119). It is hard not to suspect that Lalaby eventually makes the same jump in this novel. *Once in a Promised Land*, as its title implies, plays with the conventions of fairy tale. It also tries to show how apparently distant political events can disrupt normalcy, even the most serene and suburban of personal and domestic lives. It ends up surrendering to the need for a fairytale happy ending and allowing the personal and domestic not just to resolve but to swamp the public and political.

"'Happily ever after' only happens in American fairy tales," we are told at the conclusion of *Once in a Promised Land.* "*Wasn't this an American fairy tale?* It was and it wasn't" (335). Lalaby's novel is not as promisingly hybrid as that final declaration suggests, however. Crisis is dissipated, dispersed in obedience to conventions that are partly those of fairy tale, partly those of melodrama, and partly those of domestic romance. In *Harbor,* the conventions are different. Essentially, Lorraine Adams uses the narrative structure of a thriller to tell her story of illegal immigrants from Algeria caught up in the paranoid atmosphere of America after the terrorist attacks. The story begins with Aziz Arkoun, a young Algerian, arriving in 1999 in Boston after stowing away in the hold of a tanker for 52 days. He is fleeing from a country where, as he puts it, "The generals torture us for being terrorists. The terrorists kill us for not being terrorists" (153). In his life up until now, "the one clear thing was running" (227); and he continues on the run, hiding out with a succession of other immigrants from the Third World, some illegal like him and some not. Adams introduces us to a world that is at once subterranean and heterogeneous: on Coney Island Avenue where Aziz stays for a while, for instance, "most everyone spoke Urdu, enough spoke Arabic and a few had some English" (145). And he is forced into a serious of menial jobs, all of which, he sardonically observes, "lacked titles" (75). He picks up snatches of English, learns to read American body language and comes to realize that he is invisible. "days – no weeks – went by without a person speaking to him, and longer still, without someone's eyes meeting his own" (62). He is unseen, but he sees. "The pretty new nothing that was America – he wanted to watch that" (63); and he does so, becoming at once seduced and repelled by the complacent serenity and surfeit of his new surroundings, so different from his war-torn and impoverished place of origin. "Life" for him, he concludes, "was a series of dramas in which the goal was a place to talk, truly talk, and say whatever it was that haunted you at night alone" (111). But safe harbor of that kind eludes him, just as it does the other immigrants he encounters.

Among these other immigrants is another Algerian who arrives in America as a stowaway. Ghazi, like Aziz and like most of the others, finds himself caught between cultures. "Al Pacino was his favorite actor" (232), the narrator discloses; and "when he wasn't watching Pacino, he was in the public library" where "he tried to read the Qu'ran" (232–3). Torn between movies and mosques, he thinks of going for noon prayers but decides instead to go to "a matinee of *Saving Private Ryan*" (258). Like Aziz, Ghazi seeks some kind of anchorage in the United States: "America," we learn, "became the place he would come clean, stay clean, make it clean" (254). He is drawn, however, into petty crime and credit card fraud as a way of getting by. Ghazi is not a devout Muslim, still less a militant. He, and most of his neighbors and companions feel a healthy contempt for the "mosque-heads" and the call of jihad. "Irhabiya, khanjiya muja-hadeen, jihadists, terrorists. Same, same, same, same" (261), one of them dismissively declares. Nevertheless, Ghazi is eventually drawn to the idea of terrorism in a gesture of existential despair. "It was hard to kill yourself, at least in a way that would show your father and dick-kissing brothers you were a man," (259–260), Ghazi reflects. But maybe he would do so, become a suicide bomber in Algeria or Afghanistan or "maybe Chechnya" (269). So Ghazi flirts with the idea of terrorism, although he never acts on these random impulses. Another character, Rafik, makes money out of terrorism. A dealer in stolen goods, he handles material for explosives along with designer suits, drugs, and other contraband. "If people wanted to believe this jihad shit, so be it," Rafik tells himself. "They created opportunities for those smart enough to take them. You couldn't stop it, so you might as well make money off it" (267). Ghazi is a desperate dreamer, Rafik is a cynical crook, neither is a committed terrorist. Nor is Aziz, who is innocent to the point of bewilderment. Almost a child, his schemes of making money include selling coffee on the streets in paper cups scrawled with popular American sayings translated into Arabic. After 9/11, however, even the innocent quickly become an object of sus-picion; Aziz and his friends are no longer unseen – on the contrary, they become the subject of an intense scrutiny that misinterprets their every move.

"Arab, Muslim – however you slice it, trouble" (275): that remark made by a member of the FBI team that begins investigating Aziz and his friends neatly summarizes their starting position. Another remark sums up their method. "We don't have to *know* them," one member of the FBI team observes of Aziz, Ghazi, and the others. "We can't ever. We can just piece something here with something there and draw logical conclusions" (280). The approach is, in every sense, piecemeal, unhelped by the fact that the FBI team have trouble with Arab names and so with identifying or distinguishing between the various subjects of their investigation. And the conclusions are far from logical: for no good reason, the FBI team eventually conclude that Aziz is "at the center of the conspiracy" (267). Rafik escapes, Ghazi for his crimes of intention is sentenced to life imprisonment. With the help of a good lawyer, the innocence of Aziz is established but, as an illegal immigrant he is deported and disappears into the "blurriness" (291) of a country torn apart by civil conflict. The strength of *Harbor* lies here: in its ruthless exposure of the inadequacies of surveillance. It also lies in its calculated measuring of the distances of language and culture that separate the watchers from the watched. Because of those distances, the book suggests, the polyglot subculture of the immigrants may be seen in the literal sense after 9/11 – by investigators, by the media, by mainstream America generally – but, fundamentally, it remains unseen. Aziz Arkhoun, and people like him, remain invisible as anything other than objects of suspicion; as possible terrorists or conspirators, they come into the line of vision but as human subjects they are still outside it. The problem is that, as human subjects, Aziz and his friends never come into the line of narrative vision either. One reviewer of *Harbor* complained that the innocence of Aziz was so thinly realized that he came across as clueless.[8] Other immigrants are also lightly drawn so that, ironically, the reader may well share the FBI investigators' confusion about who, beyond the two or three main characters, is who.

The thinness of conception extends beyond the representation of the immigrant community. "The scenes with the FBI," another

---

[8] Hepzibah Anderson, "Life's no tea party for immigrants in Boston," *The Observer*, 26 March, 2006 (http://www.guardian.co.uk/books/2006/mar/26/fiction. features1).

reviewer complained, ",sound a bit too much like a thriller film;"[9] character depth and nuance are effectively sacrificed to the pursuit of atmosphere and the development of a sometimes labyrinthine plot. The problem here stems from the narrative strategy. Adams is an investigative reporter who has chosen the form of the thriller to dramatize serious issues raised by 9/11 and the "war on terror" and disseminate them to a wider audience. Unfortunately, what this leads to is a story that pulls in two different directions, because of the split between "serious" theme and "popular" form. The "popular" form is ruptured at times by the demands of the "serious" theme, when Adams feels compelled to underline the wider issues at stake. The "serious" theme, in turn, tends to float free, unanchored in the story and undermined by the exigencies of a complex plot. That plot, being only a pretext in the end, is fractured by the pressures of the message; while the message, having been imposed rather than emerging out of the exigencies of the narrative, never quite slots into the plot – and, more often than not, slides away into over-insistence and preachiness. The result is a novel that promises more than it performs. This is a different kind of novel from *Once in a Promised Land* – for one thing, the ending is far from happy – but it is similarly hampered by a narrative form that does not quite work. The conventions of the thriller exact too high a price: imposing a sense of closure on crisis, coating the strange with a veneer of familiarity – and so leaving the strange new world of terror and counter terror strangely invisible.

Other kinds of invisibility are at work in *Self Storage* and *The Kite Runner. Self Storage* is a gently sentimental novel that uses New Age pieties to celebrate resistance to the "war on terror." The narrator, Flan Parker, lives in what she calls "a wonderfully international community" (18), a university housing complex, with her husband and two children. "In our courtyard alone", she tells the reader, "there were also families from Wales, from Guatemala, from Afghanistan. Our

[9] Wendy Brandmark, "Harbor, by Lorraine Adams," *The Independent*, 10 March, 2006 (http://www.independent.co.uk/arts-entertainment/books/reviews/harbor-by-lorraine-adams).

blond family was an anomaly" (18). Flan makes some extra money by selling secondhand goods acquired from the auctions of forgotten and abandoned storage units. The narrative catalyst here is the crisis initiated in this small community by 9/11 and its aftermath. The Afghan couple in Flan's corner of the complex become the targets first of some petty vandalism (eggs are twice thrown at their house), then of suspicion and gossip ("Do you think he's a terrorist?" (92)), and then of official persecution. The husband is arrested and detained, simply because he is from Afghanistan. And, after she is involved in a car accident, driving without an American licence on her way to visit her husband in detention, the wife, Sodaba, is threatened with arrest and perhaps deportation. Flan rescues Sodaba, hiding her in an empty storage unit and subsequently arranging for her to go on the run. Then, when she herself becomes the target of FBI investigation for helping Sodaba, Flan with her family takes to the open road. "I pointed the car toward the freeway," she concludes her story, "The freeway that led to New York and New Orleans, Moab and Seattle, Miami and Fargo and Dallas and Philadelphia and every place in between" (250). "We would find our way," she adds, "whatever direction we might choose" (251). So the crisis of 9/11 and its aftermath is subsumed in the romance of the open road, becoming a kind of narrative device for enabling the narrator, as she puts it, to find the "Yes" in her life. The Afghan characters here are narrative instruments, the beneficiaries of Flan's liberating gestures. And the public crisis – the fall of the Twin Towers, the Patriot Act, internment at Guantanamo Bay and elsewhere, the invasion of Iraq – operates as, at most, a topic of conversation between characters and a backdrop to a story that is, first and last, about the protagonist finding herself. Right at the beginning of this story, Flan declares that "one image keeps coming back" to her, of Sodaba "hunched inside the storage locker." "The front of her burqua" she recalls, was momentarily "flipped up off her face; it hung down the back of her head like a nun's habit." "That was the first time, the only time," Flan confesses, "I saw any part of her face" (4). This momentary, partial sighting is the closest both the narrator and the novel get to seeing its main Afghan character. And it is, of course, not close at all.

In *The Kite Runner*, Khaled Hosseini uses a different but not unrelated strategy for disappearing crisis. The narrator here is a young Afghan man called Amir. His mother, when the story opens, is dead; his father, a rich businessman, is often preoccupied and, in Amir's hearing, confesses to his closest friend Rahim Khan, that he can hardly believe Amir is his son. Amir finds company and consolation in Hassan, a young man of roughly the same age who is at once loyal friend and servant. Hassan protects Amir from sadistic neighborhood bullies; in turn, Amir entertains Hassan by reading him heroic Afghan tales. Then, during a kite-flying contest that should be Amir's moment of triumph, Hassan is attacked by some of the upper-class gang that terrorize the neighborhood and raped by their brutal leader, Assef. Amir witnesses the attack but fails to intervene, a failure that will haunt him the rest of his life. The story shifts through time, incorporating the Russian invasion and the triumph of the Taliban, and space, as Amir and his father flee first to Pakistan and then to the United States. Eventually, however, Amir returns to Afghanistan on a rescue mission. Hassan has been killed by the Taliban, so has his wife; their son Sohrab has been placed in an orphanage and then, as Amir discovers, seized by the Taliban for their own sexual purposes. The agent of evil is again Assef, who has now become an enthusiastic member of the Taliban, and, having raped Hassan, is now raping his son. Against the odds, Amir manages to rescue Sohrab and take him back to America where he and his wife – who cannot have their own children – adopt him. Sohrab has been traumatized by his experiences but, when Amir takes him kite-flying, a momentary smile on his face promises recovery. Recovery in Afghanistan, too, is promised by the overthrow of the Taliban. And Amir has redeemed himself, paid the price for betraying Hassan by saving Hassan's son.

The Kite Runner, when it was published, was said to be the first English language Afghan novel, which may or may not be the case. What is certain is that, like *Self Storage*, it uses public crisis as a device and a backdrop – in this case, to an intensely personal and essentially melodramatic tale about guilt and redemption. The good in this book are impossibly good: Hassan, in particular is a saintly innocent who, as Amir reluctantly recognizes, is ready to make any sacrifice for him.

The evil, in turn, are irredeemably evil. Assef grows up from being a thug and a rapist who admires Hitler to being a religious fanatic who believes he has received a "message from God" (248) and, in the name of that belief, is willing to practice indiscriminate torture and commit mass murder. Prone to evil laughter and wearing dark glasses, "the tall Talib in white" (241), as he eventually appears, even looks the part: a combination of folk devil and Hollywood villain. Public events, when they intervene in the narrative, tend to be hastily summarized: 9/11, the American invasion of Afganistan, the fall of the Taliban and the establishment of a new regime, for instance, are all summarized in rather less than a page. What the novel dwells on, first and last, is a tale rather like the ones Amir told Hassan when they were boys: a tall tale about a boy who becomes a man through an act of redemptive heroism. Amir, on his rescue mission, tells a taxi driver who helps him that he feels like a tourist now in Afghanistan. The driver snaps back, "You? You've *always* been a tourist here, you just didn't know it" (204). It is hard to escape the conclusion that *The Kite Runner* has a similar relationship to Amir's country of birth and the series of crises that link it to his country of residence. This is a fiction that views the critical public events it invokes through a kind of touristic lens, from the safe distance of fairy tale.

To draw cognitive maps that are extraterritorial can involve a double strategy, as even a less successful novel like *The Kite Runner* demonstrates. It can mean a renewed commitment to hospitality, a more generous and heterogeneous definition of home. It can mean leaving the domestic space for riskier foreign encounters: mapping "America's extraterritorial expansion," as one commentator has put it, "exploring the ... impact of American global reach" and "the cracks in its necessarily incomplete hegemony" (Rothberg, A Failure of Imagination, 159). Or it can, and frequently does, mean both. The centripetal tendency emphasizes the fundamentally plural character of American society: the United States as a multiculture, a cultural mosaic the different fragments of which are separated by only the most porous and permeable of boundaries. The centrifugal tendency pushes beyond the borders of the nation-state to reveal another kind of porousness and permeability: measuring the asymmetrical power of America to influence world events, to infiltrate, shape, and be shaped by other national cultures. Books such as *Monkey Bridge, Prisoners, The Foreign Student, The Gangster We Are All Looking For,* and *Grass Roof, Tin Roof* accommodate both tendencies. So, less conclusively, do *Once in A Promised Land, Harbor,* and *The Kite Runner.* They relocate and reorient our notion of "home" and "abroad" by situating the stories they tell in an internationalized America and in an international space that, if not entirely Americanized, is nevertheless within America's orbit – which is to say, within the reach of, and affected by, American economic, political, and cultural power. Other books, however, take the transnational turn by moving out of the territory of the American nation-state altogether. They pivot away from the American homeland and direct all our attention to America's extraterritorial expansion through trade, tourism, war, cultural or political or even military invasion. These books include two collections of short stories, *Sightseeing* by Rattawutt Lapcharoensap and *Lucky Girls* by Nell Freudenberger, and a novel, *Tree of Smoke* by Denis Johnson.

"Pussy and elephants," observes one of the characters in *Sightseeing* of the tourists who frequent her native Thailand:

> That's all these people want ... You give them history, temples, pagodas, traditional dance, floating markets, seafood curry, tapioca desserts, silk-weaving cooperatives, but all they really want is to ride some hulking gray beast like a bunch of wildmen and to pant over some girls and to lie there half-dead getting skin cancer on the beach during the time in between. (2)

One of the achievements of this collection of stories by Rattawut Lapcharoensap is to deconstruct the familiar image of Thailand summed up in these remarks: to reveal it as a complex society standing at the interface between the First and the Third Worlds and under the influence, in particular, of American money and culture. There is corruption at work in this society. In the story, "Draft Day," for example, the young narrator watches with discomfort while his friend gets drafted into the military, knowing he is safe because his parents have pulled strings so that he will not have to do so. There is change and there is violence. So, in the story "Cockfighting," an equally young narrator – this time, female – describes how her father was forced out of the brutal traditional sport referred to in the title by a ruthless young gang leader, and how the sport then gradually died away in her neighborhood. In passing, she also recalls her mother telling her about her own youth. "Those were barbarous times, you know" the daughter remembers her mother saying:

> We lived like monkeys. We didn't have television. We didn't have cars. We danced naked around bonfires at night. We wore diapers to catch our menses. You should be thankful for the times ... You should be thankful for the modern age. (178)

Above all, there is the sense of culture deeply colored and profoundly changed by the impact of other cultures and especially by the culture of the one remaining superpower in the world. The "modern age" to which the mother in "Cockfighting" refer is, for the most part, an American one.

Other cultures do come into play, of course. There are, for instance, the tourists from all parts of the world. "This is how we count the days," the young narrator of "Farangs," the opening story in the collection, explains, "June: the Germans come to the island ... July: the Italians, the French, the British, the Americans ... August brings the Japanese. By September they've all deserted, leaving the Island to the Aussies and the Chinese'" (1–2). "Farangs," we learn is a disparaging term for foreigner. And among the many other foreigners encountered here, along with the tourists, are immigrants and casual workers. In the story, "Priscilla the Cambodian," for instance, another young narrator makes friends with the girl of the title: a refugee living in a shantytown close to the half-built housing development where he and his family live. His father and mother are less welcoming. "Refugees meant one thing and one thing only" to them, the narrator explains. "It meant we'd be living in the middle of a slum soon" (100). They blame the Cambodians for the deterioration of their neighborhood; and the father eventually helps burn the shantytown down. What sticks in the mind here, however, is not the burning of the village

125

where Priscilla and her family live, but her gesture of friendship when she leaves. Her teeth are capped with gold because, when the bombs were falling in Phnom Penh, her father, a dentist, had the family gold smelted and crowned each tooth. Before leaving, Priscilla wrenches one of her teeth out for her ashamed friend. "This is for you" (120), she declares. What also sticks in the mind is not just the heterogeneous character of the neighborhood here, with Thais, Cambodians, and others living, however uneasily and at times violently side by side, but the degree to which that heterogeneity is compromised by global culture, forms of living that are in the final analysis American. The housing estates where the young narrator of "Priscilla the Cambodian" and some of the other stories live are in many ways like a working-class American suburb. The boys ride bikes, worry about whether they will get any girls and declare anything they care for "awesome." Priscilla, we learn, was named after the wife of Elvis Presley; and one of the few possessions her mother has managed to salvage during her flight from Cambodia is "an LP showing Elvis's fat farang mug framed by those thick bushy chops" (100). A kind of icon, the LP is never played because the family do not own a record player, although the mother sometimes does renditions of some of the songs. The relationship these characters have with a country they have never seen, is sometimes fraught and always problematic. So, in the second story, "At the Café Lovely," the young narrator recalls how his father was killed when a malfunctioning crane dropped "a crate the size of our house full of little wooden toys waiting to be sent to the children of America" (26) on him in the factory where he worked. Closer to home, he also remembers how a birthday trip "to the new American fast-food place at Sogo Mall" (27) ended in humiliation when he regurgitated everything he had ate, hamburger, fries, pickles, and cheese, "all over that shiny American linoleum floor" (29). He had dreamed of looking "like those university students" he had seen "through the floor-to-ceiling windows, the ones who laughed and sipped at their sodas" (27), but the dream turned sour, almost literally, and turned his stomach. The dream, however, remains; the relationship with American culture and money and dreaming may be fraught; however, it seems indelible and inescapable. Nothing makes that clearer than the opening story.

126

Like most of the stories in *Sightseeing*, "Farangs" is told by a young man. The son of a Thai woman who now runs a small motel, and an American soldier known only to him as Sergeant Marshall Henderson, the boy is, to the perception of both Thais and Americans a "mongrel" (5). "Ma doesn't want me bonking a farang," he confides, "because once, long ago, she had bonked a farang herself" (5), who had impregnated her, left her promising to send for her to follow him to the United States but never did. Nevertheless, every tourist season, the young man falls in love with American girls: "girls with names like Pamela, Angela, Stephanie, Joy" (18), with "tiny, perfectly even rows of teeth" (4), on show when they laugh – which they frequently do. One of the girls," the narrator recalls, "sent me a postcard of Miami once," asking him to look her up "if you ever make it out to the US of A" (18) – "which was nice of her," perhaps but rendered meaningless by the fact that "there was no return address on the postcard" (18–19). In the brief period of present time the story occupies, the young narrator falls in love with another American girl called Lizzie. They meet on the beach when Clint Eastwood, the narrator's pet pig, named after the American movie star, runs up to her and sniffs her. "It might be real love," he tells his mother. "Like Romeo and Juliet love" (2). He takes his "American angel" (15) for an elephant ride to "MR. MONGHOKON's JUNGLE SAFARI" (8) run by the uncle of his friend, Surachai. Later, the evening of the same day, he takes her on a dinner date that turns into a disaster when Lizzie's American boyfriend, Hunter, unexpectedly appears. Hunter insults him, the narrator leaves, seeking solace in the company of Surachai; and, remembering and rehearsing a time when he and Surachai pretended to be "the Island's Miraculous Monkey Boys" (19) for the entertainment of tourists, they climb up into a mango tree. From there, they see Hunter, Lizzie and some other young Americans appear on the beach below them. The Americans, catching sight of Clint Eastwood grazing on the beach, give chase to the pig. The narrator and Surachai, to distract Hunter and his companions, throw mangoes down from the tree. Some of the mangoes hit Lizzie but, by this time, the narrator does not care. "Swim, Clint, Swim," the narrator thinks, as the pig scuttles into the sea. He can only dream of escape, for him as well as his pig.

What is remarkable about this story is how tangled and highly nuanced the young narrator's relationship is to his dual inheritance. He is an exotic curio, in many respects, to the American girls he meets and the tourists whom, as a Miraculous Monkey Boy, he entertains: but he is also a "bastard" (7), in the eyes of his Thai neighbors and someone who, like those neighbors, has had his imagination colonized by the "US of A." Sergeant Henderson gave him the pig that is his closest and most constant companion. It is the only real memento he has of the man who left both him and his mother behind. He has, clearly, named Clint Eastwood in honor both of his American father and of the American hero of "*Dirty Harry, Fistful of Dollars, The Outlaw Josey Wales, The Good, the Bad and the Ugly*" (3) and all the other films that dictate the terms of his dreaming. The fact that – as the narrator seems hardly aware but Lapcharoensap surely is – two of the films whose titles he reels off to Lizzie, while explaining the name of his pet pig, are Westerns made by an Italian director in Spain only adds to our sense that the story is investigating cultural faultlines, not just American cultural hegemony but what Clifford Geertz has called "the international hodgepodge of postmodern culture" (82). And the nuances, the investigation of hegemony and heterogeneity, extend to the language of this story. The narrator, for instance, tells his friend's uncle that the sign advertising his elephant riding business is "grammatically incorrect," offering to make the corrections for "a small fee." But the uncle "just laughed," we are told, "and said farangs preferred it just the way it was, thank you very much, they thought it was charming" (8). In turn, the language of the narrator himself, in conversation with those "farangs" is often elaborately formal, contrasting with the slapdash simplicity of his usually American interlocutors. So, talking about the movie star Clint Eastwood, Lizzie declares, "He's a very good actor:" to which the narrator responds "Yes. Mr. Eastwood is a first-class thespian" (4): a form of agreement ("Yes") that only underlines the verbal chasm here – and, beyond that, the gap between the unselfconscious self-confidence of the American girl and the uneasiness, the stiff formality that characterize this half-Thai, half-American boy.

In effect, the narrator of "Farangs" is a wavering hero, inhabiting a territory that is itself "wavering" in the sense that it is on the borders between colonized and colonizer – a place defined by a subtle, self-reflexive relationship between Third and First Worlds. The central figure in the "classical form of the historical novel," Georg Lukacs argues, brings together "the extremes whose struggle fills" the narrative and "whose clash expresses artistically a great crisis in society;" "through the plot," Lukacs goes on, "at whose center stands this hero, a neutral ground is sought and found upon which the extreme opposing social forces can be brought into a human relationship with one another" (*Historical Novel*, 36). In his own modest way, the narrator of "Farangs" performs this function, transforming a social and historical encounter into a deeply personal one. And the Thailand of this and other stories in *Sightseeing* is precisely what Lukacs terms a "neutral ground," a site where differing and often opposing cultural forces can come into contact with one another, resulting in congruence sometimes and sometimes collision. After making love to his "American angel," the narrator tries to share himself and his past with her. "I told her about Sergeant Henderson," he explains, "the motel, Ma, Clint Eastwood." Lizzie makes an effort to reciprocate. "she told me about her Ohio childhood, the New York City skyline, NASCAR, TJ Maxx, the drinking habits of American teenagers" (12). This slightly comic, slightly poignant moment measures both the connections and the distances between these two young people, as they try to engage more than physically, to negotiate their way through "the international hodgepodge of postmodern culture" and achieve, if not intimacy, then at least some kind of rapprochement. If engagement is made, however, it is fleeting and imperfect. The narrator is left at the end of the story looking out across an ocean that seems to reflect his own dilemma and division. "I told Lizzie," the narrator recalls of his conversation with her,

> about how the Sergeant and my mother used to stand on the beach, point east, and tell me that if I looked hard enough, I might be able to catch a glimpse of the California coast rising out of the Pacific horizon. (13)

By the end of the story, his "American angel" like his American father, is lost to him. And the sea that connects him to America also divides him from it. Look as hard as he might, he cannot catch a glimpse of the fresh green breast of a new world rising out of the ocean. It remains for him a dream and a desire, something running through his blood and racing through his imagination that is nevertheless elusive, out of sight. It is there and not there, a part of and apart from him; he longs for escape ("Swim, Clint, Swim") but he does not really know whether the escape he longs for is from or to America.

"Travelling is for people who don't know how to be happy" (80), observes a character, an Indian housekeeper, in one of the stories in *Lucky Girls*. And the travelers in these stories, especially the American and female ones, do very little to prove her wrong. Their lives are mired in strangeness; they seem unmoored, adrift between the old life and the new, America and Asia. And, despite the claim of one American character that "You can bring your home with you" (153), most of these travelers seem to be homeless searching for safe harbor, a shelter, in a world that offers them none. One Indian character reflects, with envy, that Americans seem to be at home wherever they go. "Americans could go all over the world and still be Americans," he thinks; "they could live just the way they did at home and nobody wondered who they were, or why they were doing things the way they did" (153). But that, Nell Freudenberger quietly suggests, is a misreading. The distinction, in a globalized world, between home and away, the "foreign" and the "domestic" may be fine to the point of vanishing altogether. Americans, of a certain class, may enjoy an enviable mobility and have the opportunity of moving around in a global environment dominated by their language, their culture, and their money. But that does not seem to diminish the sense of drift they experience as they move from place to place, the feeling of being unanchored, denied the chance to get their bearings. It is as if Freudenberger's tourists and travelers, especially the Americans, have been provided with a map for their journeys that has only minimal points of reference – that is largely blank, waiting for them to fill it in. It is also as if home is everywhere and nowhere for them. A telling image occurs in one of these stories. In an Indian marketplace, two characters, an Indian man and an American girl, encounter "a poster man" setting out his wares "on a frayed blue tarpaulin." One poster, in particular, grabs their attention:

> Across the bottom of a composite photo – an English cottage superimposed on a Thai beach, in the shadow of Swiss mountains dusted with yellow and purple wildflowers and bisected by a torrential Amazonian waterfall – were the words HOME IS WHERE, WHEN YOU GO THERE, THEY HAVE TO LET YOU IN. (131)

In a "floating world," as the novelist Cynthia Kadohata christened it, people become nomads, required, whether they like it or not, to embrace the intermediate space between cultures. They are neither entirely "here" nor "there," wandering or floating contrapuntally across a liminal ground, occupied by overlapping and in the end interdependent histories. As they wander from place to place, the inhabitants of this liminal ground, like the "lucky girls" of Freudenberger's stories, effectively challenge the notion of both a common heritage and fixed boundaries so central to the grand narrative of the American state. But that does not dilute the pathos, the poignancy of their personal condition. So, looking at the poster, and its definition of home as here, there, and everywhere, all these characters can think is that it is "difficult… to imagine a more depressing sentiment" (131).

The condition of drift, of course, varies in its details from story to story in *Lucky Girls*. In the title story, for instance, an American woman who has been involved in a five-year affair with a married Indian man feels bound, following his sudden death, to her memories of him and to her adopted country. But the ties that bind her to India, past and present, are loose and tangled ones. When she first met the man who would become her lover, Arun, her Indian friends had dressed her "in a dark pink sari." "We spent so much time making me look like them," she recalls, "that no one had a chance to teach me to walk in the sari, which turned out to be more difficult than I had imagined" (5). She was gently reprimanded by Arun for wearing an Indian outfit: "because clothes," he explained, "mean something here. Historically. And when you wear them it's for romance, glamour – you don't mean anything" (7). The reprimand, together with the awkwardness she feels in unfamiliar clothing, make her wonder if her friends were playing a practical joke in dressing her up – "like dressing up a cat or a dog" (7). And as she negotiates her way through the labyrinth of Indian costume and customs, she is constantly seduced and stymied both by her Indian lover and by India. Taken by Arun to see the Taj Mahal, she is afforded only a fleeting glimpse of its white domes, because it is Monday and the palace is closed. Flattered by Arun's mother when she visits – "You're not beautiful, but you're strong-willed" (9), the mother tells her. "You're like me – like a daughter of mine would be" (25) – she is nevertheless reminded of her difference and her distance. Most Indians have "never seen a woman like you," Arun's mother informs her, "living so well on her own" (5). And when Arun becomes fatally ill, the mother discourages her from visiting. "I ask you not to see him," the mother brusquely declares, "as it would upset the family, who are with him all the time" (20). "Was it Arun, or India," the narrator asks herself after his death. "Or was it that, for me, Arun was India?" (26) Whatever the answer, she feels both drawn and distant; whatever connects her to land and lover also holds her back. "I tried to picture Arun's face" after he is gone, she confesses, "but I couldn't – the image wouldn't stay clear" (26). That shifting elusive memory, the wavering image of Arun, then metamorphoses into another elusive memory, the "white slice of dome" that she caught sight of briefly during her abortive visit to the Taj Mahal. India is and is not there for her, despite the fact that she now claims it as her home; Arun is and is not there in her recollections, despite the fact that she now claims him as the love of her life. Of both, she can catch only glimpses, "like an eye behind a half-closed lid" (27).

"An American family" (3), Arun's mother observes sardonically, when the narrator of "Lucky Girls" explains that her mother and father live apart and she rarely sees them. In other stories, we are allowed more detailed insight into an American family than this throwaway remark can provide; the details, however, hardly challenge the judgment the mother is clearly making. So, in "The Orphan," the reader is introduced to a wealthy New York family in Thailand. The mother and father, on the verge of divorce, are visiting their daughter, who is working in a home for AIDS victims; she has made a frantic phone call home to say that her Thai lover has raped her. Once they arrive in Bangkok, however, the rape charge is withdrawn or, at least, glossed over. "It was a misunderstanding," the daughter Mandy explains. "It was a cultural thing, actually" (35). "Maybe I kind of liked it," she later adds, by way of extenuation. "Have you thought of that;" "have you even heard of rape fantasies?" (45) There is a great deal of bleakly comic play here with the "cultural thing," and with the distances that separate each member of the family from all the others. Bangkok seems a strange otherworld to the mother of the family, Alice. A city she previously thought of as being "famous for pollution, prostitution, and AIDS" (34) looks like "a city underwater" (33) to her when she first sees it on the taxi ride from the airport: "like Los Angeles," in some ways, but, in others, "like a dream of Los Angeles" (33). The father, Jeff, who conceals his smug sense of American cultural and political superiority behind a mask of casual urbanity, mocks Alice's unease with her daughter's brutal boy-friend even though he shares it. Their son, Josh, who joins them in Bangkok for this dysfunctional family reunion, mocks the kitsch décor of the Thai tourist spots they visit ("This is what democracy looks like" (60), he remarks of one touristy restaurant) and tells his parents about a college club he has joined called the Cool Rich Kids, dedi-cated to giving their trust funds away to "the more radical causes that people your age wouldn't support. Like prison abolition, for example" (47). There is plenty of talk in this family, but little real conversation. There is plenty of travel around Bangkok, but no real contact with the place. The family breathe an air of lost connections. Reflecting on "the incredible privacy of people's experience," Alice wonders why she and her family "fight at all, why they don't just allow each other to spiral off into their own interpretations: four people watching a movie about a family like themselves" (55).

"We're all so far-flung," the father of the family admits in "The Orphan," adding as a kind of deadpan joke, "New York, Bangkok, Waterville" (62). Most of the characters in *Lucky Girls* are equally "far-flung:" far from each other, far from home whether they are in America, Asia, or Europe, far even from themselves – in a condi-tion of permanent exile. The mother of the narrator in one story, "Outside the Eastern Gate," for instance, wonders if she was "meant to be born somewhere else, to different parents." "I sometimes think," she confesses, "... that there is a girl somewhere – in a village on the slopes of the high Himalaya – who would be happy to exchange her life for mine" (99). Her mother "used to say," the narrator recollects, "that going back to America was like waking up out of the most beautiful dream you ever had" (67). So she wanders the world, before returning to America eventually and killing herself. The narrator, in turn, at once mocks the memory of her mother and is mystified by her. Why, she continually asks herself, did her mother leave her behind when she set off from India to Afghanistan over the Khyber Pass? She feels herself, however, as she grows older, becoming her mother. Each passing moment of lostness, every time she feels afloat or adrift, is, she confesses, like "a piece of my mother coming alive inside me" (80). Similarly, in another story, "The Tutor," a young American girl called Julia is struck by what her Indian tutor, Zubin, sees as "homesickness" (114). Having traveled through Europe and Asia with her father, she wants to return to the United States and specifically to the Bay Area. Zubin is recruited, in fact, to help her pass her SAT tests for Berkeley. "I miss it" (113), she says of San Francisco and its surrounds. The irony is that she has hardly ever lived there, and not at all since the age of three; like so many characters in *Lucky Girls*, she is missing a home she has never really known. Zubin recognizes this strange missing of a place, roots you have never actually had, because he has experienced it himself: in his native India and in America, where he went to college. An aspiring writer, he admits that when he is "here" in India, "I want to write about America, and when I'm in America, I always want to write about being here" (153). Life, it seems, is always elsewhere.

The connection between Julia and Zubin, the recognition of likeness, only goes so far, however. Zubin, like some of the Thai characters in *Sighteeing*, is certainly drawn to America, and in particular American girls like Julia. "He wanted one of these," we learn of his first encounters with American girls in college: "He watched them from his first-floor window, as close as fish in an aquarium. They hurried past him, laughing and calling out to one another, in their boys' clothes" (114). They seem to inhabit a different element, but he is seduced by them. Eventually, he finds his own "American girl" (114) in the United States and even sleeps once with another "American girl" (111) – as he thinks, generically, of Julia – when he is back in India. But there is always that distance, signaled by the fallback on the generic description and the suggestion that the "American girl" is as distinct from him as fish is from flesh. There is always amazement, too, at what he sees as the oddity, the random enthusiasm, energy and appetite (literal and figurative) of Americans. In the United States, among his American college mates, Zubin feels at times "as if he were surrounded by enormous and powerful children" (114). And in India, he thinks precisely of Julia when he reads a science fiction story by Ray Bradbury about a girl who "had come to Venus from earth." "She was different," he notes, "and because it was a science fiction story (this was what he loved about science fiction), it wasn't an abstract difference" (149). The connection and disconnection between these two people in a floating world, is neatly measured by the autobiographical essay Zubin writes for Julia to help her pass her college entrance exams: an essay of which, of course, she is supposedly the author. "How do you even know about this stuff?" Julia asks in amazement after she has read it. "About being an American, I mean. How do you know about that?" "This part," she adds. "About forgetting where you are? D'you know that *happens* to me? Sometimes coming home I almost say the wrong street – the one in Paris or in Moscow." "*Because I am not any different,*" Zubin wants to tell her. "*If we are what we want, I am the same as you*" (156). That feeling, or rather conviction, that they are no different, that they share the same longing for home, is never voiced, however. And it is cruelly undercut by the narrative a little later, when Julia continues to ponder over the essay when she is alone. She is uneasy about his linking of "two topics" in the essay, she concludes: that is, her own and the Bradbury story. And she is even uneasier about something else, in fact slightly bemused by it:

> … the part where he talked about all the different perspectives she'd gotten from living in different cities and how she needed just one place where she could think about those things and articulate what they meant to her. She wasn't interested in "articulating." She just wanted to move on. (159)

135

If the liminal space between "domestic" and "foreign" culture, or in this case American and Asian, creates a deterritorialized landscape – and in *Lucky Girls*, in particular, an occasional shared sense of placelessness – it does not obliterate difference. The fragmented and discontinuous reality of America "at home" or "abroad" generates fissures and dissonances, a sense of distance and disorientation, as well as elaborate and sometimes almost indecipherable circuits of connection. At the end of "Lucky Girls," the American narrator remembers a time when she lay in bed with her Indian lover and heard what she believed to be the cry of an exotic bird – a mockingbird, perhaps, a myna or nightingale – that seemed to complete the scene and her mood, her sense of union with her Indian surroundings and her lover. When she told her lover this, however, he laughed. The noise she had heard, he explained, was made by the night watchman; "I'd seen him on his bicycle," she then remembered, "a skinny young man in an olive green civil servant's uniform, with a wooden stick across his hip" (26). So, like so many characters in Freudenberger's book, she has discovered that she has the wrong map for the fluid ambience she inhabits. She has tried to get her bearings, believes fiercely that she is at one with a place and person, then learns she is mistaken.

"Once upon a time there was a war" (602). This remark is made almost at the end of *Tree of Smoke*. It reminds us that this book is preoccupied with a very different kind of American invasion from the ones described in *Lucky Girls* and *Sightseeing*. It also alerts us to the storybook romanticism, a special kind of American dreaming, that was at the heart of the war in Vietnam – which is the principal subject of the novel – and the second war in the Gulf – which was being waged when the novel was written and is clearly there, present in its narrative subtext. "There was once a war in Asia," we are then told, "that had among its tragedies the fact that it followed World War II, a modern war that had managed to retain or revive some of the glories of earlier wars. This Asian war however failed to give any romances outside of hellish myths" (603). The author of these remarks is William "Skip" Sands, who writes these lines in a letter when he knows that his encounter with the "hellish myths" of combat is coming to an end. The cornerstone in a large cast of characters and our guide through a labyrinthine plot, Skip undergoes a kind of initiation during the course of a journey that is not so much to the end of night as through a night that never seems to end. The novel begins in the Philippines in 1963, the year of the assassination of President Kennedy. Skip has joined the CIA after leaving college. He has joined, in part, out of family loyalty: his father died at Pearl Harbor, his uncle is a colonel in intelligence. But his main motivation is a naïve, unquestioning patriotism. At the sight of an American flag flying in Manila, the narrator discloses, Skip "tasted tears in his throat:"

> In the Stars and Stripes all the passion of his life coalesced to produce the ache with which he loved the United States of America – with which he loved the dirty, plain, honest faces in the photographs of World War Two, with which he loved the sheets of rain rippling across the green playing field toward the end of the school year, with which he cherished the sense-memories of the summers of his childhood, the many Kansas summers … (64)

As much as Skip loves America, however, it is not the place he chooses to live. That is a common theme with the characters in this novel. They talk about America but prefer to live elsewhere, wherever war, any war, takes them. They think of home, occasionally, but they never long for it. They are homeless nomads, wandering through the labyrinth of battle: for them, the United States is a symbol (the flag), a cause ("freedom"), a way of life they may seek to impose on others (in Asia and, implicitly, the Middle East) across the globe but it is never somewhere they really want to go or feel they belong.

Vietnam is the setting for most of *Tree of Smoke*: a site of collision between cultures and a world of chaos onto which the American forces seek to impose their own idea of order. As Skip negotiates his way through the "hall of mirrors" (337) that is the war zone, engaged in "deals struck in a half dozen languages, sinister rendezvous, false smiles, eyes measuring the chances" (192), he comes to lose all his illusions about being involved in a crusade. The words that recur to register the reality of battle are ones that measure its dreamlike, performative character, the site of combat and military encounter as a place where people die without really knowing why they fight. The war is a "dream" (462), it is "bogus" (471), it is a series of "lies" (462); it is a "demented little show" (197), it is "bullshit" (469), it is "folly on folly" (365), "a crazy circus" (368). As Skip ponders all that is happening in Vietnam – the Tet offensive, the My Lai massacre – and back in the United States – the assassinations of Martin Luther King and Robert Kennedy – everything assumes the same dreamlike, fictive quality. "These events seemed improbable, fictitious" (328) to him, we are told; history has become a nightmare from which he cannot awake. The "brilliant actuality of childhood," "the homeland from which he was exiled" seem "gone, stupidly gone;" and he feels "gone" as well, "departed, exposed, transfigured" (329–330), lost in the miasmal mist of conflict. By the end of the novel, having been chosen as "the fall guy" (499) for a series of intelligence errors that were not his, he is awaiting execution in Malaysia for gun running. It is 1983. "After I left Vietnam," he explains in one of his letters, written from a Malaysian jail, "I quit working for the giant-size criminals ... and started working for the medium size. Lousy hours and no fringe benefits, but the ethics are clearer" (604). He wanted to be "the Wise American, or the Good American," not "the Quiet American" let alone "the Ugly American," instead he came "to witness himself as the Real American and finally as simply the Fucking American" (603–4). "I'm dying and I'm glad" (546), he confesses. The mission on which he embarked twenty years earlier has become a mirage, the rhetoric of crusade seems now just a mask for criminality; and Skip appears to regard himself as just as false, as fictive, as the military adventure to which he dedicated himself. He has reached the heart of darkness. It is another, minor character, however, called Jimmy Storm, who comes closest to describing that heart. "Ain't no big shit whether we win or lose this thing," Jimmy declares:

> We live in the post-trash, man. It"ll be a real short con. Down in the ectoplasmic circuitry where humanity's leaders are all linked up unconsciously with each other and with the masses, man, there's been this unanimous worldwide decision to trash the planet and get on a new one. (194)

At the center of the web of deceit that is this war is Skip's uncle, Francis Xavier Sands, known to most people as the colonel. The colonel is a darkly mythic figure, a cross between Joseph Conrad's Mister Kurtz and John Wayne, a veteran of World War II and an expert in psychological operations. "The land is their myth," he declares of the Vietnamese. "We penetrate the land, we penetrate the national soul" (194), "we penetrate their heart, their myth, their soul" (212). The slippage between terms of military and sexual conquest is typical of an "iron figure" (439) who, we are told, has lived "a life of blood and war and pussy" (329). It also slyly links the project of the colonel to the larger national project: the myth of American exceptionalism and manifest destiny first projected on to the penetration, the conquest of the American West and now projected on to other locations beyond the borders of the United States. The particular strategy the colonel chooses for penetrating the soul of Vietnam is what gives the novel its title: "a self-authorised national deception operation" (337), as it is called at one point, involving the recruitment of a double agent. The image of the "tree of smoke" is borrowed from the Bible: as with so many other American adventures, a sense of divine mission as well as sexual conquest, characterizes the colonel's special project – which turns out, in the end, to be just that – a project, a plan that hardly gets beyond the "hypothetical" (454), the recruitment and planning stage. And it is here, in particular, in the colonel's planning, his outlining of his unauthorized scheme for penetrating the soul of Vietnam that the contemporary resonances are loudest. "*The final step*," the colonel insists when promoting the "tree of smoke" operation among the few people – including Skip – personally recruited for this purpose, "*is to create fictions and serve them to our policy-makers in order to control the direction of government*" (254). "Tree of smoke" means many things in this novel. It is a specific plot hatched without authority by a cold war warrior who believes that "the truth is the legend" (587). It is the phantasmagorical landscape of Vietnam where, masked in the clouds of war, "everything living is double" (478), not just the double agents. It is the subterfuge of counter insurgency, intelligence: "We're on the cutting edge of reality itself," one agent proudly declares of "Psy Ops," "right where it turns into dream" (189). It is the fog of war itself. And, the point is inescapable, it is the series of intelligence stories – weapons of mass destruction, axis of evil, links between Saddam Hussein and Al Qaeda – that led to one crucial, contemporary example of the use of fictions to control the direction of policy.

Like the colonel, Skip, we are told, eventually "preferred myth to the truth" (450). And one particular myth he comes to prefer concerns the colonel himself. The story is that the colonel is dead. It remains far from certain, however, if he is dead or if he is still alive – or, for that matter, if he is dead, how exactly he died. He was killed by a prostitute in Da Nang. His throat was slit by the brother of his mistress in the Mekong Delta. He was tortured to death or assassinated by enemy agents. Many Vietnamese tell the story that the colonel did die but underwent a miraculous resurrection: flooding "heaved" his coffin "to the surface" of the ground where he was buried and, when the coffin was then opened, "a beautiful black-haired American pilot… a naked young Colonel Francis" (450) was found inside. A few Americans, in turn, favor a more material version of life after death. "No man," Jimmy Storm insists, "He faked this shit … He's on a mission and we're fucked. We can't help him" (471).

Like everything in the colonel's life, and everything in the novel, the story of the colonel's death is shrouded in "veils upon veils" (450). Convinced that the colonel is still alive, Storm even makes a pilgrimage to the supposed place of burial but leaves, we learn, "knowing nothing" (450); "Skip preferred the myth. It told the truth" (450). But which myth to believe? What fiction to follow? Those are questions that he, like so many other characters in the book find it difficult, even impossible to answer. "He'd written himself large-scale," Skip reflects of his uncle, "followed raptly the saga of his own journey, chased his own myth down a maze of tunnels and into the fairyland of children's stories and up a tree of smoke" (451). So the colonel is buried in a series of stories. In (apparent) death as in life, he is compounded of fictions, as was the war to which he devoted himself and for which, quite probably, he sacrificed his life. Skip is unable to disentangle one fiction from another; he is also unable to disentangle himself from his uncle and the "tree of smoke" into which Frances Xavier Sands has disappeared. "He died," Skip says of his uncle much later, from the jail where he is awaiting execution, "and his spirit entered me" (609). And what that spirit does is leave him, like Storm, knowing nothing. Like other survivors of the war, he lives in his own kind of placeless, intermediate space – one very different from those encountered in *Sightseeing* and *Lucky Girls* but similarly on the edge, interstitial – and unable really to live inside the United States or outside its borders.

Outside the borders of the United States, for all their lives, are the Vietnamese who are confronted with yet another invasion from the West. And among those Vietnamese is the Nguyen family. Nguyen Hao, one of the principal Vietnamese characters in the novel, believes that the colonel is his ticket of escape from the hell his homeland has become. He has been unsuccessful in the family business, and sees working with the Americans as the only chance of survival for him and his wife. Hao works for the colonel as a driver, his nephew Minh, a helicopter pilot, serves as the colonel's personal pilot, his childhood friend Trung is chosen to be the double agent in the operation known as tree of smoke. Trung had left for North Vietnam to join the revolution, but he has returned, he claims, disillusioned with communism. What attracted him to communism, Trung tells Skip, was the Marxist theory of "the withering away of the state." "I thought Marx would give us back our families and villages." "That's what I saw at the end of the future," when he was a Marxist Trung explains; "the French are gone, the Americans are gone, the Communists are gone, my village returns, my family returns. But they lied" (393). In place of this vision of a return to the local, all Trung has now is a residual interest in America. "We know your history. We study your novels, your poems," Trung informs Skip. "Long before your military came to Vietnam, America was important in the world. The world's major capitalist nation. I like Edgar Allan Poe very much" (391). From a belief that the nation state will eventually be supplanted by the community to something that is not so much a belief as an acceptance – of American hegemony, the power of the most powerful nation state in the world: that is the journey that Trung has made on the way to being enlisted in the operation known as tree of smoke. A belief in a world without borders to the extent that it is atomized, brought home to the local, is supplanted by a radically different kind of borderlessness, that of

141

global capitalism. Trung never gets a chance to be a double agent and never gets to America; eventually, in another career move that is mostly a matter of luck and opportunism, he becomes a Communist apparatchik in Ho Chi Minh City. Hao and his wife, relocated in Kuala Lumpur, dream of moving to America soon: a dream bolstered by the news that his nephew Minh is already there. "He'd had word" of Minh, we learn, "through a Vietnamese family who ran a restaurant in Singapore, longtime emigrants who'd set a worldwide network going to make connections among a scattered class" (542–3). So the Vietnamese in this novel, far from returning to the local, become part of what Anthony Giddens would call a "radicalised modernity" (49), characterized by diversity, fragmentation, dispersal, mobility, and differentiation on a global scale. The United States of America is and is not the site of their desire. It is, because it is America that dictates the main terms of their culture ("We study your novels, your poems") and is in their line of sight as their final destination. It is not, because the America they know and seek is a deterritorialized space, a function of a global information network that is everywhere and nowhere – in short, a virtual America.

Literally, the final word in *Tree of Smoke* is given to its only female voice, a Canadian nurse called Kathy Jones who has a brief affair with Skip in the Philippines and then sleeps with him in Vietnam. A widow, and a once religious woman who works with war orphans, she sees Vietnam as "a fallen world" (291). Without faith any longer, she nevertheless falls back on the language of religion to try to measure her despair. "I know that this is Hell, right here, planet Earth," she writes to Skip, "and I know that you, me, and all of us were made by God only to be damned." "Or I guess as a Catholic," she adds, "you might ask yourself if this is a journey through Purgatory … Five or ten times a day, you"ll stop and ask yourself, When did I die?" (542). The last words given to Kathy, and to the story, "All will be saved. All will be saved" (614) may sound redemptive, but they smack more of desperation, the will to believe, than genuine belief. What stays in the mind, with Kathy's story, is what stays there with the story of every one of these characters: not hope but a dark anxiety, dread – and, above all, the sense of war as both brutally material and hallucinatory, dreamlike. War, the novel suggests, makes life more "real" – in the sense that it brings its participants closer to the pressures of history and the physical acts of living and dying – and more "unreal" – in that it cuts them off from everyday routine, propelling them into an unfamiliar realm, a world of potential and often actual nightmare. Those involved in the American war in Vietnam all seem haunted by their lives, compelled to move through their experiences half-asleep and half-awake – forced to bear witness to what is called, at one point, the "monstrous birth" (288) of combat. This is the world after the fall: a fallen and strangely fictive, or at least mythic, space that is the consequence of another kind of fiction, the rhetoric that has plunged these characters into the destructive element – the "lies," the verbal smokescreen deployed by those in power "to control the direction of government." *Tree of Smoke* interrogates the myths of (specifically American) nationalism and the project (again, specifically American) of national hegemony. But it offers no comforting vision either of multicultural harmony or extraterritoriality: an America redeemed by being seen simultaneously from inside and outside. Instead, what it offers is an inside/outside perspective that challenges missionary rhetoric, the binary oppositions of nationalist discourse, by insisting on their status as destructive fictions, but that accepts, at the same time, their extraordinarily seductive power – and the fact that promoting a suspension of disbelief (willing or otherwise) is the fundamental way nation-states conduct their business.

5

Imagining the Crisis
in Drama and Poetry

When an aircraft crashed into the second tower at the World Trade Center, a group of fourth and fifth grade schoolchildren were watching from their classroom window at Manhattan's PS-3. It was left to their teacher, who had only started work at the school four days earlier, to help the children deal with their feelings about the event they had witnessed. What the teacher did, in the days and weeks that followed, was to recruit a drama therapist and a group of professionals from a youth theatre organization. With their help, and following a series of theatre workshops, an original play was gradually developed based on the role plays created by the children. Performed in front of parents and friends by the schoolchildren themselves, the play offered a kind of participatory ritual of catharsis, one that was, in every sense, communal.[1] That was one function that drama began to perform after 9/11: therapy – a way for different generations to come together and to begin coming to terms with trauma. Drama has always performed multiple functions, however; and other plays written and performed following the terrorist attacks have combined the therapeutic strategy with the investigative. Some writers and producers of drama

---

[1] "Drama Therapy for Children Coping with 9/11," Newsletter at fanlight.com, 22 January, 2004 (http://www.fanlight.com/pipermail/newsletter_fanlight.com/2004-January/000009.html).

After the Fall: American Literature Since 9/11, First Edition. Richard Gray.
© 2011 John Wiley & Sons, Ltd. Published 2011 by John Wiley & Sons, Ltd.

have, in fact, been more interested in searching out the reasons for, or analysing the process leading up to, the terrorist attacks. And sometimes it has been difficult to distinguish between investigation and paranoia; the search for information has looked more like a willing embrace of conspiracy theory. So, a television mini-series titled *Path to 9/11*, produced in 2006 and evidently funded by the religious right, lays much of the blame for the failure to realize the dangers posed by militant Islam in general and Osama bin Laden in particular, at the door of the Clinton administration. The path to 9/11 "is paved with lies," according to the makers of the series; and the lies it seeks to expose are those of prominent political liberals who failed to act in the face of a clear threat.[2] At the other end of the political spectrum is a drama titled *The Reflecting Pool* by Jarek Kuppsc, issued as a DVD in 2008, which shows an investigative journalist teaming up with the father of a 9/11 victim to unravel the truth lying hidden behind the official 9/11 report. The "truth," in this case, is not that Bill Clinton and his advisors were derelict in their duties, failing to nip terrorism in the bud, but that various members of the Bush administration were. The White House, the investigators discover, knew that an attack was imminent; and the 9/11 Commission Report ignored or omitted vital evidence in order to protect those in power at the time the Twin Towers fell.[3]

Drama as therapy, drama as information or propaganda – and drama, also, as cathartic spectacle: a notable theatrical event of 2006 was a dance-theatre piece called *Love Unpunished*, performed by the Pig Iron Theatre Company. The setting for this piece is stark: three short zigzags of stairs. The action is ritualistically simple: actors repeatedly travel down (and then up a backstage ladder to get back in position),

[2] "Clinton Aides Attack 9/11 Drama," BBC News, August 9, 2006 (http://news-vote.co.uk/mpapps/pagetools/print/news.bbc.co.uk/1/hi/entertainment); "Scoop: "Path to 9/11" Docu-Drama On TV1 Is Propaganda." September 10, 2006 (http://www.scoop.co.nz/stories/HL0609/S00123.htm).
[3] "'The Reflecting Pool' A New 9/11 Investigative Drama That Challenges The Official Version of 9/11 Events Released on DVD," 911Truth.org Resource Center, March 20, 2008 (http://www.911truth.org/article.php?story=200803191 83203726).

each time slightly varying the speed, rhythm, and other details of their trip. As with all good symbolism, the reference is undeclared but clear. This is the World Trade Center immediately after the attacks; and the actors are all those who tried to escape from the burning buildings by running down the stairs. There is no attempt to cope with crisis by talking about it here, still less any investigation of motive or the paths leading up to the critical moment. This is neither more nor less than a stylized commemoration, a dramatic recovery of the moment itself – and, along with that, of the process of repetition compulsion that is its inevitable, dreadful consequence. It focuses simply on the act, the event, rather than possible explanatory contexts, but it focuses it in a way that is clearly intended to provide some kind of cathartic release through silent, ritualistic re-enactment. "The piece tries to let you sit with really simple repetitions about simple details and unlock a kind of compassion," one of the artistic directors of Pig Iron has explained. "It's an attempt to speak quietly underneath all the shout-ing." Silence, in short, becomes the only possible strategy for voicing trauma – an event that, in this case at least, is quite literally beyond the reach of words.[4]

The silent witnessing of *Love Unpunished* contrasts sharply, not just with the search for scapegoats that characterizes *Path to 9/11* and *The Reflecting Pool* but also with plays such as *Portraits* and *Omnium Gatherum* that focus, not on spectacle, the ritualistic and performative, but on words, words, words, in an almost obsessive embrace of the verbal. *Portraits* by Jonathan Bell, which was first produced in 2003, is a series of monologues about seven different Americans, dealing with how they were involved with and affected by 9/11. Two of the characters and their stories are based on actual people and events, the others are invented out of the wealth of journalistic detail that Bell had available to him. The involvement of these characters varies from the distant and peripheral to the direct and immediate. A man is rescued from having an affair, a woman must cope with being a

[4] "A Philadelphia Theater, Set in Its Free-Form Ways," *The New York Times*, September 6, 2006 (http://www.nytimes.com/2006/09/06/theater/06love.html?fta=y).

widow because her husband lost his life trying to help others escape, another woman already widowed sees her son escape, another man heads from Boston to Ground Zero to assist in any way he can and still another anticipates harassment because he is an American-born Muslim. There is also a narrator, an artist who moves from detachment to sympathy as he searches for the potentially tragic meaning of events. But the overall effect of the piece is closer to documentary than to tragedy. "Let us not fall into the caverns of brutality and darkness," the narrator implores, "let the light into your life" (23). The static quality of *Portraits*, however, and the tendency of the monologues to spill over into the portentous, mean that very little light is shone on the traumatic events Bell attempts to address. Feelings are gestured towards, trauma is announced rather than re-enacted. *Portraits* is a play that does little more than talk about what it might have been like to be at or near a critical moment; it declares, but it does not bear witness to trauma; in short, it fails to dramatize.

Omnium Gatherum by Theresa Rebeck and Alexandra Gersten was also first produced in 2003 and is equally reliant on speech more than action. It is, however, more of a witty conversation piece. It is also a *comedie a clef*. Set at a dinner party held in the wake of 9/11, many of the characters are clearly based on actual people. The hostess is obviously inspired by Martha Stewart, the television host and entrepreneur, and the guests include thinly disguised versions of the journalist Christopher Hitchens, the novelist Tom Clancy, and the scholar and critic of Middle Eastern affairs Edward Said. Among the other guests are an uneasily upwardly mobile African American, a firefighter who worked heroically on September 11 and managed to survive – and a surprise guest who adds a note of radical disruption to the proceedings. Essentially, what the audience is offered is a debate, a high octane discussion from very different perspectives of a variety of vital issues: among them, the morality or otherwise of American imperialism, the opposing cases for Israel and Palestine, the nature of heroism as defined by cultures of the East and the West, the motivations behind Islamic terrorism. "Such a lively debate," the hostess declares at one point. "Wonderful, really. Bravo to everyone" (61).

But the debate is not so much wonderful as weirdly unnerving and erratic, shifting constantly in mood and tone. All the characters are constantly changing conversational shape, sometimes contradicting themselves, and always sensitive to the combustible atmosphere that surrounds them. There is also a pervasive sense of dread beneath even the moments of banter – and there are plenty of those. "It isn't a dinner party until someone mentions the Grim Reaper" (44), one of the characters declares. There is the smell of death here; there is also a sense of crisis and decay. This particular set of people, mostly from the bourgeoisie, may have a casual grace, a discreet charm on the surface, and a beguiling way with words. But what the play captures most memorably is the incipient panic, the fear that lurks beneath and occasionally bubbles to the surface. This is a play that takes a dramatic form deployed by directors like Jean Renoir and Luis Bunuel to expose the hypocrisy of the ruling class – a social gathering of the elite – and manages to offer something different: a revelation of the fear that haunts the West and the United States in particular after 9/11 – a fear that is all the more corrosive and debilitating because it is hardly ever acknowledged

Drama as therapy, information, investigation or propaganda, drama as ritual or spectacle, or as debate or documentary; drama also as democratic forum or hybrid. One of the consequences of 9/11 has certainly been to democratize and/or hybridize art. "About a week after the tragedy, the playwright and poet Jeff Meyers has written,

> I became aware of a type of "samizdat" literature proliferating via the Web. E-mailed essays and photocopied articles circulated amongst my friends and family. We all became eager links in an Internet daisy chain of opinion, criticism, and rumination that went beyond the messages fed to us by the mass media. (20)

Meyers wrote this from the perspective of the West Coast (he is based in Seattle). On the East Coast, and specifically in Manhattan, the innumerable missing person signs that were put up all over the city, made up what Jay McInerney called a "makeshift gallery ... the

149

faces of the missing glancing back hopefully and artlessly in photographs taken at weddings and graduation ceremonies, now hanging above impromptu shrines of flowers and candles" (144). The World Trade Center itself formed what one architectural critic has called "a screen that conceals the body" (Wigley, 75), which relegated all those who worked there to a similar anonymity, a faceless mass in the service of a centerless multinational power. "When the facades came down," however, "the faces of the invisible occupants who were lost came up" (Wigley, 82). The posters pasted up all over New York City "formed a new kind of façade, a dispersed image of diversity in place of the singular monolithic screen" (Wigley, 83). The effect was to individualize in death those whose individuality had been denied in life. It was also to democratize. As another commentator has put it, the missing person posters "dramatised one of the central themes of modern democratic culture: *life stories.*" Just like the play developed and performed by those Manhattan schoolchildren who witnessed the fall of the second tower, life stories reveal "how heroically extraordinary… ordinary life can be" (Berman, 5).

The hybridizing of art, in turn, has taken many forms since 9/11. In *11 septembre mon amour*, for example, the French writer Luc Lang mixes autobiography and fiction and juxtaposes the voices of those about to die, calling their loved ones on the telephone to express their love and say goodbye, with the rhetoric of the media and the political administration. The authentic intimacy of individual speech is, in effect, set against the vacuous rhetoric of newscasts and the politician Lang insists on calling "Double V Bouche." In *Windows on the World*, another French writer Frederic Beigbeder constructs a story of doubling and repetition that is simultaneously a fictive hall of mirrors and a confessional, circulating around two narrators – a Texan trapped in the Windows on the World restaurant in Trade Center One on September 11 and a writer called Beigbeder who, to help him imagine his characters' experience, goes off every morning to Le Ciel de Paris, the restaurant at the top of La Tour Montparnasse, the highest skyscraper in Paris. And in *In the Shadow of No Towers*, Art Spiegelman charts what he calls "that faultline where World History and Personal History collide" (1) – in other words, his personal witnessing of the destruction of the World Trade Center – by producing a graphic novel that combines his own cartoons, responding to 9/11 and the "war on terror," with classic figures from the early days of newspaper cartoon serials. At once an encounter with trauma (Spiegelman had what he calls a "ringside seat" (2) to the collapse of the towers), a savage polemic (he felt, he explains "equally terrorised" (2) by Al Qaeda and his own government) and a form of therapy (the classic cartoon characters supply a refuge, emotional rescue and so, in the words of one commentator, "account for both distance and resistance" (Versluys, 66)), the book mixes moods and modes, defamiliarizes and loops back on itself to cope with the presence of absence, the "shadow of no towers." *11 septembre mon amour*, *Windows on the World*, *In the Shadow of No Towers*: these are all forms of the hybrid that take narrative and visual shape. Their equivalent in terms of performance is a play like *Language Rooms*, first produced in 2010. Here, in a play set in a secret US detention center in an unnamed country, Yussef El Guindi, brings the immigrant experience, the comedy of office politics, and the war on terror into intimate and sometimes violent collision.

At the center of *Language Rooms*, a play that is equally a tragedy, a comedy, and a piece of political agit-prop, is Ahmed, an Arab-American interrogator charged with extracting information by any means necessary from fellow Muslims suspected of terrorism. His life begins to unravel when he realizes that his colleagues harbor the same resentment and suspicion towards him as he feels towards his interview subjects. The world we enter here is a microcosm of a society that has surrendered to surveillance, paranoia, and secrecy. The task of the interrogators is to pry secrets from their subjects that can then be used in covert military operations. But the investigators themselves are under surveillance too: they have no privacy, are expected to obey orders without question, and are actually told that they can have no secrets from the head of their team. Ahmed comes under particularly close surveillance after he misses a Super Bowl party held at the detention center and refuses to use the communal shower. "I wanted this to be a kind of corporate environment," El Guindi has said of *Language Rooms*. "The whole issue of office politics was a way for me

151

to introduce Ahmed's questions of fitting in ... and moving from that to the larger issues of fitting in as a citizen."[5]

The play is full of bizarre touches: as Kevin, the head of the interrogation team, grills Ahmed about his loyalties, he takes off his shirt, carefully irons it and puts it back on. It also flirts with the kind of doublespeak that characterizes both managerial and political rhetoric. "I love you, my friend," Kevin tells Ahmed. "If I give you the third degree, it's to confirm those feelings." After demanding total obedience and conformity, Kevin even suggests to Ahmed that "it's important to be authentic" and to be an individual; "loyalty," he slyly suggests, "has been overstressed." Whether this is sincerely meant or manipulation, an attempt to draw Ahmed out, is never clear. It is wrong probably, however, to invoke the notion of sincerity at all in this context; the dividing line between the authentic and the artificial, here and elsewhere in *Language Rooms*, if it exists at all, is invisible. Kevin certainly plays on Ahmed's ambiguous connection to the people he interrogates. If Ahmed hates his interview subjects, Kevin suggests, his fellow Arabs – as he surely does, the rider is – then perhaps he also hates his other fellow Americans; perhaps he hates being an American just as much as he evidently hates being of Arab origin. He is guilty of anything and everything, in this densely conspiratorial atmosphere, where not sharing a shower or participating in a Super Bowl party seem of equal weight with being a traitor; and being a traitor can, in any event, seem a matter of verbal slippage. *Language Rooms* is full of dialogue and debate that slips between the surreal and the political, absurd pantomime and verbal sleight-of-hand, black comedy and bleak tragedy, the little slights and squabbles of everyday life in the office and the tactics of surveillance and counter-surveillance embedded in global conflict. "Think *The Office* meets *24*,"[6] one reviewer said

[5] *Language Rooms* is, at the time of writing, an unpublished manuscript. For more details, see, Anneke Esch-Van Kan, "Amazing Acrobatics of Language: The Theatre of Yussef El Guindi," *American Studies Journal*, 52 (Winter 2008) (http://asjournal.zusas. uni-halle.de/157.html); doollee.com: The Playwrights Database (http://www.dool lee.com/PlaywrightsE/el-guindi-yussef.html).
[6] Tirdad Derakhshani, "A funny, ferocious drama post-9/11," *The Philadelphia Inquirer*, March 9, 2010 (http://www.philly.com/imquirer/magazine/20100309).

of its first production. It is much more than that, however; it is densely, complexly hybrid. El Guindi copes with the trauma of 9/11 and its social and political spillage through a kind of mimetic approximation: a form that incorporates traumatic experience not so much discursively or thematically, on the surface, as stylistically, deep down in its tensions of mood and dramatic texture.

Of all the dramas written and performed in response to 9/11 and its aftermath, however, one of the simplest – and as far removed from the complexly layered character of *Language Rooms* as possible – has so far proved the most popular: *The Guys* by Anne Nelson. Written in just nine days and first performed almost immediately after it was written, it was conceived as a staged reading. There are two characters: Nick, a New York City Fire Department captain who just happened to be off duty when his crew was called to the World Trade Center on September 11, and Jean, a reporter born in Oklahoma but now living in New York City, who feels powerless in the face of the 9/11 crisis. The premise of this play, which has an artless, impromptu quality to it, is simple. Nick has been asked to speak at memorial services being organized for those of his men who died as a result of the terrorist attacks. He is, however, at a loss for words – or, at least, words suffi-cient for the purpose. Somehow, in the strange serendipity of the days following 9/11, he is thrown together with Jean, who listens to his guileless accounts of his fallen colleagues and then fashions them into eulogies. Through talking about the dead and making them come alive again in memory and eulogy, the two characters achieve a kind of catharsis. So, clearly the intention is, do the audience. Many of the familiar tropes of post-9/11 writing are rehearsed. We are told, for instance, that September 11 marked a turning point in history, or, as Jean puts it, "the end of the Postmodern era" (8). And Jean dreams of rewinding history. "Let's just play the tape backwards," she suggests, so that "the planes fly backwards … and land backwards in Boston. Everyone gets out of the plane and drives backwards home" (35). But no attempt is made to understand the crisis. "I lie awake at nights think-ing, 'What was the reason?'" Nick confides, seeking an explanation for the terrorist attacks. And Jean speaks for the play when she replies simply, "No reason" (28). Later on, Jean resists the idea that 9/11 has a global significance. "Everybody, all over the world, was talking about it," she recalls, "... And they all ... thought it was about them! But it's not! It's about us" (30). Admittedly, this declaration is followed by a tentative query, a request for confirmation ("Isn't it?"(30)). But that hardly qualifies the intense focus of the play on actual consequences rather than possible causes, the suffering of victims. The strength of the play resides in its simplicity: in its belief in the "wonders" that "lie hidden in the people around us" (25) including those who died at the World Trade Center, and in its conviction that talking, telling about those wonders is both necessary and therapeutic since, as Jean puts it, "People need to tell their stories" (29). That simplicity, however, is also its weakness. "The firefighter needs a writer" (9), the audience is told at the beginning of the action; and Nick and Jean never really develop beyond those stereotypical roles. The four men who form the basis of their conversation and the subjects of the eulogies are never developed beyond the stereotypical either: one is a veteran, one an apprentice who died on his first day at work, and so on. Of one of the victims, Nick declares that he was "just an ordinary guy ... but you can't say that in a eulogy" (27). On the whole, though, that is all that is said about the victims of 9/11 in *The Guys*. For good or ill, the play belongs in the honorable tradition of American populism that celebrates the "ordinary" rather than the individual.

Superficially, *The Mercy Seat* by Neil LaBute, first performed in 2002, bears a resemblance to *The Guys*. It also has just two characters, and is set in New York City just after the attack on the World Trade Center (in this case, the day after). It, too, studiously avoids addressing the larger issues: LaBute has, in fact, insisted that *The Mercy Seat* is "not a play that concerns itself with the politics of terrorism" (ix). There, however, the resemblance ends. This acerbic, sophisticated drama focuses on power and betrayal, in the process deconstructing the belief lying at the heart of *The Guys* that, in a crisis, people can and will rise above themselves and pull together. Ben Harcourt is in the apartment of his boss and mistress, Abby Prescott, a woman twelve years older than him. It is September 12, 2001. The day before, rather than going to his office in the World Trade Center, Ben visited his mistress. He has not since gone home to his wife and children, who probably believe that he is dead: a cellphone rings intermittently throughout the play, and the implication is that it is Ben's family trying to find out if he has survived. Ben does not answer the phone. Instead, he considers the opportunity 9/11 offers him to run away with Abby and start a new life with a new identity. For him, much to the surprise and consternation of his mistress, the crisis is "a meal ticket" (12) – as she sardonically terms it. "I'm saying the American way is to overcome, to conquer, to come out on top," Ben explains. "And we do it by spending and eating and screwing our women harder than anyone else" (16).

Ben is a survivalist. "No matter what's happened or is going on," he tells Abby, "we still go the movies and buy gifts and take a two-week vacation, because that's-the-way-it-is." (16). Abby, although caught up in the intricate power game of their relationship, is much more ambivalent – and not just because she does not want to sacrifice a successful career to go on the run. When it comes down to it, she wants Ben to tell his family "the truth" (64). The twist in the tale is that eventually Ben reveals a different truth from the one Abby imagines: almost at the end of the play, he tells Abby that, on September 11, he was planning to break up with her. The revelation does not, however, lead to a resolution of his self-imposed dilemma. As *The Mercy Seat* finishes, Ben is still toying with the choices that the crisis has made available to him. Like some dark parody of the traditional American hero, he is still caught between the alternatives of, on the one hand, a return to home and family and, on the other, escape into anonymity. *The Mercy Seat* may not be a political play in the conventional sense. But it does explore the politics of personal and sexual relationships, what LaBute calls "a particular kind of terrorism: the painful, simplistic warfare we wage on those we profess to love" (ix). And, in exposing the seamless egotism of Ben, it not only subverts the consolatory myths of shared victimhood and communal suffering on which a play like *The Guys* depends. It also identifies "the American way" as opportunism. LaBute has explained that he tried, in this play, "to examine how selfishness can still exist during a moment of national selflessness" and to look at "the 'ground zero' of our lives, the gaping hole in ourselves that we try to cover up with clothes from Gap, with cologne from Ralph Lauren" (x). Like *The Guys*, *The Mercy Seat* may concentrates on the consequences of terror rather than causes. It does so, however, for a radically different purpose. "Don't make this thing that's happened, this whole ... unbelievable thing ... just about you" (26), Abby tells Ben. Unfortunately, he does. That, LaBute suggests, is "the American way."

Recent *Tragic Events* by Craig Wright was first produced less than a year after 9/11. Like *The Guys* and *The Mercy Seat*, it circulates around the events of that day; like *The Mercy Seat*, too, it is set in an apartment; it is, however, very different from either. This apartment is in Minneapolis, Minnesota; and this play is more like *Language Rooms*, in that that it yokes heterogeneous elements together and also flirts with the bizarre. Just as, in a media saturated age, reviewers of *Language Rooms* tried to explain its strange brew of genres by describing it as a mix of *The Office* and *24*, so one of the critics who reviewed *Recent Tragic Events* suggested that "It's as if Pirandello had been hired to do the season finale for *Friends*."[7] Certainly, the basic premise is out of situation or screwball comedy: a blind date that goes horribly wrong. Along with the couple, brought together by a colleague, there is a wacky neighbor and his even wackier woman friend called Nancy, mostly silent, who insists on wandering around in an outfit that leaves her private parts publicly exposed. To that extent, this is cable TV comedy rather than terrestrial TV, let alone the world of Doris Day. But then *Recent Tragic Events* also spirals off into big philosophical questions and the surreal. Part of the edginess and uncertainty here, too, is that is never clear to what extent the surreal humor subverts the asking of big questions and to what extent it complements or even reinforces it. Is this all serious, in short, or is it a joke? Or is there, in a postmodern, post Monty Python world, a difference? Whether asked seriously or in the jest, however, the questions addressed here are neatly summed up in the epigraph to the play: a passage from Schopenhauer that makes the distinction between two "fundamentally different

---

[7]   Ben Brantley, "A First Date Blindsided By a Cosmic Event," *The New York Times*, March 2, 2010 (http://theater.nytimes.com/mem/theater/treview/html?res=9406 E6D8103DF93AA157).

kinds of connection," two ways of explaining the link between events. There is, Schopenhauer suggests, the "objective, causal connection of the natural process" and there is the "subjective connection which exists only in relation to the individual who experiences it." This is a sophisticated play on the ancient debate between fate and free will. Are we the authors and heroes of our own singular narratives? Are we the product of an elaborate concatenation of circumstance? Or are we, in some way that, as Schopenhauer intimates, "surpasses our powers of comprehension," a miraculous combination of both? That is something that the play sets out to consider, to play with and turn over in our minds, if not to resolve. And all of this circulates around the events of 9/11; appropriately enough, because it was then, in particular, that, – to recall that remark of Art Spiegelman's quoted earlier – personal and world histories, the personal, subjective narrative and the larger, "objective...natural process" came into sudden collision.

The story in *Recent Tragic Events* is simple. An airport bookstore manager called Andrew arrives at the home of Waverly, an advertising executive, for a blind date arranged by a mutual acquaintance whom both of them despise. The date of their meeting is September 12, 2001; and Waverly is distracted by the fact that her twin sister, Wendy, a student in New York, has not been heard from since the terrorist attacks. As the evening wears on, Waverly and Andrew become aware of a series of bizarre coincidences that seem to connect or "twin" them. Andrew, in particular, comes to believe that he met Wendy in New York and, challenged by Wendy as to whether she should take a job with a firm based at the World Trade Center ("she said talking to strangers was like flipping a coin," Andrew recalls "it's how she makes decisions, and tonight, I was the coin"(35)), he recommended that she should accept the offer. Coincidence or providence? Chance or something more deeply intricate and convoluted? The play plays with the possibilities, different ways of reading what has happened and continues to happen; it also plays with the expectations of the audience. Before the beginning of the first act, we are told by a character playing the Stage Manager that the action will depend on a coin tossed by "a volunteer from the audience." There are two sets of variables and, "every time something occurs" in the play "that was determined by this coin toss, a tone will be heard" to signal a transition. The characters will continue "in blissful ignorance" but the audience will know that "those particular moments could potentially have occurred differently" (9). So far, so (apparently) clear. But then, before the beginning of the second act, the Stage Manager reappears to say that this was, of course, a ruse: "the tone of 'chance'" was only sounded in the first act "whenever the playwright indicated it *should* be sounded;" "everything that occurred on stage only happened because *that was the only way it ever could have happened*" (37). If there was any "blissful ignorance" at issue here, it belonged as much to those watching as to those being watched. What compounds the philosophical gamesomeness now, in Act Two, is the sudden appearance of someone called Joyce Carol Oates, related to Waverly and deeply admired by Andrew, who has been detoured to Minneapolis after the terrorist attacks. This Joyce Carol Oates, we are assured by the Stage Manager before Act Two begins, is "an entirely fictitious" character, even though she bears the name of a famous and famously prolific author – a fictitious character "who has happened *by chance* to write a massive body of work which *just so happens* to correlate word for word to the works of the *real* Joyce Carol Oates" (37–8). And, the Stage Manager patiently explains, "just so nobody gets the idea that the 'Joyce Carol Oates' portrayed in this play is supposed to be *the Joyce Carol Oates*, this part is going to be played by a sock puppet" (38), worn on the hand of the actress playing the otherwise mostly silent Nancy. It is the puppet that makes a long, impassioned speech in support of a belief in free will: "everything about my experience tells me I'm free," the puppet proudly declares; "human beings are free ... free to fly planes into buildings and free to help people who are hurt when it happens." (51–2). "It sounds like you think you're a puppet" (51), the sock puppet scornfully declares to another character, the wacky neighbor Ron, when he resists this suggestion. "Without freedom, Ron, there's no such thing as human nature!" (52) So, this second act takes the theme of chance dictating events, and the big questions about causal connection posed already in act one, and turns them on their head – or, rather, inside out – and then fractures them.

Which brings us to 9/11: the philosophical elephant in the room in this play. *Recent Tragic Events* asks the question inevitably asked at critical moments in history. Are we in control of events or do events control us? Are we the authors of our story or merely the characters and/or, still worse, the impotent spectators whose biggest mistake is to believe we have some say in things we are merely witnessing? What is the degree of our responsibility for, or our complicity in, the larger experiences that shape our lives? What is at stake here? Chance (the apparently accidental meeting of Andrew and Wendy in New York City, the flip of a coin)? Coincidence (the bizarre fact that, as it turns out, Andrew and Waverly have so many things in common, the twinning of Waverly and Wendy)? An obscure pattern, an elaborate, barely decipherable series of circumstances – like those that bring together a group of utterly disparate characters, including a sock puppet, in a particular space at a particular and particularly momentous moment in time? Or the authority over circumstance that finds its paradigm in the authority of the author ("the tone of 'chance'…was sounded whenever the playwright indicated it *should* be sounded")? There are no answers here, only a proliferating series of questions. A sock puppet makes the major speech in favor of free will. A wacky downstairs neighbor makes the major claim that the attack on the World Trade Center was determined and "inevitable." "Take a nation with the most hypertheroid self-concept in the history of the world," Ron declares,

> kick everybody's ass for a hundred and fifty years … build a pair of ultrafucking tall buildings in the most prominent city in the world … and do NOTHING to protect them from the air, in a world of billions of assholes; and then act *surprised* when something bad happens … (49)

"*That's* fucked up," he concludes, but that seems no more conclusive than anything else in this play. The author of these remarks is left, at the end of *Recent Tragic Events*, simply to switch off the TV and turn off the lights, while the Stage Director reminds us that he is doing just that because it is in the script. He seems to be no more in control of the story than anyone else.

Or, then again, perhaps he is. A running joke in this strange, surreal drama involves the characters, sometimes in chorus, falling back on the vague, gestural term, "the thing," to describe the event that occurred only the day before the present action – an event that seems to haunt all their lives. The gestural character of the word is a symptom, a clue to their sense of bewilderment, their impotence, their inability to think of an adequate term for their condition. As Waverly says, thinking about those who died in the Twin Towers, including quite possibly her sister, "It makes no sense" (23–4). "I used to wake up every morning and think 'What am I gonna *do?*'" Waverly confesses at one point a little prior to this. "Today I woke up and thought, 'What's going to *happen to me?* It's kinda different'" (15). It *is* "kinda different;" there *is* a difference between the idea of agency ("What am I gonna *do?*") and the idea of victimhood ("What's going to *happen to me?*"). Although Waverly is hardly aware of it, it is a difference that is both philosophical and – given the gap in thinking, the fissure opened up by 9/11 – historical, throwing down a challenge to the way Americans think about themselves and their nation. It is also a difference that *Recent Tragic Events* attempts to measure – in blackly, bleakly comic terms that are themselves "kinda different."

With *Back of the Throat* by Yussef El Guindi and *The God of Hell* by Sam Shepard, the focus shifts from the immediate crisis of September 11, 2001, to the longer term trauma engendered by the "war on terror." Yussef El Guindi, also the author of *Language Rooms*, is one of a small group of Arab-American playwrights who have gained a higher profile since the terrorist attacks. Others are associated with the Silk Road Theatre Project in Chicago, founded after 9/11 to concentrate on plays about countries along that historical route from China to Europe, and with Nibras, an Arab-American theatre collective, similarly set up after 9/11, in New York. El Guindi has explained that, after the attack on the World Trade Center, he "started to imagine what could happen"[8] if FBI agents were to visit his apartment. Several of his Arab-American friends had become subject to suspicion, and

---

[8]   Dinitia Smith, "For Arab-American Playwrights, a Sense of Purpose," *The New York Times*, February 11, 2006 (http://www.nytimes.com/2006/02/11/theater/newsand features/11throhtml).

targets for investigation, because of their ethnicity. And he became interested, in both a political and a personal sense, in the processes of investigation, interrogation, and even torture unleashed by the "war on terror." The result was *Back of the Throat,* premiered in 2005: in which an Arab-American writer called Khaled is suddenly visited in his apartment by two FBI agents, a smooth talker named Bartlett and a tougher specimen who goes by the name of Carl. Khaled begins by being eager to please but also slightly anxious. "This isn't as casual as you make it out to be" (18), he suggests. The agents, in turn, begin by being polite and reassuring. "If you're innocent, you're innocent," Bartlett tells Khaled. "You don't have to work at it" (15). But gradually the mood darkens. "Facts aren't the only game in town" (41), Bartlett declares; and Khaled finds himself suffering guilt by rumor and association – and, in particular, association with someone named Asfoor, a supposed terrorist (although, like so much in the play, this is never definitely established) with whom Khaled has been linked by some less than reliable evidence. But guilty of what? It is never really clear. "What are you accusing me of?" Khaled asks plaintively. "This is like some fifties B movie. *I Married a Communist*" (27).

As *Back of the Throat* charts a downward spiral from polite conversation to intimidation and torture, it also seesaws wildly between dark seriousness and equally dark comedy. One of the more blackly comic moments, for instance, comes during an argument over how to pronounce Khaled's name. Bartlett starts with Haled and finally gets it right, commenting that "it's that back of the throat thing" (13). As that moment illustrates, this is a play about the power and problems of language. The agents create their own reality through their dialogue with one another and with Khaled. Khaled struggles to find the right language with which to confirm his sense of his own innocence. And, throughout the play, Yussef El Guindi slips between different forms of language, constructing and deconstructing the relationships between these three characters, inventing and then uninventing possible scenarios of what is going on here. Khaled is never proven innocent to the audience, let alone to the agents. But that is part of the point, since it is difficult if not impossible to work out just what form, in this context, definite proof of innocence would assume. In this environment,

161

where facts are not the only game in town and the suspicion of conspiracy is rife, it is a question, not of truth, but of whose story gets told. The final speeches of any length in the play are given to Bartlett and then, in an apparent time shift, to Asfoor. Bartlett explains the choices available to Khaled. He can claim he is innocent, "in which case proving it might be difficult." Or he can confess that he is guilty – and so, Bartlett suggests, "score … points" "by telling us now" "because we'll find out soon enough." Or he can admit that he is "innocent of being guilty." Which would mean, Bartlett explains, "You didn't know what you were getting into. Stumbled into it. Through deception. Other people's. Your own stupidity." "And that would be okay too," Bartlett helpfully adds. "We can work with that. We can work with you to make that seem plausible" (49–50) History, Bartlett is suggesting, is coextensive with story. Reality is something acted out, a master narrative constructed by the agents of empire, those in authority; it is a matter of language. A language that Khaled does not have, although Bartlett is certainly trying to help him have access to it – and in the process, incriminate himself. It is also a language that, in the final speech of the play, Asfoor confesses that he longs to learn. "I must learn the language that is everywhere," Asfoor declares. "Language that has fallen on our heads and made us like – like children again." "And one day … I might even teach it," he adds, "I will teach language back … I will make them speak words they never spoke before. I will make them like children too … And soon my language will fall on their heads. Like theirs falls on ours. Exploding in our brains 'til we can't even dream in peace" (50). The elision between words and bombs here offers a powerful rider, both metaphorical and literal, to the speech of Bartlett that immediately precedes it, and to the verbal dynamics of the entire play. In the war between terrorist and counter terrorist, words become weapons, vital agents in the reconstruction of reality and the destruction of the real. Language as communication, in short, is replaced by language as power.

In *The God of Hell,* first staged in 2004, Sam Shepard also starts with the narrative premise of unexpected visitors. The setting here is the American heartland of Wisconsin. Emma and Frank are dairy farmers. They are visited, first, by a mysterious stranger called Haynes. When

Haynes shakes hands with Emma, bolts of electricity are emitted from his fingers. Then, while Haynes is briefly staying with the couple in the basement of their house, they receive another visitor, a purveyor of flags, bunting, and other patriotic paraphernalia called Welch. "Whole country's made of salesmen" (23), Welch declares, as he alternately smooth talks and tries to intimidate Emma and Frank. Manically energetic, Welch staples flags and bunting all around the house, while questioning the couple about how many rooms the house has and who might be staying in the basement. Gradually, it becomes clear that he is a government agent and that Haynes is his prey. Haynes, it seems, has escaped from a secret nuclear facility called Rocky Buttes, having been contaminated by plutonium. Welch is out to get him back and, in response to any objections or protests, simply insists, "We can do whatever we want ... We're in absolute command now. We don't have to answer to a soul, least of all a couple of Wisconsin dairy farmers" (43). "This guy is taking over our house" (48), Emma complains. She, in particular, tries to resist. But Haynes is tortured into submission; and Frank seems persuaded that Welch will lead him to a brave new world. "We're going to Rocky Buttes," Welch tells Frank. "Whole different landscape. Wide open. Just like the Wild Wild West. Not a tree in sight. Endlessly flat and lifeless" (59). All Emma can manage, in response to this, is to run outside the house and start ringing the alarm bell. She sees the danger, evidently, but all she can do is what, in this play, Shepard is also clearly trying to do: sound the alarm.

The God of Hell takes its title from two punningly linked sources, Pluto, the god of the underworld, and plutonium, the element evidently manufactured at Rocky Buttes that might signal the end of the world. Its dramatic strategies involve a combination of broad, black satire and deadpan surrealism and it directs its satire far and wide. Among its targets, for instance, are the patriotic cant of the "war on terror," the myth of the Midwestern heartland (Frank and Emma are, it turns out, the only people left in the area who still actually farm), the destruction of privacy in post-9/11 America, the demolition of civil rights in pursuit of terrorism, the threats posed by nuclear power and nuclear weapons. Emma and Frank are "out of touch," Welch sneers. "Living completely in the long-ago. Stuck in some quaint pioneer morality" (43). Shepard rehearses one of his favorite themes here, the loss of the true West and the emergence of a new West that commodifies and corrupts. But the catalyst for this rehearsal is now the events of September 11, 2001 and their consequences: the destruction of America, not so much by acts of terrorism, as by the relentless processes of counter terrorism. The choice of a family farm as setting is carefully calculated, as is the focus on a middle American couple like Frank and Emma – two people who seem proud of the fact that, as Emma puts it, "Nothing ever happens here" (29). The traditional location of the American Dream turns out to be a place of surreal nightmare as Shepard invokes the old myth of the American West, on the one hand, while, on the other, he subverts it. Emma and Frank turn out to be, not the happy farmers of legend, but the unhappy victims of a literal invasion of their land and lives. If they are, as Thomas Jefferson supposed in his famous celebration of the rural heartland of America, the chosen people of God then that God is the God of Hell.

Two large-scale works that fall into the nascent genre of post-9/11 drama are *Where Do We Live* by Christopher Shinn and *Pugilist Specialist* by Adriano Shaplin. *Where Do We Live*, which received its world premiere in London in 2002, has a large cast of fifteen characters, people who are lovers, friends, rivals, and business partners. They are also neighbors, since the play is set mostly in a New York City apartment block. Ostensibly, what Shinn is concerned with here is a young, gay man called Stephen, his relationships and, in particular, the relationship with his black neighbors. In fact, it is a deeply symbolic look at life in New York just before and just after September 11, 2001: the play begins in late July and ends in early October, with the terrorist attack occurring between the second and third acts. Stephen, a writer, has a reasonably comfortable life. He is in love with Tyler, a sleek young actor. Temperamentally, the two have little in common. Stephen is serious about his liberal politics, while Tyler has the benefit of a trust fund that insulates him from having to take anything too seriously. There is, it seems, bound to be a clash. What provokes it is Stephen's interest in his neighbor, Timothy, a middle-aged black man who begins borrowing cigarettes from Stephen and then small sums of money. To complicate matters further, there is the young black man

Timothy lives with, his nephew Shedrick, who deals drugs. Shedrick, or Shed as he is known, wants to escape from the drugs trade but has not managed it. And Shed lets Stephen know that he resents the white man's charity and despises his homosexuality. Other characters add to the rich mix of class, race, and gender issues and the intricate network of conflicts created by these four characters. There is, for instance, a young English woman called Lily also living in Timothy's apartment, a white drugs supplier, Dave, who likes to think of himself as being in touch with black idiom and life, and a young gay Asian man who sees Stephen's rejection of his advances as one more sign of his having "no access" to society and being "totally ignored" (84). And through them, as well as through a kaleidoscopic series of scenes and a variety of often overlapping conversations, Shinn explores the state of the city and the nation at a critical moment in the history of both.

During a crucial interchange in the play, Tyler, with some irritation, asks Stephen why he wants to help his neighbors. Stephen's reply is simple: "I *live* here!" (63). Shed says something similar to Stephen during another conversation. "You know how it is, we all live together, we all neighbours" (13). Then, shortly afterwards, talking to Timothy and Lily, Shed adds to that observation. "There's things in life that go on," Shed explains, "like where you live, what you have, those things never go away." Other things might "go away," he suggests, like "having sex" or "getting high." But "this place gonna stay." So, "if you gotta focus on one thing in life you pick the thing that stays" (16). *Where Do We Live*, as these remarks suggest, explores the ethics of place and community: not in any traditional or nostalgic way but by seeing "where you live" as a site of multiple encounters. The constant shifting of scene, the overlapping action and conversations have a vital function here; they register the place where the play is situated as another border territory, where people of radically different cultural, class, and ethnic backgrounds meet, argue, and engage with each other. The threat to this place, it is clear, comes from the forces of division: from terrorism to narrow nationalism, acts of violence and attitudes of bigotry, bombs that destroy and social policies that cut people off from one another. *Where Do We Live* is a subtle analysis of the state of a city, and by implication a society, in crisis, its potential as a cultural interface, and its problems if that potential is ignored. The tensions at work here are caught in an exchange that ends the play. One character, called Howard, celebrating the beginning of the "war on terror," opts for nationalism, the imperatives of special mission and manifest destiny. "A toast, what do you say?" he suggests. "To the USA!" Stephen responds in a way that at once agrees with and resists that suggestion. "To where we live" (97), he says.

In *Pugilist Specialist*, which was first performed in 2003, Adriano Shaplin shifts the focus directly to the forces of division. The major players here are four marines assigned the task of assassinating a Middle Eastern leader known as "Big 'Stach" (for "Big Moustache") and "The Bearded Lady." The fifteen scenes of the play cover the first military briefing of the marines, their lunch at a mess hall, their reconnaissance training, their deployment close to the target, a last-minute change of plan and immediate execution of that plan. *Pugilist Specialist* is an ensemble piece, written with certain specific actors in mind, members of the Riot Group based in San Francisco, although it has been performed by others. And its text, Shaplin has warned, is process rather than product – or, as he puts it, "just one unfixed, unfinished component of a dialogue between author and ensemble, performance and audience" (12). The core conflict that takes place in this fluid theatrical landscape is between Lieutenants Emma Stein and Travis Freud. Stein is a tough but clearheaded explosives expert known for her carefully organized bombings of enemy sites. Freud is a misogynistic sniper who loves to kill. At the close of the play, when Stein and Freud have finally entered the mansion of the target to plant a bomb as planned. Freud suddenly receives instructions via radio to kill Stein instead of "The Bearded Lady." The leader of the operation, Colonel Johns, claims that he never expected the team to get close enough to the target to kill him. Johns cannot let Stein finish the mission, he tells the fourth member of the team, Lieutenant Harpo. "We need the target more than we need her … No more targets, no more history" (80). Following the killing of Stein, one last scene consists simply of a taped recording of the radio conversation between the surviving team members. In that conversation, Johns tells Freud to leave the corpse of Stein in the mansion and switch

166

off the tape recorder. The play then ends with the sudden and abrupt cutting off of the tape.

That abrupt ending – a conclusion that does not in any conventional sense conclude – is characteristic. *Pugilist Specialist* thrives on indeterminacy. There is threat here, violence but there is also confusion. Character, motive, purpose are illegible, just about impossible to read. "What did this guy actually do," Stein asks about "Big 'Stach," and receives the answer, "Who cares?" followed by the throwaway comment, "He's just your average neighbourhood philistine" (27). Within the play, none of the marines is ever fully informed about his or her mission. Information is consistently with-held or fragmentary, while the marines themselves are under con-stant surveillance since a microphone records all their conversations. Similarly, the audience is left guessing, invited to read character and motive but denied the evidence required to read them properly. The dialogue is elliptical and allusive, rendered foggier by a per-sistent use of clipped military jargon. The names of the characters seem eponymous, significant (Freud, Stein, Harpo) but, in the end, appear to signify nothing but themselves; they simply tease us with the possibility, the deferral of meaning. And those characters, while they try to guess each other's motivation and invite the audience to do so too, hide behind military postures or even draw attention to their own opacity. Stein, for instance, suggests that women in the military like her can only survive by strenuously protecting their privacy. "Secret is my armour," she declares. "Silence is my camou-flage" (35). Even the critical moment in the play is unreadable. After the killing of Stein, it remains unclear whether the change of plan was really a spontaneous decision on the part of Colonel Johns or whether Stein had been the target all along, in retaliation for her leaking sensitive information to the *New York Times* after a previous operation. "A strong narrative arch is essential to any military vic-tory" (54), Colonel Johns declares at one point. But *Pugilist Specialist* resists a "narrative arch" of this kind. It deconstructs the "strong," monolithic narratives of nationalism and substitutes for them the dramatic language of illegibility and indeterminacy – a language that actively challenges the discourse, the story on which notions

167

of "military victory" are based. Interrogating the "war on terror" in general and the invasion of Iraq and pursuit of Saddam Hussein in particular, *Pugilist Specialist* is at once one of the subtlest and one of the most subversive of those plays that try to address the post-9/11 crisis: taking its characters, and its audience, into a landscape where ignorant armies clash by night.

★ ★ ★

"Politics kills poetry," wrote Tim Scannell, before launching into an attack on what he saw as the politicization of cultural activity in general and poetry in particular. Scannell was talking in broad terms about what he believed was a sinister development: the relentless growth of "ideological coilings which throttle"[9] poetic activity. But he was writing in 2002; and there is no doubt that this gave his argument a peculiar resonance. That resonance was picked up by, among others, another poet, Daniela Giosoffi who retorted, "many of us do not wish to write merely 'art for art's sake' – especially after the 'blow-back' of 9/11!"[10] The relationship between poetry and politics has always been a problematic one. On the one hand, there are those who argue that poetry, being a human activity, is inseparable from community, society, and so from politics. On the other, there are those who argue that the sources of poetry are pre-historical, pre-societal, and that the individual voice stands apart from, even in resistance to, politics in its own musical space. A subtler variation on this debate is offered by those who insist that the poet attends, first and last, to language but, in doing so, performs an essentially political act, since language, perception and the construction of our social lives are intertwined. Building on this, there are also those who suggest that, in attending to and renewing the language, the poet is in effect interrogating and subverting the dominant political rhetoric – or what Ezra Pound called "the fogged

[9] Tim Scannell, "Poetry and Politics," 29 May, 2002 (http://www.cosmoetica. com/S10-TS1.htm).
[10] Daniela Gioseffi, "Poetry and Politics After 9/11: An Editorial," PoetsUSA.com (http://users.tellurian.net/wisewomensweb/PoetsUSA/Gioseffi_Ed.html).

language of the swindling classes."[11] But although the debate over the relationship between poetry and politics has always been there, it has certainly acquired a new edge and relevance with the terrorist attacks and the "war on terror." As various observers announced an end to irony[12] (which appeared to be shorthand for literary indirection), poets found themselves challenged more than ever to reveal exactly where they stood in that debate – and, in doing so, to respond to the simple question of how to write poetry after 9/11.

"There were, in the immediate aftermath, poems everywhere," the editors of an anthology of post-9/11 poetry by New York poets have recalled:

> Walking around the city you would see them – stuck on light posts and phone stalls, plastered on the shelters at bus stops and the walls of subway stations. In neighborhood newspapers the letters-to-the-editor pages were full of them. Downtown, people scrawled poems in the ash that covered everything. And on the brick walls of police stations and firehouses, behind the mountains of flowers and between photos of the dead, poetry dominated. Eventually, a fire chief actually issued a statement: Thank you for the food and the blankets and flowers but please – no more poetry. (Johnson and Merians, ix)

This was a different take on the function of poetry at a time of crisis from the ones offered by Scannell and Giosoffi. This was poetry as a spontaneous overflow of feeling, written in the belief that only poems could say what needed now to be said. For some observers, poets included, this use of poetry as a populist instrument – a vehicle for expressing the sentiments of people who, in many cases, had never written poems before – was a measure of the failure of public discourse after the terrorist attacks. So the poet Dana Gioia argued that the sudden outpouring of poetry after 9/11 was proof of the

[11] Marjorie Perloff, "Writing Poetry after 9/11," *American Letters & Commentary* (2002), 18–23 (http://marjorieperloff.com/articles/poetry-9/11/)
[12] Roger Rosenblatt, "The Age of Irony Comes to an End," *Time*, September 16, 2001 (http://www.time.com/time/magazine/article/0,9171,1101010924-1751112, 00.html).

"media's collective inadequacy to find words commensurate with the situation;" "the media may have provided information," Gioia wrote, "but it was still left for poets to present language equal to the histori- cal moment" (Gioia, 160, 164). The problem, however, is that many of the poems written in response to the fall of the Twin Towers, and its aftermath, do not actually question or resist the consensual, con- ventional response in the way Gioia suggests they do. On the con- trary, they tend at best to express the bewilderment caused by that traumatic event and, at worst, to repeat the clichés generated by the media. Very often, they do both. Here is the opening of a typical poem called "The Eleventh of September" by Roger J. Robicheaux, from a website titled "America's Tragedy:"

> We mourn their loss this day this year
> Those now with God, no danger near
>
> So many loved ones left do stand
> Confronting loss throughout our land
>
> My heart goes out to those who do
> No one can fathom what they view.

According to the epigraph to this poem, it was "read before the United States Senate by Senator John Kerry on September 4, 2002." It goes on to hope for "peace of mind," to ask God to "guide" "our soldiers now at war" ("The finest force you"ll ever see/ All freedom grown through liberty") and concludes by saying that the eleventh of September is a day that "must live in infamy." The technical clumsiness of the lines is matched by the naivete of the sentiments and routine character of the language. That is characteristic of nearly all the poems on this and similar websites. So is the way outrage at the obscene acts of the ter- rorists spills over into a celebration of the "war on terror" – the speed, in short, with which genuine grief, however awkwardly expressed, modulates into compensatory feelings of revengeful triumphalism. Writing poems like this may have been a necessary act of catharsis for those who wrote them, but, reading them, adds nothing to our understanding of, or our ability to come to terms with, the events they memorialize. What is on offer here is symptom not diagnosis. All that is registered, really, is the confusion, and the desperate resort to the familiar – the clichéd, the stereotypical – that is often the result of shock.

If poems like "The Eleventh of September" prove anything – beyond, that is, the necessity of writing as therapy – it is that authenticity is an effect. The immediate expression of a feeling does not guarantee authenticity of communication. It mostly guarantees the opposite, since a vital and necessary tool here is mediation. Dependence on pre-established verbal structures does not enable authenticity of expression. It mostly disables and discourages it, since a further vital and necessary tool is language that slices through those pre-established structures in order to defamiliarize: to deconstruct what we thought we knew and to reconstruct it in terms that shed new light on sequences of thought and feeling that would otherwise go unexplored and – in literary terms, at least – unexperienced. The simple question of how to write a poem after 9/11 is not, when it comes down to it, simple at all: not just because of the fundamental challenge posed by the writing of trauma but because of the equally fundamental series of challenges posed by the writing of anything, especially but not exclusively poetry. And very different answers to that question are given by half a dozen poems about the attack on the World Trade Center that have generated a great deal of interest and controversy: "Curse" by Frank Bidart, "Somebody Blew Up America" by Amiri Baraka, "History of the Airplane" by Lawrence Ferlinghetti, "The Pilots" by Tom Clark, "first writing since" by Suheir Hammad and "Alabanza: In Praise of Local 100" by Martin Espada.

"Curse" is addressed to those who brought down the Twin Towers. It is a beautifully cadenced cry of rage. The poem ends by declaring, "Out of the great secret of morals, *the imagination to enter/the skin of another*, what I have made is a curse." The aim here is to get under the skin, certainly, but not in order to search out motives, to try to find out why the terrorists performed a monstrous act. This is about, not possible causes, but actual consequences and necessary responses. Getting under the skin, in this context, involves a dream of revenge: imagining an appropriate suffering, what punishment and pain might

171

begin to be an adequate measure of that monstrosity. "Curse" is a latterday jeremiad. A long free verse line, incremental repetition, and elaborate verbal music are all deployed, not just to denounce, but to damn those who reduced the Twin Towers to rubble. "May what you have made descend upon you," the poet prays, as he imagines the terrorists buried under "*one hundred and ten/floors,*" dreams of the eyes of their victims eating "like acid" into "the bubble of rectitude" they breathe in, or being eaten up and spat out ("you are not food") by the other dead who surround them. The hell that the poet wishes for them is a disorienting mix of the literal and the surreal, as the poet slips between the landscapes of twenty-first century New York City and a subterranean world where the dead eat the dead which recalls the paintings of Hieronymus Bosch. If one of the great functions of poetry is to allow a voice to victims, then "Curse" memorably performs that function. It does not attempt to fathom the possible reasons why horror occurs. It simply proclaims, and declaims against, that horror. Austere, resistant to subtlety, the seeking out of complex argument or metaphorical elaboration, it suggests that the least inappropriate response to trauma is the cry of the traumatized, setting down what they might feel in starkly simple but deeply rhythmic terms.

In "Somebody Blew Up America," Amiri Baraka uses formal devices that are, in many ways, similar to those of Bidart: a fluctuating free verse line, incremental repetition, plain speech, and a pointedly direct address to the reader. This, however, is a far longer poem: several hundred lines as opposed to seventeen. And the perspective is radically different, a difference that is caught in the key word in either poem. Bidart uses the word "may" over and over again, as he prays for what "may," he hopes, fall on the heads of the terrorists as punishment. For Baraka, the key, repeated word, the verbal linchpin of the poem is "who." "All thinking people/ oppose terrorism/ both domestic/ & international," his poem begins, "But one should not/ be used/ To cover the other." "Somebody Blew Up America" is, in effect, concerned with the ubiquitous presence of "terror" in American life: not just the acts of terrorism perpetrated by Al Qaeda and acts of counter terrorism performed by the American Government but terror as an agency of power. So "terror" becomes a blanket term for the apparatus of the state, the machinery of corporate control, the various means by which, according to Baraka, the rich – both individuals and nations – ensure that it is only they who will inherit the earth. This reading of 9/11 as another chapter in a continuing narrative of oppression does not mitigate its obscenity. What it does do, however, is situate the events of one day in what looks like an endless cycle of violence breeding further violence. This is history as a story authored, which is to say totally controlled by, those in authority: in the United States and elsewhere in the world, in the present but also the imperial past. That history is read here, and communicated, as a series of rhetorical questions. "Who bought the slaves, who sold them," the poet asks, "Who have the colonies/ Who stole the most land/ Who rule the world;" "Who own the oil/ Who need peace/ Who you think need war." The relentless series of questions weaves a web of suspicion, a sense of forces at work below the surface of events that are all the more unnerving for remaining shadowy, resolutely unnamed. "Somebody Blew Up America" verges on the paranoid in its conspiratorial reading of 9/11 and its multiple contexts; at times, it even topples over the edge, as when it appears to implicate the state of Israel in the terrorist attacks. What rescues the poem, however, is the tidal force of its rhetoric, as well as that energy of purpose which characterizes so many radical American texts. At the end, the word "who" on which the poem turns metamorphoses into "whoooo," the cry, we are told, of "an Owl exploding/ In your life in your brain in your self," an owl with the capacity to see in the darkness and hunt down its prey. Rage there is in "Somebody Blew Up America," certainly, bewilderment and a sense of betrayal, but there is also, finally, hope. "We hear the questions rise," the poem concludes. Those questions might, the suggestion is, lead to the right answers so that, like the owl, "we" too can see through the dark – the darkness of history that is blanketing both past and present crises – and discover just who that "somebody" is.

"History of the Airplane" starts out as just that. Using a long, loping line, and beginning each verse paragraph with a rapt, bardic "And then," Lawrence Ferlinghetti achieves an almost prophetic eloquence as he charts the story of the dream and development of flight from the invention of the airplane to the moment when two airplanes smashed into the World Trade Center. If "Curse" is a kind of jeremiad, and "Somebody Blew Up America" offers a conspiratorial reading of history, then "History of the Airplane" tells a sadly familiar story of dreams turning into nightmares. The Wright brothers, we are told, believed they had invented something that "could make peace on earth" when their "wonderful/ flying machine took off" into "the kingdom of birds." "The parliament of birds," however, was "freaked out by this man-made bird/ and fled to heaven." So, the oppositions of the poem are swiftly established: the dream of flight and its destructive actuality, a condition of peace associated with actual or mythical birds and the reality of war identified with what humanity has mostly done with its newly discovered ability to rise above mother earth. Lindbergh circling above Versailles, the site of the peace conference after the First World War, hoping "to sight the doves of peace" but failing to do so. The "Famous Flying Clipper" setting off in the opposite direction from Lindbergh, across "the terrific Pacific" and frightening "the pacific doves" as it made "the world safe for peace and capitalism." The planes that laid waste to Hiroshima; "the great man-made birds with jet plumage" flying higher than any "real birds" that "seemed about to fly into the sun and melt their wings/ and like Icarus crash to earth;" "the high-flying/ bombers that now began to visit their blessings on various Third/ Worlds," while those who sent them claimed "they were searching for the doves of peace." The poem is a litany of high-flying aspiration incessantly crashing down into desolation and waste: a catalogue of failure that is all the more striking thanks to a cunning mix of the mythical (the parliament of birds, the dove of peace, Icarus) and the historical (Two World Wars, imperialist wars in the Third World), fanciful puns ("pacific doves," for instance, plays on "Pacific" and "peaceful") and flat, streetwise idiom ("freaked out"), the elevated ("And then") and the mundane ("peace and capitalism"). All this then spirals down on the event that is at once the occasion and the conclusion, the core of the poem: the moment when, as Ferlinghetti puts it, "the Third World struck back," storming "the great planes" and flying them back to earth and "into the beating heart of/ Skyscraper America." In a "blinding flash," "America became a part of/ the scorched earth of the world:" so that now "a

174

wind of ashes blows across the land" and, as the last lines of the poem have it, "Cries and whispers/ Fill the air/ Everywhere." What the poet offers us, as a conclusion to his history of flight, is, like the rest of the poem, at once annunciatory and apocalyptic. In a series of images that link up with both Eliot's Waste Land and Slavoj Zizek's desert of the real – and that, perhaps makes a nod to Ingmar Bergman along the way ("Cries and whispers") – he announces what looks like the end of history and the end of time: a doom that is an image in reverse, and in negative, of the original dream of flight – and all the more terrible for being predictable.

"The Pilots" is a much quieter and more reflective poem than the ones by Ferlinghetti, Baraka, and Bidart. Tom Clark considers the terrorists and their families. "Ziad Jarrah danced at his female cousin's/ Wedding," the poems begins. "Having lost his son," the poet tells us later, "Mohammed Atta's/ Father rages against the Americans." The terrorists are located in places and moments of domesticity: "Marwad Al-Shehhi lived behind that gate," we are told, and a friend of Mohammed Atta weeps to recall "their shared childhood hours." The poem walks a delicate tightrope between acknowledging the humanity of those it considers – the humanity they shared, after all, with their victims and with us, the readers – and insisting on the inhumanity of their actions, the degree to which an acknowledgment of shared humanity was wiped out, obliterated in their minds by their dedication "to the cause." A comparison with "The Last Days of Muhammad Atta" by Martin Amis is instructive here. In his short story, Amis imagines the final hours of one of the terrorists from the moment he wakes up on September 11 to the instant the plane he is in hits the north tower. Scrupulously attentive to the minutiae of his subject's life, Amis nevertheless transforms Muhammed into a bigot and a monster. Amis's terrorist suffers from a "detestation of everything" (153), a "pan-anathema" (161, 162). He is unable to enjoy himself; he lacks all curiosity, he loathes music and is utterly humorless. He cherishes "extreme hostility" (154) towards women and firmly believes that adultery should be "punished by whipping" and sodomy by being "buried alive" (155). He kills because he hates life and everyone living, including himself. Amis dehumanizes and, in doing so, puts the obscene acts of the terrorists beyond our understanding; they are acts performed by "them," a demonized other. Clark humanizes: not so as to excuse or even extenuate the acts of the terrorists but in order to begin at least to try to understand them: to place them within the range of our shared history – what the poem calls "the algae and flotsam of guilt and time/ And fear." It is precisely the dreadful contradiction that human beings commit inhumane acts that the poem explores: how the corruption of conscience can lead "intelligent/ Looking," "dedicated, serious" young men to commit themselves to horror. The poem reaches no conclusions: except to suggest that to try to understand and articulate this contradiction is our duty. With "life our school, knowledge of suffering our teacher," the poet concludes, our project as human being is or should be to "build sentences of such transparency" as to unearth "a grammar of humanness" concealed beneath "pictures of the dead." Our aim, in short, should be to acknowledge our *potential* complicity: to turn the unspeakable into speech by acknowledging that it is men and women like ourselves who have committed acts that sometimes seem too terrible for words.

That notion of an event too terrible for words is also at the heart of "first writing since," a poem of seven sections, each of which includes two or more stanzas written in a deliberately loose, apparently improvised form of free verse. The author of this piece, Suheir Hammad, is a Palestinian American; and what she offers here reads like a confessional or series of diary entries, outlining the impact of the terrorist attacks on herself, her family and the various, unnamed people she meets or imagines on the streets of New York City. Not unusually among post-9/11 poems, "first writing since" begins by questioning the legitimacy or even possibility of writing about trauma. "there have been no words/ I have not written one word," Hammad confesses. What one observer has astutely called "the paradoxical temporality of this opening" (Rothberg, There is No Poetry in This, 153) gives us speech speaking of a moment before speech. This is the period of latency: the moment of disbelief, denial ("please god, let it be a mistake," "let it be a nightmare"), accompanied by the awful, shameful relief felt by those who managed to be out of harm's way ("thank you for my/ lazy procrastinating late ass, thank you to the germs that had me/ call in sick"). The poem moves deftly and sinuously between the autobiographical and the choric, as it intersperses Hammad's voicing of her own responses with the voices of others – the victims, their families and loved ones as well as the lucky ones ("thank you") who escaped. What is especially remarkable here is how, in giving voice to the victims, the poet uses a mask or screen by quoting or alluding to the posters of the missing that sprung up all over New York City. The allusiveness means that she and we encounter the shock of 9/11 through a strategy of mimetic approximation: there is proximity but also distance. The voices of those who suffered are heard, but at a remove, they are mediated; the poet brings us closer to the victims, but she does not allow us to confuse our position with theirs. So we are offered what one authority on trauma has called an "empathic unsettlement," "a kind of virtual experience through which one puts oneself in the other's position while recognizing the difference of that position and not taking the other's place" (LaCapra, 78). What is equally remarkable is how, as the poem develops, Hammad moves beyond this to explore other forms of unsettlement: her own position as a Palestinian American (the "double trouble" of being an outsider and an insider), the unfathomable motives of the terrorists ("I do not know how bad a life has to break in order to kill"), the many victims of violence outside the United States ("if there are any people on earth who understand how new york is/ feeling right now, they are in the west bank and the gaza strip"). Gravitating from the terrorism of 9/11 to the "war on terror," Hammad confesses, "I have never felt less american and more new Yorker – particularly/ brooklyn, these past days." And the net effect of these moves below (New York, Brooklyn) as well as above (Palestine) the national radar is to place a question mark over the either/or oppositions of nationalist discourse. Challenging the distinction between native and foreign from her own perspective as an American and an Arab, the poet responds to the suspicion that "there is no poetry in this" by asking us to see the experience of trauma itself as the link between cultures. Interrogating the rhetoric of being either for "us" or against "us," she invokes bonds that are once local and transnational. "first writing since" is a poem

177

that moves from trauma to a vision of social transformation. Along the way, it makes a two-pronged assault on the oppositional rhetoric of both terrorist and counter terrorist. The only opposition countenanced here is the one announced in its closing lines: "you are either with life or against it/," Hammad declares; "affirm life."

In "Alabanza: In Praise of Local 100," Martin Espada, like Bidart, Baraka, and Ferlinghetti, uses a flowing free verse line and idiomatic speech, incremental repetition and insistent rhythms. There are further connections with the Baraka poem, in particular. In "Somebody Blew Up America," as elsewhere in his poetry, Baraka deploys the aesthetic tools of the black community, African American verbal and rhythmic forms, to embed his voice in a broader tradition and so communicate the sense that the poet is speaking for more than just himself. Similarly, in "Alabanza," Espada rehearses the oral traditions of Hispanic culture, as well as the long line of Whitman, to pay tribute to "the 43 members of Hotel Employees Local 100, working at the Windows on the World restaurant who lost their lives in the attack on the World Trade Center." Like other poets steeped in the Hispanic tradition, Espada creates a cultural space in his poem where convergence and *mestizaje* or mixing can take place. Within this space, he skillfully walks a tightrope between commemoration and celebration, honoring all the victims of 9/11 by focusing on one specific loss. The key word repeated here is "praise," as the poet honors certain individuals lost on September 11, 2001: "the cook with the shaven head," the busboy, "the waitress who heard the radio in the kitchen/ and sang to herself about a man gone." Weaving together an intricate network of images, a metaphorical web spun around intimations of light, craft, and music, Espada realizes what is called, at one point in the poem, "the chant of nations:" a song dedicated to workers drawn from all over the world to work at a place where they "could squint and almost see their world." What is particularly memorable about this poem is how its sense of the World Trade Center, and by implication the United States, as a cultural interface is slowly but relentlessly globalized: the closing lines shift to the war in Afghanistan but continue the theme of intercultural dialogue. What is just as memorable is the oracular tone of the poem, mixing grief and joy, elegy and prophecy, in a voice that seems to come out of a community rather than a single person. "When the war began," the poem concludes, "two constellations of smoke" drifted towards and spoke to each other. "One said with an Afghan tongue:/ Teach me to dance. We have no music here." To which, we are told, the other replied, "with a Spanish tongue:/ I will teach you. Music is all we have." In this magical realist moment, the different worlds invaded by terrorism and counter terrorism converge, their point of convergence being not only "smoke," the fog of war, but also "music" and "dance," the liberating energies of rhythm, peace, and poetry. "Alabanza" is a poem that enacts as well as announces its belief in a hybrid space as the only one in which the location of cultures can properly occur; it performs and also praises an act of cultural encounter. To that extent, it is as much about the fundamental possibilities of community as it is about the fierce actualities of crisis. Not only that, by inserting the terrorist attacks in a "chant of nations," it makes that attack and its aftermath, if not fully understandable, then at least susceptible to understanding. It pieces the fragments of traumatic events together into a meaningful story and, in doing so, offers one answer to the question of just what form a post-9/11 poetry might assume.

On one level, "Alabanza: In Praise of Local 100" is a variation on the elegy; and a commemorative approach is one that has been favored by many poets choosing to write in response to 9/11. So, in "September 28, 2001", Michael Atkinson talks of those killed at the World Trade Center as "treasure buried/ in the underworld beneath a new mountain;" in "Our New York Room in the 1930s Remembered in September 2001", Willis Barnstone pays tribute to those "thousands gone" both before, during and after 9/11; and in "Elegy for the Victims and Survivors, World Trade Towers, N.Y., 2001," Mark Irwin honors both those who were killed and those left behind, uniting them in one community, a "Stadium of sorrow." In "Umeja: Each One of Us Counts", Rita Dove similarly recalls and honors the dead, whatever their origins, allegiances or the manner of their dying." "One went the way of water/." The poem begins, "one crumpled under stone;" it then goes on to chronicle the multiple forms that crisis and death can assume and to insist, above all, that the dead should not be forgotten. "*Remember us*," is the refrain of the poem, and the project of remembering is at its heart. This is a memorial to all those who have fallen and continue to fall in the ongoing war between terrorist and counter terrorist, "those absent ones," as they are called here, "unknown and unnamed." "Umeja" does not name the dead, but it does permit them to be counted and known. In "The Olive Wood Fire", by contrast, Galway Kinnell begins by writing of the named and particular: his son Fergus, remembered as Kinnell "would carry him from his crib" to a "fire of thousand-year-old olive wood." In dream or reverie, however, the poem then gravitates towards something more mysteriously anonymous. "Half-asleep" by the fire once, with his son in his arms, the poet tells us that he thought he heard a scream: perhaps "a flier crying out in horror/ as he dropped fire" or "a child thus set aflame." So the poem moves, subtly but inexorably, from the peace of home and hearthside to the trauma of war, from a sleeping child to a dying one, and from the fire that nourishes to the fire that annihilates. This movement from domesticity to dread, and from intimacy to horror, is one that characterizes a number of poems that try to address September 11, 2001 and its aftermath: among them, "Pittsburgh, 9/10/01, 7.30 p.m." by Melissa Altenderfer, "Making Love After September 11, 2001" by Aliki Barnstone, "September Ever After" by Karl Elder and "Dragons and Sharks" by Kelly Levan. Commemorating the dead, Kinnell's poem and all these others reveal how closely woven the fabric of our lives is, at all times but especially at moments of crisis. Even at the most apparently tranquil and intimate moments, war and the horror and pity of war are not far away.

The elegiac, perhaps understandably, is in fact one of the forms most often favored by those poets who have tried to write about 9/11. "It's impossible to understand it's impossible," writes Norman Stock in "What I Said"; and, not being able to "understand" the crisis, many poets have felt compelled simply to commemorate its consequences. "What can I tell you about history," asks Anne-Marie Levine in "Four November 9ths" "– history teaches." To which Shelley Stenhouse in "Circling" adds the rider, "It's so strange to be caught/ in history, to be making history." Caught up in history, in events that they find it difficult or even impossible to "tell you about," many poets feel that what they can do – and it is a great deal – is to honor the dead. So, Stenhouse offers the simple statement, "Patti was a good person and she died." Sometimes, the commemorated death is that of a community. In "The Old Neighborhood," for example, Andrea Carter Brown pays tribute to the vanished vendors of the World Trade Center in precise ethnic detail. "Where are they now?" she asks. "And how?" At other times, the commemoration is intensely personal. In "She Would Long," Jean Valentine imagines the mother of a girl lost on September 11, 2001 who yearns to "dig herself into the graveyard" with "her daughter's ashes/ in her nose in her mouth." Whatever the focus, however, there are common feelings of loss and longing: a sense that everything has changed and, quite often, the desperately articulated wish that it had not, that things could still be the same.

"Oh how to piece together a life/ from this scandal and confusion," Harvey Shapiro declares in "Nights". "It's we the living who must run for cover." And the "cover" frequently sought is that of commemorative measure: measuring what has been lost, measuring the gap between before and after 9/11, measuring the horror by meditating on an alternative history in which that horror never happened. In "Grudges", Stephen Dunn tries to measure the loss. "Before you know it something's over/," he reflects. "Suddenly someone's missing at the table." So does Rachel Hadas in "Sunday Afternoon." For her, "recollection of what's been lost" is enshrined in the relics left behind by those who have vanished: "a mildewed quilt," perhaps, or "a tattered T-shirt." George Murray, in "The Statue", in turn, reflects on the terrible logic of things dictated by 9/11. "It was a good but rocky world/ as recently as yesterday –," he observes, adding with mordant irony, "it is there to see in all the papers of record." And Tim Suermondt, in "Squad 1," takes the measure of what might have been: imagining a small boy playing at fireman in whose game "everyone was saved/ from the inferno," all the firemen emerging from the Twin Towers with "small birds on each/ of their massive shoulders." Another kind of consolation is sought and found for a moment by Miranda Beeson in "Flight". The poet recalls or imagines how, on the day the Twin Towers fell, an "iridescent exhausted finch" found its way to her home, having apparently survived the attack. Somehow, she sadly reflects, "the survival of this slight speck/ of feathered imperfection" appeared "more important than anything else:" more important, even, than the man "in his business suit/ who fell through the air without/ the benefit of wings." Poems like these offer "cover" of a kind, perhaps, in wishful thinking or wonder at a small miracle of survival. But the cover is only partial and, in the long run, illusory. "You can grieve a long time," Bill Kushner confides in "Friends". And all these poems, in their different ways, are acknowledgments of that sad fact, and announcements of grief. They commemorate by trying to turn what Hugh Seidman in "New York" calls "the involuntary wail/ that changes soul" into articulate speech.

"Ground Zero" by Robert Creeley is also a memorial poem, but of a very different kind. What it maps, as its title implies, is the bleak impersonality, the vacancy of loss. The scarred, empty landscape left by the destruction of the Twin Towers becomes a visual equivalent of trauma, the moral and emotional vacuum that opens up after a moment of crisis. And it maps it mostly by indirection and stealth. The language is terse and anonymous, the spaces between the words appearing to be as eloquent as the words themselves. The verbal music, in turn, is plangent. This is a verbal tapestry of mourning that is as remarkable for what it leaves unsaid as for what it actually says. As such, it is symptomatic of two vital tendencies in these poems of commemoration, to do with verbal and visual absence. In "To the Words", W.S. Merwin dismisses the instruments of his trade as poet, calling them "ancient precious/ and helpless ones." That is a common theme. "I cannot imagine," complains Kimiko Hahn in "In the Armory", as he thinks of those searching for their loved ones after 9/11, "It is too much." "Words are so small. Words have no weight,/" Elizabeth Spires confesses in "The Beautiful Day", "And nothing will ever be the same." Perhaps the unspeakable cannot be spoken, these poems suggest; perhaps the horrors of 9/11 and after can only be imagined on the borders of language, a verbal absence inscribing a human one. Or, alternately, as other poems intimate and "Ground Zero" demonstrates, an appropriate measure of loss is empty space, a visual vacancy. "All you have to do is/ look up and it's not there," observes David Lehman in "9/14/01:" "it" being what Nancy Mercado, in "Going to Work", calls the "twin ghosts" of the World Trade Center towers. In "Blackout", Jonah Bornstein takes the darkness alluded to in the title as a metaphor for the "world shadowy/ and silent" that came into being with the collapse of those towers. Bart Edelman, in "Empty Rooms" focuses on a more domestic form of vacancy: the empty spaces, the rooms and cupboards "where yester-day's clothes hung" before the victims of terrorism "vanished." While in "View Interrupted," Ann Lolordo returns the reader to Ground Zero: the "twin shadows" of the Towers are "replaced by light," she tells the reader, an "uninterrupted view" to the Empire State Building "is what you see." "We cannot live in Eden anymore," Spires suggests in "The Beautiful Day." "We peer beyond the ruin of that day/ and see… what do we see?" The answer maps the geography of absence: "Just smoke and rubble/ A vacancy terrible to behold."

The sense of apocalypse hovering just below the surface of commemorative pieces like "Ground Zero" and "The Beautiful Day" is openly acknowledged in some other post-9/11 poems. "Thunder and lightning and our world/ is another place," observes Lucille Clifton in "Tuesday 9/11/01," "no day/ will ever be the same no blood untouched." "Everything is burning – everything –," David Ray announces in "Preparing the Monument:" a bleak thought on which Aaron Smith and Jean Valentine offer their own variations. So Smith confesses, in "Silent Room," that there is not enough to convince him after 9/11 that "everything I am isn't burning," while Valentine admits that she can see "nothing" anywhere "In the Burning Air" that appears to surround her. "Black leaves," in turn, and "the limbs of the city/ Warping towards heaven," the burning of the natural and the built environment, characterizes the landscape of destruction mapped by David St John in *The Face*; while in "Late Blooming Roses," David Baker describes the week after September 11 as a week of "black clouds, rain, spit-/ mist of fog,/ the streets/ gripped with terror," and in "The Equation," Steve Kowit sketches an almost Gothic portrait of "Horrific towers of smoke," "belching flames" and a "haze of rubble." In "No," Joy Harjo stresses the com-munity of suffering, the shared grief of all those caught up in the war between terrorist and counter terrorist: a theme that Maxine Hong Kingston also explores in "Memorial Service," where she suggests that, because of the multicultural character of America, "all our wars are civil wars." And Harjo's poem situates that community in a scarred landscape that "all those who had no quarrel with each other" now inhabit, a landscape overshadowed by "the terrible black clouds" of conflict. There is a surreal dimension to the portrait of apocalypse Harjo paints; and that surrealism is even more marked in "Gulf War" by Carolyn Kizer and "Green Plants and Bamboo Flute" by Brenda Hillman. Kizer borrows, in fact, from Paul Verlaine, whom she quotes in her epigraph and then translates in the first line: "The whole green sky is dying. The last tree flares." This is a poem written, apparently, at the end of the world, "under a canopy of poisonous airs," its elegantly rhyming lines only serving to emphasize the man-made chaos it portrays. With "Green Plants and Bamboo Flute," confusion is even worse confounded. "Oaks tear up the storm floor,/" the poem begins, "Nothing left to warn/ The poisoned rat has poisoned the owl." A series of surreal images function here as a precise register of the sense that, under the pressure of war, everything is running down, descending from crisis to extinction. Or, as Anna Rabinowitz has it in "Bricolage: Versicolor" – which offers a kind of poetic abc of confusion – from "All afternoon alterities advanced" to "ZERO, O ZERO, OUR ZEALOTSTREWN ZONES."

What is remarkable about many post-9/11 poems, in fact, is the sheer range and scope of their imagination of disaster. The trope of falling is, unsurprisingly, a common one: falling towers and falling men and women. "Our towers fall into/ a dust of memos,/ plaintive notes," Nora Gallagher declares in "Lament for the World," "all life suspended, falling." Samuel Hazo, in "September 11, 2001," remembers actually seeing a few people "freefalling/ through the sky like flotsam from a blaze." And, in a gesture of even more intense immediacy, Tony Towle, in "Diptych," declares, "I imagine myself in *that* space/ falling through the exploded event." Of the "Falling Man" referred to in the title of her poem, Diane Seuss remarks, "he had no choice,/ or two bad choices. Burn/ or fall." "I didn't know the man in black pants/ who plunged headfirst/ from the top of the north tower," Lucille Lang Day confesses in "Strangers" but, nevertheless, he and those who suffered similarly seem her intimates; "I still feel them/," she says, "stirring inside me." For X.J. Kennedy in "September Twelfth, 2001," there is a poignant contrast to be drawn between, on the one hand, "Two caught on film who hurtle/ from the eighty-second floor" to their deaths and, on the other, the poet and his lover, waking to "the incredible joy of coffee/ and the morning light" the day after the disaster. A contrast and a connection: since the image of a couple who jumped "holding hands" is indelibly engraved on the memories of those who survive, reminding them of their "pitiful share of time." Time assumes different dimensions in other poems that revolve around the trope of falling. Working from the premise that everyone remembers where they were the moment when they first heard the news of the 9/11 attack, for instance, some poems concentrate on that moment. "We watch the Twin Towers of the World Center struck by our own planes," Terry Tempest Williams recalls in "Scattered Potsherds," "then collapse under the weight of terror." For Hugh Ogden, in "Northwest Maine, September 2001," the moment is remembered as a radio announcement interrupting a performance of a Brahms symphony, signaling "the end of pure harmonies." For Lucien Stryk, in "Quiet, Please," the news, he recalls, brought "bedlam in the morning," causing him to lose his footing and almost fall himself, down the stairs. Brendan Galvin, in "Fragments," remembers the news as something shouted or rather screamed to him by a passing cyclist on a road normally "given over to birdsong." Bruce Bond, in "The Altars of September," approaches the recollected moment indirectly, through the narrative of a woman who, just before she heard the news, noted "a stillness unlike any day" and "the uneasy silence of the skies." And for Rachel Vigier, in "Burnt Ground," what is momentous is "the moment – just before" and "the moment – just after," measuring the abyss between the calm of "a bright September day" and crisis.

What is common to these poems is the feeling of a terrible transfiguration of the ordinary. "And all this while I have been playing with toys," Alice Ostriker reflects in "The Window, At the Moment of Flame." Now, she feels, she has to put away childish things; the stage sets of the normal and everyday collapse in the presence of

185

a monstrous fact. And the collapse, it seems, is irreversible. In some poems, as in some drama and fiction, the fact seems not only irreversible but also inescapable, a nightmare played over and over again. Antler, in "Skyscraper Apocalypse," for example, imagines the film of the Towers "being struck, burning, imploding/ in slow motion over and over," the lovers jumping holding hands as a "freeze-frame." Similarly, Wayne Dodd, in "The Third Tower," thinks of the Towers "falling forever/ out of the future" and "Falling into memory/ into absence;" Dan Giancola tells us, in "The Ruin," that he is "glued to the tube" as "Flight/ 175 repeatedly slams/ its innocent freight/ into Tower Two" on his television screen; while Judith Minty, in "Loving This Earth," imagines the remorseless, repetitive process of destruction in terms of "the tower falling into itself over and over." Time stands still in these poems; in others, time moves inexorably from "before" to "after;" in some, towers and people fall and are gone, in others, both seem to go on falling forever. In all these poems, however, there is the feeling that, as Dodd puts and repeats it in "In The Third Tower," "nothing will ever be the same/ again" – or, as Karl Kirchwey confesses in "Nocturne, Morningside Heights," "It is too early and too late." Dodd falls back on one of the rhetorical signatures of 9/11 here (nothing will ever be the same, everything has changed, the end of irony/ innocence/ isolation). Kirchwey, in turn, falls back on that sense of fissure, existential fracture that became a commonplace response to the terrorist attacks. Both remarks, in their deliberately gestural way, map a loss of verbal and emotional coordinates; and, in doing so, like so many of these poems, slip the reader the suggestion that the fall of buildings and flesh is a shared fall into darkness.

Adding to this feeling of inexorable fall is the suspicion voiced in many of these poems that terror and counter terror are mirror images of each other. "A bomb made/ from a jetliner hits the World Trade Center," observes Daniel Bourne in "The First of October, We." "A jetplane flings/ a bomb on the Taliban in Kandahar." "These/ are the transformations of the world,/ one thing leading to another." "So kindred slaughter each other," comments F.D. Reeve in "Sunset, New York Harbor:" a sentiment that Ishmael Reed, in "America United," develops into a wholesale diatribe against any "crusade" "to hammer the infidels" in revenge for 9/11, suggesting that the counter terrorist is a "comrade in oil" of the terrorist. In "Letter to Hayden Carruth," Marilyn Hacker suggests that fundamentalism rather than oil is the link between enemies: "men maddened with revealed religion," she insists, are behind the conflict on both sides. More simply, but echoing that sentiment, Eliot Katz, in "When the Skyline Crumbles," suggests that "the war has now come home." Ursula Le Guin, in "American Wars," goes further, slipping the reader the suggestion that all American history is war; while, in "Bulletin," Diane Di Prima presents the entire world as an elaborate network of violence in which everyone is complicit. "Do not think to correct this by refusing to read," she warns, then later, "Do not think to correct this by reading." "It is happening even as you read this page," Di Prima declares. "By the time you finish reading this it will be over." Knowledge, in this context, is powerlessness. The poet can only rage impotently against the dying of the light, as "halfway around the world the bombs are dropping." In "The Blinding of Samson," Robert Bly uses the Biblical story invoked in the title to underline his growing sense of the powerlessness he feels. "Please god help/ The human beings," the poem concludes, "for men are coming to blind Samson." Those men, it seems, are in control of events and obeying the logic of war. "Things go on," Bly reflects in "The Approaching War." "The weight of history begins/ To bend us over once more." All the poet can do, evidently, or feels he can do, is watch and wearily lament the apparent failure to remember that violence only generates further violence. "The writer of this poem," Bly confides, "is forgetful like you;" and, to that extent, we are all responsible for what is happening.

As "The Approaching War" illustrates, one reason for the feeling of impotence, even exhaustion, that characterizes some of the more polemical 9/11 poems is the suspicion that all this has happened before. Not only do terrorist and counter terrorist mirror each other, the sense is, the war between them also mirrors other, earlier wars. "Collateral Damage" by John Balaban, "Army Burn Ward" by Martin Galvin, and "Twelve Meditations" by Emily Borenstein, for instance, all invite a comparison with the war in Vietnam. "The Way of It" by Ruth Stone and "Fairy Tale" by Ai go back for a potential mirror of the contemporary crisis to the Second World War; in "To the Forty-third President of the United States of America," William O'Daly goes further back to the First World War; and in "House of Xerxes," Paul Violi goes even further back to the ancient wars of the Persians, Assyrians, and others – "Today we're making history/," he sardonically concludes, "We're raising cane." "How many times," Shirley Kaufman asks in "Cyclamen," while intimating that "the... efficiency/ that kills" is inexhaustible. "Once more the urge/ to be alone in a rented car," C.D. Wright laments in "Once Again the Old Urge to Be Alone in a Car No Matter Where the Local Roads Are Going," the urge, that is, to light out from the awful inevitable cycle of wars following wars into a world elsewhere, "waking up in the full sun/... minimally deluded/ it would all stop." "For Christ's sake: Hold your fire!" Wright concludes, switching from the desire to escape to a cry that hovers between demand and prayer. The switch, however, only emphasizes the sense of despair. In "The Hearth," C.K. Williams offers a quieter meditation on the remorseless recurrence of warfare. During a moment "alone with the news" of impending battle, Williams discloses, he threw a "plastic coffee cup" on to the fire. Beginning with this homely image, the poet then reflects on other kinds of destruction: a man he knew who was "caught in a fire," an owl descending through the dark on its prey. Intimations of fire, descent, and darkness then lead into the heart of the poem: the thought of imminent warfare, "radar, rockets, shrapnel,/ cities razed." The route may be more circuitous than in Wright's poem, but the destination is not so different. By the end of the poem, the poet can only wonder "how those with power over us/ can effect such things" and seek shelter from the storm of warfare by choosing to "crouch closer" to the fire. But a retreat into the warmth of hearth and home seems no more viable, in this climate of gathering conflict, than escape on the open road "in a rented car." Neither Wright nor Williams, in the end, can find genuine comfort in a private space. The personal is there in both poems but it is a source of cold comfort if, as both poems suggest, it is indelibly linked to the public. There is no real hope here of a separate peace.

Despair shades into rage in some post-9/11 poems; a sense of impotence shifts into an implicit belief in the power of the poet as truthteller. Drawing on a tradition of poetic populism that goes back through William Carlos Williams and Carl Sandburg to Walt Whitman, some poets use simple speech and expansive rhythms to address their fellow citizens and teach them about the current crisis. Whitman is even invoked by a few of them. "Come back, Walt Whitman, we need you in the hour of our grief," Norbert Krapf begins "Elegy" from "Three Paumanok Pieces." "Come back, Camerado, wind your way back to Ground Zero where you belong." "I am at once myself & Whitman we two ghosts," Bill Kushner claims, in "In the Hairy Arms of Whitman," as he imagines the two of them together grieving for "so many martyrs," raging at "the fragments flying papers ash flesh" and "calling all the hatemongers Stand back Stand back." Even when Whitman is not called on for poetic assistance, the sense of his presence is still there in the plainspeaking, pedagogical thrust of these poems. So, in "Speak Out," Lawrence Ferlinghetti does just that, warning his audience that "the attack on the Twin Towers" is in danger of being turned into "the Third World War/ The war with the Third World." "Now is the time for you to speak/," he declares, "Before they come for you." "This is a rant," Terry Tempest Williams unashamedly admits at the beginning of "(Statement) Portrait of George W. Bush as a Cowboy, or: America's Foreign Policy of Peace." She then embarks on a diatribe against "the romance of the American cowboy" in general and what she calls "the cowboy president" in particular, while warning her fellow Americans that "the "war on terror" is first being waged at home" against them. The "rant" is followed by two short poems, "Freedom of Speech" and "Freedom from Speech," which offer a further warning: "The erosion of voice is the build-up of the war." But it is almost as if Williams feels compelled by the crisis to write a kind of antipoetry here, since that is what the age demands: to write the facts down in a clear, bold hand. Perhaps the suspicion, the sense is that after 9/11 conventional poems can no longer be written; the poet needs to speak out, or even to rant, in order to stand a chance of being heard, because austere times necessitate a new verbal austerity.

That returns us to the bass note sounded in so many, perhaps most, post-9/11 poems: the question of how to write in a time of acute crisis. Related to that is the suspicion, not just about the tools of the trade, the potentially "helpless" nature of words – their use or otherwise in saying the unsayable – but about voice and audience. "We're as silent as sparrows in the little bushes," Robert Bly complains in "Call and Answer," "What's the sense/ of being an adult and having no voice? Cry out!" The cry is muted in this poem, however, and the reason is clear: the poet may want to "cry out" or "speak out" but is often deeply uncertain about what form this crying or speaking out should assume – and, for that matter, about whether or not she or he will be heard. "Everywhere people are weeping and afraid,/" Peter Coyote writes in "Flags," "waving flags, plotting check and mate." In a climate of confusion, with the trauma of terrorism fueling a widespread desire for revenge, some poets appear to feel challenged, not just by the problem of how to imagine disaster, but by the possibility that what they say might be ignored or even suppressed. "I bought a flag and/ blended in with/ the other sheep," Adrian C. Louis confesses at the end of a poem, ironically titled "Liberty Street," that chronicles his futile attempts to stand apart from "our shivering heartland" and a climate of fear. "Write as if you lived in an occupied country," is the injunction from Edwin Rolfe that Eleanor Wilner uses as the epigraph to her poem, "Found in the Free Library." Wilner then develops the conceit that the poem is a fragment, a document discovered in the library of its title, describing how a people moved from fear to fighting. "And we were made afraid," the poem begins, before going on to chart how "we" descended into the destructive cycle of "war, and war, and war." "Found in a Free Library" does not so much end as stop short, with the bleak statement "(but here the document is torn)." The implication is clear. Crisis generates fear which generates, not just war, but also what Williams terms "the erosion of voice," with truth and the speaking of it as the first casualties of conflict.

Which is to say that there is an undercurrent of paranoid feeling running through some post-9/11 poetry, the suspicion that "they" are out to suppress individual vision and voice. "Coming man they're right behind you/," Ross Martin warns in his small hymn to paranoia titled "This Message Will Self-Destruct in Sixty Seconds," "they are right on your freakin" tail./ Go." Just who "they" are varies from poem to poem. But one figure or group recurs: not the terrorists so much as the counter terrorists, "The House of Bush" as Carol Muske-Dukes calls it in the poem of that title. Sometimes, the "frauds in office" as W.S. Merwin terms them in "Ogres" are addressed directly. So, in "Complaint and Position," Hayden Carruth uses an old American tradition of plainspeaking to the powerful to tell the then president that "we, the people" and "especially the poets" demand that he "desist" from war, "otherwise the evil you have/ loosed will destroy everything." And in "In Memoriam," Philip Whalen derides "DEAR MR PRESIDENT" as someone who knows nothing about the things that matter most, now more than ever, "LOVE AND POETRY." At other times, those who seem to be dictating the direction of events, and the terms of the culture, after 9/11 are not directly addressed but directly attacked. In "Who Cares?" by Ruth Stone, they are described as "aliens." In "Poem of War" by Jim Harrison, their leader is called "the theocratic cowboy." And in the nightmare vision of "Heaven as Anus" by Maxine Kumin, painful experiments on helpless animals performed by "the Defense Department" become an image, or more accurately an illustration, of the obscenity of power. In poems like these, there is no room for subtlety or indirection; words are being used as weapons, perhaps the only ones available to the powerless. "I don't know your exalted language/ of power," Carruth tells President George W. Bush in "Complaint and Petition." What he does know and have instead is what Robert Pinsky claims for himself in "Statement of Conscience," "an 'American voice' in the singular."

And that, surely, is what the best of the post-9/11 poems have, whether they are satirical or lyrical, declamatory or surreal, elegiac or apocalyptic. The poet tries to take the measure of crisis, not by explaining its origins or examining its consequences, but by registering one individual experience of it. "What can we do/ but offer what we have?" asks Katha Pollitt in "Trying to Write a Poem Against War:" which, whatever their focus or persuasion, is what the finest of these poems do. They seize on what Gregory Orr, in "Refusing," calls "The chance to be part of/ the poet's chorus" and insert their story in the history of the moment. In a poem like "The School Among the Ruins" by Adrienne Rich, that story is a densely layered one. "Beirut, Baghdad, Sarajevo, Bethlehem, Kabul. Not of course here," the epigraph to the

191

poem reads. Rich then weaves an intricate verbal tapestry around the image announced in the title, using the compulsions of memory to describe a sanctuary: the school as a redemptive site of work, routine, and community, a refuge from a landscape of chaos where "nightglare/misconstrues the day," "rooms from the upper city/ tumble cratering lower streets" and "fear vacuums" "the whole town." In other post-9/11 poems, the story is a simple one told plainly. So, in "The Dispute," Alice Ostriker subverts the whole notion of either terrorists or counter terrorists winning; only those who stand apart from war, she suggests, will really "win." And in "How to Write a Poem After September 11th," Nikki Moustaki advises poets simply to stick to the facts. "Say: we hated them then we loved them then they were gone/," she advises, "Say: we miss them. Say: there's a gap." Whatever the terms of their engagement with crisis, though, these poems do engage with it; they offer a verbal equivalent of a personal encounter with trauma. Or rather, a series of equivalents, since there is no single formula at work here. Poets have responded to the problem of how to write poems after 9/11 by reformulating that problem in the singular. And they have begun to resolve it in terms that are fundamental to the traditions of American poetry: by acknowledging the human presence at the heart of the historical experience and announcing that presence in a single, separate voice.

Works Cited

Adams, Lorraine. 2006. *Harbor* (2004). London: Portobello Books.

Adorno, Theodor. 1981. "Cultural Criticism and Society." *Prisms*, translated by Samuel and Shierry Weber. Cambridge: MIT Press, 17–34.

Ai. 2002. "Fairy Tale." In *September 11, 2001: American Writers Respond*, Heyen, William (editor). Silver Springs, MD: Etruscan Press, 7–10.

Altenderfer, Melissa. 2002. "Pittsburgh, 9/10/01, 7.30 p.m." In *September 11, 2001: American Writers Respond*, Heyen, William (editor). Silver Springs, MD: Etruscan Press, 16–17.

Amis, Martin. 2001. "Fear and Loathing." *The Guardian*, September 18 (http://books.guardian.uk/departments/politicsphilosophyandsociety/story/0,,553923,00.html).

Amis, Martin. 2002. "The Voice of the Lonely Crowd." *The Guardian*, June 1 (http://booksguardian.co.uk/review/story/0,12084,725608,00.html).

Amis, Martin. 2006. "The Age of Horrorism." *The Observer*, September 10, (http://observer.guardian.co.ukreview/story/0,1868732,00.html).

Amis, Martin. 2006. "The Last Days of Muhammad Atta." *New Yorker*, September 24, 152–63.

Antler. 2002. "Skyscraper Apocalypse." In *September 11, 2001: American Writers Respond*, Heyen, William (editor). Silver Springs, MD: Etruscan Press, 18–22.

Atkinson, Michael. 2002. "September 28, 2001." In *September 11, 2001: American Writers Respond*, Heyen, William (editor). Silver Springs, MD: Etruscan Press, 30–32.

After the Fall: American Literature Since 9/11, First Edition. Richard Gray.
© 2011 John Wiley & Sons, Ltd. Published 2011 by John Wiley & Sons, Ltd.

Baker, David. 2002. "Late Blooming Roses." In *September 11, 2001: American Writers Respond*, Heyen, William (editor). Silver Springs, MD: Etruscan Press, 33–34.

Bakhtin, Mikhail. 1981. "Discourse in the Novel." In *The Dialogic Imagination: Four Essays by Mikhail Bakhtin*, translated by Caryl Emerson and Michael Holquist Austin: University of Texas Press, 259–422.

Balaban, John. "Collateral Damage." In *Poets Against War* (http://www.poetsagainstwar.com/chapbook.asp).

Baraka, Amiri. "Somebody Blew Up America." In *Amiri Baraka: Poet Playwright Activist* (http://www.amiribaraka.com/blew.html).

Barnstone, Aliki. 2002. "Making Love After September 11, 2001." In *September 11, 2001: American Writers Respond*, Heyen, William (editor). Silver Springs, MD: Etruscan Press, 35.

Barnstone, Willis. 2002. "Our New York Room in the 1930s Remembered in September, 2001." In *September 11, 2001: American Writers Respond*, Heyen, William (editor). Silver Springs, MD: Etruscan Press, 38.

Baudrillard, Jean. 1998. *America*, translated by Chris Turner. London: Verso.

Baudrillard, Jean. 2002. *The Spirit of Terrorism and Requiem for the Twin Towers*, translated by Chris Turner. London: Verso.

Beckett, Samuel. 1960. *The Unnamable* (1958), *Three Novels*. London: Calder.

Beeson, Miranda. 2002. "Flight." In *Poetry After 9/11: An Anthology of New York Poets*, Johnson, Dennis Loy and Merians, Valerie (editors). Hoboken, NJ: Melville House Publishing, 6.

Beigbeder, Frederic. 2004. *Windows on the World: A Novel*, translated by Frank Wynne. London: Fourth Estate

Bell, Christine. 1990. *The Perez Family*. New York: Norton.

Bell, Jonathan. 2004. *Portraits*. New York, Samuel French.

Bell, Vereen. 1988. *The Achievement of Cormac McCarthy*. Baton Rouge: Louisiana State University Press.

Berger, James. 2003. "There's No Backhand to This." In *Trauma at Home: After 9/11*, Greenberg, Judith (editor). Lincoln, NB; University of Nebraska Press, 52–59.

Berman, Marshall. 2002. "When Bad Buildings Happen to Good People." In *After the World Trade Center: Rethinking New York City*, Sorkin, Michael and Zukin, Sharon (editors). New York: Routledge, 1–12.

Berry, Wendell. 1983. *The Gift of Good Land: Essays Cultural and Agricultural*. San Francisco: North Point Press.

Berry, Wendell. 1983. *Standing by Words*. San Francisco: North Point Press.

Works Cited

Berry, Wendell. 1986. *The Unsettling of America: Culture and Agriculture.* San Francisco: Sierra Club Books.

Berry, Wendell. 2001. *In the Presence of Fear: Three Essays for a Changed World.* Great Barrington, MA: Orion Society.

Berry, Wendell. 2002. *The Art of the Commonplace: The Agrarian Essays of Wendell Berry*, Norman Wirtzba (editor). Washington, DC: Counterpoint.

Bhabha, Homi K. 1994. *The Location of Culture.* London: Routledge.

Bidart, Frank. 2006. "Curse." In *The Oxford Book of American Poetry*, Lehman, David (editor). New York: Oxford University Press, 938–939.

Bly, Robert. "Call and Answer." In *Poets Against War* (http://www.poetsagainstwar.com/chapbook.asp).

Bly, Robert. "The Approaching War." In *Poets Against War* (http://www.poetsagainstwar.com/chapbook.asp).

Bly, Robert. "The Blinding of Samson." In *Poets Against War* (http://www.poetsagainstwar.com/chapbook.asp).

Bond, Bruce. 2002. "The Altars of September." In *September 11, 2001: American Writers Respond*, Heyen, William (editor). Silver Springs, MD: Etruscan Press, 55–57.

Borenstein, Emily. 2002. "Twelve Meditations." In *September 11, 2001: American Writers Respond*, Heyen, William (editor). Silver Springs, MD: Etruscan Press, 58–59.

Bornstein, Jonah. 2002. "Blackout." In *September 11, 2001: American Writers Respond*, Heyen, William (editor). Silver Springs, MD: Etruscan Press, 61–62.

Borradori, Giovanna (editor). 2003. *Philosophy in a Time of Terror: Dialogues with Jurgen Habemar and Jacques Derrida.* Chicago: University of Chicago Press.

Bourne, Daniel. 2002. "The First of October, We." In *September 11, 2001: American Writers Respond*, Heyen, William (editor). Silver Springs, MD: Etruscan Press, 64–65.

Brandeis, Gayle. 2008. *Self Storage* (2007). New York: Ballantine Books.

Brodsky, Joseph. 1999. "A Footnote to a Commentary" translated by Jeremy Gambrell and Alexander Summerkin. In *Rereading Russian Poetry*, Sandler, Stephanie (editor). New Haven: Yale University Press, 184–99.

Brooks, Peter. 2003. "If You Have Tears." In *Trauma at Home: After 9/11*, Greenberg, Judith (editor). Lincoln, NB: University of Nebraska Press, 48–51.

Brown, Andrea Carter. 2002. "The Old Neighborhood." In *Poetry After 9/11: An Anthology of New York Poets*, Johnson, Dennis Loy and Merians, Valerie (editors). Hoboken, NJ: Melville House Publishing, 7–8.

Works Cited

Bui, Thi Phuonag-Lan. 2009. "The Eye of Vietnam." In *A New Literary History of America* Marcus, Greil and Sollors, Werner (editor). Cambridge, MA: Harvard University Press,

Burckhardt, Sigurd. 1956. "The Poet as Fool and Priest." *ELH: A Journal of English Literary History*, 25, 290–310.

Butler, Robert Olen. 1993. *A Good Scent from a Strange Mountain* (1992). London: Minerva.

Camus, Albert. 2005. *The Myth of Sisyphus*. (1942) translated by Justin O'Brien London: Penguin.

Cao, Lan. 1998. *Monkey Bridge* (1997). New York: Penguin.

Carruth, Hayden. "Complaint and Position." In *Poets Against War* (http://www.poetsagainstwar.com/chapbook.asp).

Caruth, Cathy (editor). 1995. *Trauma: Explorations in Memory*. Baltimore: Johns Hopkins University Press.

Caruth, Cathy. 1996. *Unclaimed Experience: Trauma, Narrative and History* Baltimore: The Johns Hopkins University Press.

Choi, Susan. 1999. *The Foreign Student* (1998) New York: Harper Perennial.

Clark, Tom. 2002. "The Pilots." In *September 11: West Coast Writers Approach Ground Zero*, Meyers, Jeff (editor). Portland, OR: Hawthorne Books, 351.

Clifton, Lucille. 2002. "Tuesday 9/11/01." In *September 11, 2001: American Writers Respond*, Heyen, William (editor). Silver Springs, MD: Etruscan Press, 80.

Clover, Joshua. 2002. "Seven Letters." *September 11: West Coast Writers Approach Ground Zero*, Meyers, Jeff (editor). Portland, OR: Hawthorne Books, 125–130.

Coyote, Peter. "Flags." In *Poets Against War* (http://www.poetsagainstwar.com/chapbook.asp).

Creeley, Robert. "Ground Zero." In *Poets Against War* (http://www.poetsagainstwar.com/chapbook.asp).

Day, Lucille Lang. 2002. "Strangers." In *September 11, 2001: American Writers Respond*, Heyen, William (editor). Silver Springs, MD: Etruscan Press, 88–89.

Deleuze, Gilles and Guattari, Felix. 1983. "Rhizome." In *On the Line*. New York: Semiotext(e), 1–36.

DeLillo, Don. 2001. "In the Ruins of the Future: Reflections on Terror and Loss in the Shadow of September." *Harper's*, December, 33–40.

DeLillo, Don. 2007. *Falling Man*. London: Picador.

DeLillo, Don. 2010. *Omega Point*. London: Picador.

Works Cited

Di Prima, Diane. "Bulletin." In *Poets Against War* (http://www.poetsagainst war.com/chapbook.asp).

Dodd, Wayne. 2002. "The Third Tower." In *September 11, 2001: American Writers Respond*, Heyen, William (editor). Silver Springs, MD: Etruscan Press, 103.

Doody, Margaret Ann. 1993. "Where a Man Can Be a Man." *London Review of Books*, XXV, 20.

Dove, Rita. "Umeja: Each One of Us Counts." In *Poets Against War* (http:// www.poetsagainstwar.com/chapbook.asp).

Du Bois, W.E.B. 1970. *The Souls of Black Folk* (1903). In *The Selected Writings of W.E.B. Du Bois*, Wilson, Walter (editor). New York: New American Library.

Dubus III, Andre. 2008. *The Garden of Last Days*. New York: W.W. Norton & Company.

Dunn, Stephen. 2002. "Grudges." In *Poetry After 9/11: An Anthology of New York Poets*, Johnson, Dennis Loy and Merians, Valerie (editors). Hoboken, NJ: Melville House Publishing, 3.

Edelman, Bart. 2002. "Empty Rooms." In *September 11, 2001: American Writers Respond*, Heyen, William (editor). Silver Springs, MD: Etruscan Press, 110–111.

Edkins, Jenny. 2001. "The Absence of Meaning: Trauma and the Events of 11 September." *Interventions*, October 5 (http//www.watsoninstitute.org/ infopeace/911article.cfm?id=27).

Edkins, Jenny. 2003. *Trauma and the Memory of Politics*. Cambridge: Cambridge University Press.

Egan, Jennifer. 2003. *Look at Me* (2001). London: Picador.

Ehrhart, W.D. 1972. "Fragment: 5 September 1967." In *Winning Hearts and Minds: War Poems by Vietnam Veterans*, Rottmann, Larry, Barry, Jan, and Paquet, Basil T. (editors). London: McGraw –Hill.

Eisenberg, Deborah. 2007, "Twilight of the Superheroes." In *Twilight of the Superheroes* (2006). London: Picador, 1–42.

El Guindi, Yussef. 2006. *Back of the Throat*. New York: Dramatists Play Service.

El Guindi, Yussef. 2010. *Language Rooms*. Unpublished.

Elder, Karl. 2002. "September Ever After." In *September 11, 2001: American Writers Respond*, Heyen, William (editor). Silver Springs, MD: Etruscan Press, 115.

Eliot, T.S. 1936. *Collected Poems 1909–1935*. London: Faber & Faber.

Ellison, Ralph. 1952. *Invisible Man*. New York: Random House.

Espada, Martin. "Alabanza: In Praise of Local 100." In *Poets Against War* (http://www.poetsagainstwar.com/chapbook.asp).

197

Works Cited

Farrell, Kirby. 1998. *Post-Traumatic Culture: Injury and Interpretation in the Nineties*. Baltimore: The Johns Hopkins University Press.

Faulkner, William. 1929. *The Sound and the Fury*. London: Chatto & Windus.

Faulkner, William. 1937. *Absalom, Absalom!* (1936). London: Chatto & Windus.

Faulkner, William. 1990. *Go Down, Moses* (1942). New York: Vintage International.

Ferlinghetti, Lawrence. 2002. "History of the Airplane." In *September 11: West Coast Writers Approach Ground Zero*, Meyers, Jeff (editor). Portland, OR: Hawthorne Books, 25–26.

Ferlinghetti, Lawrence. "Speak Out." In *Poets Against War* (http://www.poet sagainstwar.com/chapbook.asp).

Fernandez, Roberto. 1988. *Raining Backwards*. Houston: Arte Publico.

Fitzgerald, F. Scott. 1945. "Echoes of the Jazz Age" (1931). In *The Crack-Up*, Wilson, Edmund (editor). New York: New Directions.

Fitzgerald, F. Scott. 1995. *Tender is the Night* (1934). London: Wordsworth Editions.

Fitzgerald, F. Scott. 1995. *The Great Gatsby* (1925). London: Penguin.

Foer, Jonathan Safran. 2006. *Extremely Loud & Incredibly Close* (2005). London: Penguin.

Franzen, Jonathan. 2002. *The Corrections* (2001). London; Fourth Estate.

Freud, Sigmund. 1957, "Mourning and Melancholia." In *Standard Edition of the Complete Psychological Writings of Sigmund Freud*. London: Hogarth Press, Vol. 14, 253.

Freud, Sigmund. 1974. *Moses and Monotheism: Three Essays*, translated by James Strachey. London: The Hogarth Press.

Freudenberger, Nell. 2005. *Lucky Girls* (2003). London: Picador.

Gaines, Ernest. 1972. *The Autobiography of Miss Jane Pittman*. New York: Bantam Books.

Gallagher, Nora. 2002. "Lament for the World." In *September 11, 2001: American Writers Respond*, Heyen, William (editor). Silver Springs, MD: Etruscan Press, 124.

Galvin, Brendan. 2002. "Fragments." In *September 11, 2001: American Writers Respond*, Heyen, William (editor). Silver Springs, MD: Etruscan Press, 129–130.

Galvin, Martin. "Army Burn Ward." In *Poets Against War* (http://www.poet sagainstwar.com/chapbook.asp).

Garcia, Christina. 1992. *Dreaming in Cuban*. New York: Alfred A. Knopf.

Gardner, Mary. 1995. *Boat People*. New York: W.W. Norton & Company.

Works Cited

Geertz, Clifford. 1988. *Works and Lives: The Anthropologist as Author*. Stanford: Stanford University Press.

Giancola, Dan. 2002. "The Ruin." In *September 11, 2001: American Writers Respond*, Heyen, William (editor). Silver Springs, MD: Etruscan Press, 132.

Giddens, Anthony. 1990. *The Consequences of Modernity*. Stanford: Stanford University Press.

Gioia, Dana. 2004, "'All I Have Is a Voice:' September 11 and American Poetry." In *Disappearing Ink: Poetry at the End of Print Culture*. St Paul, MN: Graywood Press, 163–167.

Gray, Richard. 1990. *American Poetry of the Twentieth Century*. London: Longman.

Greenberg, Judith. 2003. "Wounded New York." In *Trauma at Home: After 9/11*, Greenberg, Judith (editor). Lincoln: University of Nebraska Press, 21–35.

Gwynn, Frederick L. and Blotner, Joseph (editors). 1959. *Faulkner at the University: Class Conferences at the University of Virginia 1957–1959*. Charlottesville: University of Virginia Press.

Hacker, Marilyn. "Letter to Hayden Carruth." In *Poets Against War* (http://www.poetsagainstwar.com/chapbook.asp).

Hadas, Rachel. 2002. "Sunday Afternoon." In *Poetry After 9/11: An Anthology of New York Poets*, Johnson, Dennis Loy and Merians, Valerie (editors). Hoboken, NJ: Melville House Publishing, 93–94.

Hahn, Kimiko. 2002. "In the Armory." In *September 11, 2001: American Writers Respond*, Heyen, William (editor). Silver Springs, MD: Etruscan Press, 164.

Halaby, Laila. 2007. *Once in a Promised Land*. Boston: Beacon Press.

Hamburger, Michael. 1969. *The Truth of Poetry*. London: Weidenfeld and Nicholson.

Hamid, Mohsin. 2007. *The Reluctant Fundamentalist*. London: Hamish Hamilton.

Hammad, Suheir. 2003. "first writing since." In *Trauma at Home: After 9/11*, Greenberg, Judith (editor). Lincoln: University of Nebraska Press, 139–143.

Harjo, Joy. "No." In *Poets Against War* (http://www.poetsagainstwar.com/chapbook.asp).

Harrison, Jim. "Poem of War." In *Poets Against War* (http://www.poetsagainstwar.com/chapbook.asp).

Hartman, Geoffrey. 1998. "Shoa and Intellectual Witness." *Partisan Review* February 1, 37–48.

Works Cited

Hartman, Geoffrey, 2003. "On That Day." In *Trauma at Home: After 9/11*, Greenberg, Judith (editor). Lincoln: University of Nebraska Press, 5–10.

Hazo, Samuel. 2002. "September 11, 2001." In *September 11, 2001: American Writers Respond*, Heyen, William (editor). Silver Springs, MD: Etruscan Press, 170–171.

Hemingway, Ernest. 1964. *A Farewell to Arms* (1929). In *The Essential Hemingway*. London: Penguin.

Henry, William A. III. 1990. "Beyond the Melting Pot." *Time* April 9, 26–35.

Herman, Judith. 1992. *Trauma and Recovery*. New York: Basic Books.

Hillman, Brenda. "Green Plants and Bamboo Flute." In *Poets Against War* (http://www.poetsagainstwar.com/chapbook.asp).

Hirsch, Joshua. 2004. "Post-traumatic Cinema and the Holocaust Documentary." *Trauma and Cinema: Cross-Cultural Explorations*, Kaplan, Ann E. and Wang, Bang (editors). Hong Kong: Hong Kong University Press, 93–121.

Hirsch, Marianne. 2003. "I Took Pictures: September 2001 and Beyond." In *Trauma at Home: After 9/11*, Greenberg, Judith (editor). Lincoln: University of Nebraska Press, 69–86.

Hosseini, Khaled. 2004. *The Kite Runner* (2003). London: Bloomsbury.

Irving, Washington. 1962. *The Sketch Book* (1820). New York: New American Library.

Irwin, Mark. 2002. "Elegy for the Victims and Survivors, World Trade Towers, N.Y., 2001." In *September 11, 2001: American Writers Respond*, Heyen, William (editor). Silver Springs, MD: Etruscan Press, 209.

James, C.L.R. 1993. *Beyond a Boundary* (1966). Durham, NC: Duke University Press.

James, Henry. 1967. *Hawthorne* (1879). New York: Macmillan.

Jameson, Fredric. 1981. *The Political Unconscious: Narrative as a Socially Symbolic Act*. Ithaca, NY: Cornell University Press.

Jarrell, Randall. 2006. "The Death of the Ball Turret Gunner." *The Oxford Book of American Poetry*, Lehman, David (editor). New York: Oxford University Press.

Johnson, Denis. 2008. *Tree of Smoke* (2007). London: Picador.

Johnson, Dennis Loy and Merians, Valerie. 2002. *Poetry After 9/11: An Anthology of New York Poets* Hoboken, NJ: Melville House Publishing.

Kadohata, Cynthia. 1989. *The Floating World*. New York: Viking.

Works Cited

Kahane, Claire. 2003. "Uncanny Sights: The Anticipation of the Abomination." In *Trauma at Home: After 9/11*, Greenberg, Judith (editor). Lincoln: University of Nebraska Press, 107–116.

Kalfus, Ken. 2007. *A Disorder Peculiar to the Country* (2006). London: Simon and Schuster,

Kaplan, Ann E. and Wang, Bang. 2004. "From Traumatic Paralysis to the Force Field of Modernity." In *Trauma and Cinema: Cross-Cultural Explorations*, Kaplan, Ann E. and Wang, Bang (editors). Hong Kong: Hong Kong University Press, 1–22.

Karlin, Wayne. 1988. *Lost Armies* New York: Henry Holt and Company.

Karlin, Wayne. 2000. *Prisoners* (1998). Willimantic, CT: Curbstone Press.

Katz, Eliot. 2002. "When the Skyline Crumbles." In *Poetry After 9/11: An Anthology of New York Poets*, Johnson, Dennis Loy and Merians, Valerie (editors). Hoboken, NJ: Melville House Publishing, 23–26.

Kaufman, Shirley. "Cyclamen." In *Poets Against War* (http://www.poetsagainstwar.com/chapbook.asp).

Kennedy, X.J. 2002. "September Twelfth, 2001." In *September 11, 2001: American Writers Respond*, Heyen, William (editor). Silver Springs, MD: Etruscan Press, 221.

Kermode, Frank. 1961. *The Romantic Image* (1957). London: Penguin.

Kingston, Maxine Hong. 2002. "Memorial Service." In *September 11: West Coast Writers Approach Ground Zero*, Meyers, Jeff (editor). Portland, OR: Hawthorne Books, 348.

Kinnell, Galway. "The Olive Wood Fire." In *Poets Against War* (http://www.poetsagainstwar.com/chapbook.asp).

Kirchwey, Karl. 2002. "Nocturne, Morningside Heights." In *Poetry After 9/11: An Anthology of New York Poets*, Johnson, Dennis Loy and Merians, Valerie (editors). Hoboken, NJ: Melville House Publishing, 60.

Kizer, Carolyn. "Gulf War." In *Poets Against War* (http://www.poetsagainstwar.com/chapbook.asp).

Komunyakaa, Yusef. 1988. "Maps Drawn in the Dust." *Colorado Review*, 15 (Spring-Summer), 13.

Kowit, Steve. 2002. "The Equation." In *September 11, 2001: American Writers Respond*, Heyen, William (editor). Silver Springs, MD: Etruscan Press, 224–225.

Krapf, Norbert. 2002. "Three Paumanok Pieces." In *September 11, 2001: American Writers Respond*, Heyen, William (editor). Silver Springs, MD: Etruscan Press, 231–236.

Works Cited

Kremer, Lillian. 1989. *Witness Through the Imagination: Jewish American Holocaust Literature* Detroit: Wayne State University Press.

Kumin, Maxine. "Heaven as Anus." In *Poets Against War* (http://www.poetsa gainstwar.com/chapbook.asp).

Kushner, Bill. 2002. "Friends." In *Poetry After 9/11: An Anthology of New York Poets*, Johnson, Dennis Loy and Merians, Valerie (editors). Hoboken, NJ: Melville House Publishing, 10–11.

Kushner, Bill. 2002. "In the Hairy Arms of Whitman." In *Poetry After 9/11: An Anthology of New York Poets*, Johnson, Dennis Loy and Merians, Valerie (editors). Hoboken, NJ: Melville House Publishing, 14–15.

La Capra, Dominick. 2001. *Writing History, Writing Trauma*. Baltimore: Johns Hopkins University Press.

LaBute, Neil. 2003. *The Mercy Seat*. New York: Faber and Faber.

Lang, Luc. 2003. *11 Septembre, mon amour*. Unpublished.

Lapcharoensap, Rattawut. 2006. *Sightseeing* (2004). London: Atlantic Books.

Laub, Dori. 2003. "September 11, 2001 – An Event without a Voice." In *Trauma at Home: After 9/11*, Greenberg, Judith (editor). Lincoln: University of Nebraska Press, 204–15.

Lauck, Jennifer. 2002. "September 11 from Abroad." *September 11: West Coast Writers Approach Ground Zero*, Meyers, Jeff (editor). Portland, Oregon: Hawthorne Books, 297–308.

Le Guin, Ursula. "American Wars." In *Poets Against War* (http://www.poetsa gainstwar.com/chapbook.asp).

Lehman, David. 2002. "14/9/01." In *Poetry After 9/11: An Anthology of New York Poets*, Johnson, Dennis Loy and Merians, Valerie (editors). Hoboken, NJ: Melville House Publishing, 89.

Lehman, David. 2002. "The World Trade Center." In *Poetry After 9/11: An Anthology of New York Poets*, Johnson, Dennis Loy and Merians, Valerie (editors). Hoboken, NJ: Melville House.

Levan, Kelly. 2002. "Dragons and Sharks." In *September 11, 2001: American Writers Respond*, Heyen, William (editor). Silver Springs, MD: Etruscan Press, 240–241.

Levine, Anne-Marie. 2002. "Four November 9ths." In *Poetry After 9/11: An Anthology of New York Poets*, Johnson, Dennis Loy and Merians, Valerie (editors). Hoboken, NJ: Melville House Publishing, 53–54.

Lolordo, Ann. 2002. "View Interrupted." In *September 11, 2001: American Writers Respond*, Heyen, William (editor). Silver Springs, MD: Etruscan Press, 247.

Works Cited

Louis, Adrian C. 2002. "Liberty Street." In *September 11, 2001: American Writers Respond*, Heyen, William (editor). Silver Springs, MD: Etruscan Press, 251.

Lowell, Robert. 2006. "For the Union Dead." *The Oxford Book of American Poetry*, Lehman, David (editor). New York: Oxford University Press, 634–636.

Lubin, Orly. 2003. "Masked Power: An Encounter with the Social Body in the Flesh." In *Trauma at Home: After 9/11*, Greenberg, Judith (editor). Lincoln: University of Nebraska Press, 124–131

Lukacs, Georg. 1963. *The Meaning of Contemporary Realism*, translated by John and Necke Mander. London: Merlin Press.

Lukacs, Georg. 1969. *The Historical Novel*, translated by Hannah and Stanley Mitchell. London: Pelican.

Mallarme, Stephane. 1956. *Mallarme: Selected Prose, Poems, Essays and Letters*, translated by Bradford Cook. Baltimore: The Johns Hopkins University Press,

Marcuse, Herbert. 1969. *Eros and Civilisation: A Philosophical Inquiry into Freud* (1956). London: Penguin.

Mars-Jones, Adam. 2006. Review of *The Road*. *The Observer*, November 26, 19.

Martin, Ross. 2002. "This Message Will Self-Destruct in Sixty Seconds." In *Poetry After 9/11: An Anthology of New York Poets*, Johnson, Dennis Loy and Merians, Valerie (editors). Hoboken, NJ: Melville House Publishing, 56–57.

McCarthy, Cormac. 1989. *Blood Meridian* New York: Alfred A. Knopf.

McCarthy, Cormac. 1992. *All the Pretty Horses* New York: Alfred A. Knopf.

McCarthy, Cormac. 1994. *The Crossing*. London: Picador.

McCarthy, Cormac. 2006. *The Road*. New York: Alfred A. Knopf.

McInerney, Jay. 2006. *The Good Life*. London: Bloomsbury.

Mercado, Nancy. 2002. "Going to Work." In *Poetry After 9/11: An Anthology of New York Poets*, Johnson, Dennis Loy and Merians, Valerie (editors). Hoboken, NJ: Melville House Publishing, 55.

Meriwether, James B. and Millgate, Michael (editors). 1968. *Lion in the Garden: Interviews with William Faulkner, 1926–1962*. New York: Random House.

Merwin, W.S. "Ogres." In *Poets Against War* (http://www.poetsagainstwar.com/chapbook.asp).

Works Cited

Merwin, W.S. 2002. "To the Words." In *September 11, 2001: American Writers Respond*, Heyen, William (editor). Silver Springs, MD: Etruscan Press, 3.

Messud, Clare. 2007. *The Emperor's Children* (2006). London: Picador.

Meyers, Jeff (editor). 2002. *September 11: West Coast Writers Approach Ground Zero*. Portland, Oregon: Hawthorne Books.

Minty, Judith. 2002. "Loving This Earth." In *September 11, 2001: American Writers Respond*, Heyen, William (editor). Silver Springs, MD: Etruscan Press, 232–233.

Mishra, Pankaj. 2006. "The Politics of Paranoia." *The Observer*, September 11 (http://books.guardian.co.uk/departments/politicsphilosophyandsoci ety/story/0,1874132.html).

Mishra, Pankaj. 2007. "The End of Innocence." *The Guardian*, May 19 (http://www.guardian.co.uk/books/2007/may/19/fiction.martin. amis).

Morrison, Toni. 1987. *Beloved*. London: Chatto & Windus.

Morrison, Toni. 1992. *Playing in the Dark: Whiteness and the Literary Imagination*. Cambridge: Harvard University Press.

Morrison, Toni. 2003. "The Dead of September 11." In *Trauma at Home: After 9/11*, Greenberg, Judith (editor). Lincoln: University of Nebraska Press, 1–2.

Moustaki, Nikki. 2002. "How to Write a Poem After September 11th." In *Poetry After 9/11: An Anthology of New York Poets*, Johnson, Dennis Loy and Merians, Valerie (editors). Hoboken, NJ: Melville House Publishing, 95–96.

Mukherjee, Bharati. 1990. *Jasmine* (1989). London: Virago.

Muller, Gilbert H. 1999. *New Strangers in Paradise: The Immigrant Experience and Contemporary American Fiction*. Lexington: The University Press of Kentucky.

Murray, George. 2002. "The Statue." In *Poetry After 9/11: An Anthology of New York Poets*, Johnson, Dennis Loy and Merians, Valerie (editors). Hoboken, NJ: Melville House Publishing, 84–85.

Muske-Dukes, Carol. "The House of Bush." In *Poets Against War* (http:// www.poetsagainstwar.com/chapbook.asp).

Nelson, Anne. 2003. *The Guys*. New York: Dramatists Play Service.

O'Daly, William. "To the Forty-third President of the United States of America." In *Poets Against War* (http://www.poetsagainstwar.com/chap book.asp).

O'Neill, Joseph. 2008. *Netherland*. London: Fourth Estate.

Works Cited

Ogden, Hugh. 2002. "Northwest Maine, September 2001." In *September 11, 2001: American Writers Respond*, Heyen, William (editor). Silver Springs, MD: Etruscan Press, 292–293.

Orr, Gregory. "Refusing." In *Poets Against War* (http://www.poetsagainstwar. com/chapbook.asp).

Ostriker, Alice. "The Dispute." In *Poets Against War* (http://www.poetsa gainstwar.com/chapbook.asp).

Ostriker, Alice. 2002. "The Window, At the Moment of Flame." In *Poetry After 9/11: An Anthology of New York Poets*, Johnson, Dennis Loy and Merians, Valerie (editors). Hoboken, NJ: Melville House Publishing, 86.

Paz, Octavio. 1965. *L"Arc et la lyre*. Paris: Gallimard.

Pilkington, Tom. 1997. "Fate and Free Will on the American Frontier." *Western American Fiction*, XXXVII.

Pinsky, Robert. "Statement of Conscience." In *Poets Against War* (http:// www.poetsagainstwar.com/chapbook.asp).

Pollitt, Katha. "Trying to Write a Poem Against War." In *Poets Against War* (http://www.poetsagainstwar.com/chapbook.asp).

Ponge, Francis. 1967. "My Creative Method" (1947–48), translated by Lane Dunlop. *Quarterly Review of Literature*, 15, 140–158.

Powers Richard. 2004. *The Time of Our Singing* (2003). London: Vintage.

Price, Reynolds. 2006. *The Good Priest's Son* (2005). New York: Scribner.

Rabinowitz, Anna. 2002. "Bricolage: Versicolor." In *Poetry After 9/11: An Anthology of New York Poets*, Johnson, Dennis Loy and Merians, Valerie (editors). Hoboken, NJ: Melville House Publishing, 79–83.

Radstone, Susanna. 2003. "The Way of the Fathers: Trauma, Fantasy and Serptember 11." In *Trauma at Home: After 9/11*, Greenberg, Judith (editor). Lincoln: University of Nebraska Press, 117–123.

Ragan, Paul. 1993. "Values and Structure in *The Orchard Keeper*." In *Perspectives on Cormac McCarthy*, Arnold, Edwin T. and Luce Jackson, Dianne C. (editors). University of Mississippi Press.

Ray, David. 2002. "Preparing the Monument." In *September 11, 2001: American Writers Respond*, Heyen, William (editor). Silver Springs, MD: Etruscan Press, 320–321.

Rebeck, Theresa and Gersten, Alexandra. 2003. *Omnium Gatherum*. New York: Samuel French.

Reed, Ishmael. 1988. "America: The Multinational Society." In *Writin' is Fightin': Thirty-Seven Years of Boxing on Paper*. New York: Atheneum, 56–68.

Works Cited

Reed, Ishmael. 2002. "America United." In *September 11, 2001: American Writers Respond*, Heyen, William (editor). Silver Springs, MD: Etruscan Press, 322–328.

Reeve, F.D. 2002. "Sunset, New York Harbor." In *September 11, 2001: American Writers Respond*, Heyen, William (editor). Silver Springs, MD: Etruscan Press, 329.

Rich, Adrienne. "The School Among the Ruins." In *Poets Against War* (http://www.poetsagainstwar.com/chapbook.asp).

Robicheaux, Robert J. "The Eleventh of September." In *September 11, 2001 – America"s Tragedy* (http://www.butlerwebs.com/tragedy/poems.htm).

Rodriguez, Richard. 2002. *Brown: The Last Discovery of America*. New York: Viking Penguin.

Rosenbaum, Thane. 2004. "Art and Atrocity in a Post–9/11 World." In *Jewish-American and Holocaust Literature: Representation in the Postmodern World* Berger, Alan L. and Cronin Albany, Gloria L. (editors). State University of New York Press, 125–136.

Rothberg, Michael. 2003. "There is No Poetry in This: Writing, Trauma and Home." In *Trauma at Home: After 9/11*, Greenberg, Judith (editor). Lincoln: University of Nebraska Press, 147–57.

Rothberg, Michael. 2009. "A Failure of the Imagination: Diagnosing the Post–9/11 Novel: A Response to Richard Gray." *American Literary History*, Spring, 152–162.

Rushdie, Salman. 1991. *Imaginary Homelands: Essays and Criticism, 1981–1991*. London: Faber.

Sartre, Jean-Paul. 1955. "John Dos Passos and 1919." In *Literary and Philosophical Essays*, translated by Annette Michelson. New York: Criterion Books.

Schopenhauer, Arthur. 1891. *On the Apparent Design of Fate on the Individual*. London: Watts.

Schwartz, Lynne Sharon. 2002. "Near November." In *110 Stories: New York Writes After September 11*, Ulrich Baer (editor). New York: New York University Press, 260–262.

Schwartz, Lynne Sharon. 2005. *The Writing on the Wall*. New York: Counterpoint.

Seidman, Hugh. 2002. "New York." In *Poetry After 9/11: An Anthology of New York Poets*, Johnson, Dennis Loy and Merians, Valerie (editors). Hoboken, NJ: Melville House Publishing, 40.

Seuss, Diane. 2002. "Falling Man." In *September 11, 2001: American Writers Respond*, Heyen, William (editor). Silver Springs, MD: Etruscan Press, 350–351.

Shapiro, Harvey. 2002. "Nights." In *Poetry After 9/11: An Anthology of New York Poets*, Johnson, Dennis Loy and Merians, Valerie (editors). Hoboken, NJ: Melville House Publishing, 78.

Shapiro, Karl. 2003. "Lord, I have seen too much." In *Selected Poems*. New York: Library of America.

Shaplin, Adriano. 2003. *Pugilist Specialist*. London: Oberon Books.

Shell, Marc (editor). 2002. *American Babel: Literatures of the United States from Abnaki to Zuni*. Cambridge: Harvard University Press.

Shepard, Sam. 2005. *The God of Hell*. London: Methuen.

Shinn, Christopher. 2002. *Where Do We Live*. London: Methuen.

Simpson, David. 2006. *9/11: The Culture of Commemoration*. Chicago: University of Chicago Press.

Smith, Aaron. 2002. "Silent Room." In *Poetry After 9/11: An Anthology of New York Poets*, Johnson, Dennis Loy and Merians, Valerie (editors). Hoboken, NJ: Melville House Publishing, 4.

Smith, Zadie. 2008. "Two Paths for the Novel." *The New York Review of Books*, 55 (22 November), 1–17.

Spiegelman, Art. 2003. *The Complete Maus: A Survivor's Tale*. London: Penguin Books.

Spiegelman, Art. 2004. *In the Shadow of No Towers*. New York: Pantheon Books.

Spires, Elizabeth. 2002. "The Beautiful Day." In *September 11, 2001: American Writers Respond*, Heyen, William (editor). Silver Springs, MD: Etruscan Press, 356–357.

St John, David. 2002. "The Face." In *September 11, 2001: American Writers Respond*, Heyen, William (editor). Silver Springs, MD: Etruscan Press, 358.

Stamelman, Richard. 2003. "Between Memory and History." In *Trauma at Home: After 9/11*, Greenberg, Judith (editor). Lincoln: University of Nebraska Press, 11–20.

Stenhouse, Shelley. 2002. "Circling." In *Poetry After 9/11: An Anthology of New York Poets*, Johnson, Dennis Loy and Merians, Valerie (editors). Hoboken, NJ: Melville House Publishing, 18.

Stevens, Wallace. 1955. *Collected Poems*. London: Faber.

Stevens, Wallace. 1957. *Opus Posthumous*, Samuel French Morse (editor). London: Faber.

Stock, Norman. 2002. "What I Said." In *Poetry After 9/11: An Anthology of New York Poets*, Johnson, Dennis Loy and Merians, Valerie (editors). Hoboken, NJ: Melville House Publishing, 34.

Works Cited

Stone, Ruth. "Who Cares?" In *Poets Against War* (http://www.poetsagainst war.com/chapbook.asp).

Stone, Ruth. 2002. "The Way of It." In *September 11, 2001: American Writers Respond*, Heyen, William (editor). Silver Springs, MD: Etruscan Press, 364.

Strom, Dao. 2003. *Grass Roof, Tin Roof.* New York: Houghton Mifflin.

Stryk, Lucien. 2002. "Quiet, Please." In *September 11, 2001: American Writers Respond*, Heyen, William (editor). Silver Springs, MD: Etruscan Press, 368–369.

Suermondt, Tim. 2002. "Squad 1." In *Poetry After 9/11: An Anthology of New York Poets*, Johnson, Dennis Loy and Merians, Valerie (editors). Hoboken, NJ: Melville House Publishing, 102.

Susskind, Ron. 2004. "Without a Doubt." *New York Times Magazine*, October 17 (http://www.ronsuskind.com/articles/000106.html).

Tate, Allen. 2006. "Ode to the Confederate Dead." *The Oxford Book of American Poetry*, Lehman, David (editor). New York: Oxford University Press, 448–450.

thúy, lê thi diem. 2003. *The Gangster We Are All Looking For.* New York: Alfred A. Knopf,

Tisdale, Sallie. 2002. "A Clamor of Symbols." In *September 11: West Coast Writers Approach Ground Zero*, Meyers, Jeff (editor). Portland, Oregon: Hawthorne Books, 49–56.

Tocqueville, Alexis de. 1966. *Democracy in America*, translated by George Lawrence (1835, 1840). New York: Harper & Row.

Towle, Tony. 2002. "Diptych." In *Poetry After 9/11: An Anthology of New York Poets*, Johnson, Dennis Loy and Merians, Valerie (editors). Hoboken, NJ: Melville House Publishing, 47.

Trilling, Lionel. 1953. *The Liberal Imagination.* Garden City, NY: Doubleday.

Twain, Mark. 1961. *Life on the Mississippi* (1883). New York: New American Library.

Twain, Mark. 1968. *The Adventures of Tom Sawyer* (1876). London: Pan Books.

Updike, John. 2007. *Terrorist* (2006). London: Penguin.

Valentine, Jean. 2002. "In the Burning Air." In *Poetry After 9/11: An Anthology of New York Poets*, Johnson, Dennis Loy and Merians, Valerie (editors). Hoboken, NJ: Melville House Publishing, 29.

Valentine, Jean. 2002. "She Would Long." In *Poetry After 9/11: An Anthology of New York Poets*, Johnson, Dennis Loy and Merians, Valerie (editors). Hoboken, NJ: Melville House Publishing, 30.

Works Cited

Van Alphen, Ernst. 1997. *Caught by History: Holocaust Effects in Contemporary Art, Literature and Theory*. Stanford, CA: Stanford University Press.

Versluys, Kristiaan. 2009. *Out of the Blue: September 11 and the Novel*. New York: Columbia University Press,

Vigier, Rachel. 2002. "Burnt Ground." In *September 11, 2001: American Writers Respond*, Heyen, William (editor). Silver Springs, MD: Etruscan Press, 387–388.

Violi, Paul. 2002. "House of Xerxes." In *Poetry After 9/11: An Anthology of New York Poets*, Johnson, Dennis Loy and Merians, Valerie (editors). Hoboken, NJ: Melville House Publishing, 71.

Warren, Robert Penn. 1955. *Band of Angels*. New York: Random House.

Warren, Robert Penn. 1976. "The Ballad of Billie Potts." In *Selected Poems: 1923–1975*. New York: Random House.

Whalen, Philip. "In Memoriam." In *Poets Against War* (http://www.poetsagainstwar.com/chapbook.asp).

White, Hayden. 1978. "Getting Out of History." In *Tropics of Discourse: Essays in Cultural Criticism*. Baltimore: Johns Hopkins University Press, 2–17.

Wigley, Marc. 2002. "Insecurity by Design." In *After the World Trade Center: Rethinking New York City*, Sorkin, Michael and Zukin, Sharon (editors). New York: Routledge, 69–85.

Williams, C.K. "The Hearth." In *Poets Against War* (http://www.poetsagainstwar.com/chapbook.asp).

Williams, Edward. 1947. "Virginia, more especially the South Part thereof Richly and Truly Valued" (1650). In of *Tracts and Other Papers Relating Principally to the Origin, Settlement and Progress of the Colonies in North America*, Vol. III, Peter Force (editor) (1636–46). New York.

Williams, Raymond. 1977. *Marxism and Literature*. London: Chatto & Windus.

Williams, Terry Tempest. "(Statement) Portrait of George W. Bush as a Cowboy, or: America's Foreign Policy of Peace." In *Poets Against War* (http://www.poetsagainstwar.com/chapbook.asp).

Williams, Terry Tempest. "Freedom from Speech." In *Poets Against War* (http://www.poetsagainstwar.com/chapbook.asp).

Williams, Terry Tempest. "Freedom of Speech." In *Poets Against War* (http://www.poetsagainstwar.com/chapbook.asp).

Williams, Terry Tempest. 2002. "Scattered Potsherds." In *September 11, 2001: American Writers Respond*, Heyen, William (editor). Silver Springs, MD: Etruscan Press, 411–415.

Works Cited

Wilner, Eleanor. "Found in the Free Library." In *Poets Against War* (http://www.poetsagainstwar.com/chapbook.asp).

Woodward, Robert B. 1992. Interview with Cormac McCarthy, "Cormac McCarthy's Venomous Vision." *New York Times Magazine* 19 April.

Wright, C.D. "Once Again the Old Urge to Be Alone in a Car No Matter Where the Local Roads Are Going." In *Poets Against War* (http://www.poetsagainstwar.com/chapbook.asp).

Wright, Craig. 2004. *"Recent Tragic Events."* New York: Dramatist's Play Service.

Wright, Richard. 1940. *Native Son.* New York: Harper.

Zizek, Slavoj. 2002. *Welcome to the Desert of the Real! Five Essays on September 11 and Related Dates.* London: Verso.

Index

After the Fall: American Literature Since 9/11, First Edition. Richard Gray.
© 2011 John Wiley & Sons, Ltd. Published 2011 by John Wiley & Sons, Ltd.

Index

212

213

Index

214

217

Index

Kingstone, Maxine Hong
"Memorial Service", 184
Kinnell, Galway
"The Olive Wood Fire", 180
Kirchwey, Karl
"Nocturne, Morningside
Heights"
Kite Runner, The (Hosseini), 114,
120, 122–4
Kizer, Carolyn
"Gulf War", 184
Komunyakaa, Yusef, 3
Korean War, 60, 91, 93
Kowit, Steve
"The Equation", 183
Krapf, Norbert
"Elegy", 189
"Three Paumanok Pieces", 189
Kumin, Maxine
"Heaven as Anus", 191
Kuppsc, Jarek
The Reflecting Pool, 146, 147
Kushner, Bill
"Friends", 182
"In the Hairy Arms of
Whitman", 189

Labute, Neil
The Mercy Seat, 154–6
Lacan, Jacques, 49
Laden, Osama bin, 85, 146
"Lament for the World" (Gallager),
184
Lang, Luc
11 septembre mon amour, 150, 151
language, 13
failure of, 1, 16, 34, 48–50, 53–4,
87–8, 128, 147, 153, 161–2,
170–71, 176, 182, 186, 190, 191

as power, 162, 188, 191
Language Rooms (El Guindi), 151–3,
156
Lapcharoensap, Rattawutt, 32
Sightseeing, 124–30, 134, 136, 140
"Late Blooming Roses" (Baker),
183
Laub, Dori, 49
Lauck, Jennifer, 9, 10
Le Guin, Ursula
"American Wars"
Lehman, David, 5
"9/14/01", 183
"Letter to Hayden Carruth"
(Hacker), 187
Levan, Kelly
"Dragons and Sharks", 180
Levine, Anne-Marie
"Four November 9ths", 180
"Liberty Street" (Louis), 190
Lindbergh, 174
literature
failure of *see* language, failure of
Location of Culture, The (Bhabha), 64
Lolordo, Ann
"View Interrupted", 183
"Lord, I have seen too much" (Karl
Shapiro), 3
Lost Armies (Karlin), 93
Louis, Adrian C.
"Liberty Street", 190
Love Unpunished (Pig Iron Theatre
Company), 146–7
"Loving this Earth" (Minty), 186
Lowell, Robert
"For the Union Dead", 99
Lucky Girls (Freudenberger), 124,
130–36, 140
Lukacs, Georg, 27, 66, 129

Index

Index

223

Index